POT-POURRI FROM A SURREY GARDEN

'Mrs Earle comes of people who for a good many generations back took their highest pleasure in their gardens, and greater pleasure than we fear the present generation of women on bykes [sic], women at golf and cricket, horsey women and new women generally are likely to share. It is an interesting book about many things… there is not a little to be learnt in it'

The Garden

'The author gossips pleasantly about the flowers in her garden and in her boudoir, and then rambles off to discuss methods of cooking potatoes… Those who can spare but little time for recreation will find the fascination of the book somewhat dangerous!' *Gardeners' Chronicle*

Mrs C. W. Earle was born Maria Theresa Villiers, in 1836. From May to October she and her husband, Captain Charles William Earle, lived in their Surrey house in Cobham, 16 miles from their home in London, where they spent the rest of the year. They had three sons.

Mrs Earle was an amateur gardener, artist, writer and hostess who entertained some of the most outspoken intellectuals of the day, including George Eliot, Aldous Huxley and Oscar Wilde. The extraordinary success of her first book, *Pot-pourri from a Surrey Garden*, published in 1897 when Mrs Earle was 61, led to four further books.

Although Mrs Earle was writing for the upper-middle classes, her views are not nearly as hard-line as those held by many Victorians of her background. Her family viewed her as a radical and she was strongly influenced by the views of her uncle, who championed the Anti-Corn Law League and the Free Trade Movement. Nevertheless, she viewed philanthropy as risking 'to stir up unintentionally class hatred by injudicious interference' – and yet she was sympathetic towards female emancipation.

Her niece, **Lady Constance Lytton**, who wrote the Appendix on Japanese flower-arranging, was to become far better known as 'Lady Con', one of the most militant of the suffragettes.

This revised edition contains her writings from all four seasons, and conveys Mrs Earle's genuine sense of wonder for her natural environment that so bewitched her Victorian readers.

Also by Mrs C. W. Earle:

More Pot-pourri from a Surrey Garden
A Third Pot-pourri
Letters to Young and Old
Pot-pourri Mixed by Two (with Miss Ethel Case)

Pot-Pourri

From a
Surrey Garden

THE CLASSIC DIARY OF A VICTORIAN LADY

MRS C. W. EARLE

WITH AN APPENDIX
BY
LADY CONSTANCE LYTTON

summersdale

POT-POURRI FROM A SURREY GARDEN

First published in Great Britain in 1897 by Smith, Elder & Co.
This edition published in 2004 by Summersdale Publishers Ltd.

Summersdale Publishers Ltd
46 West Street
Chichester
West Sussex
PO19 1RP
UK
www.summersdale.com

Printed and bound in Great Britain

ISBN 1 84024 397 X

AUTHOR'S NOTE

These 'notes' would never have been extracted from me without the encouragement I have received from all my dear nieces, real and adopted, and the very practical assistance of one of them. Now that the book is written, I can only hope that it will not prove too great a disappointment to them all.

To my sister
the Countess of Lytton

CONTENTS

JUNE

Hands and fingers after weeding—Shrub-pruning—Boxes for birds—Robins in greenhouse—'Burning Bush'—Two Polygonums—Strawberries—Geraniums and cuttings—Cactuses—Freesia bulbs—*Gloriosa superba*—Luncheon dishes— Cucumbers…

JULY

The Welsh Poppy—Astrantias—Old Green Peas—Red Currants—The Madonna Lily, *L'epée de la Vierge*—The value of the reserve garden—An English summer's day—Light soils and dry summers—Other people's gardens—Notebooks—Sunny lawns—Dutch gardens—Fountains and water-tanks— *Lobelia cardinalis*—Watering out of doors—Two hardy shrubs…

AUGUST

Gilbert White—The decline of vegetable culture in the Middle Ages—Preserving French Beans and Scarlet Runners—Scotch gardens—*Tropæolum speciosum*—Crimson-berried Elder—The coast of Sutherland—The abuse of coarse Creepers…

SEPTEMBER

Weeds we alternately love and hate—*Amaryllis belladonna*—First touch of frost—Colour-blindness—Special annuals—Autumn seed-sowing—Re-planting Carnation layers—Planting drives and approaches to small houses—'Wild gardening'—Double Violets—Salvias—Baby chickens—Pigeons…

OCTOBER

Autumn mornings and robins—Italian Daturas—The useful 'Myticuttah'—Nerines— Three Cape greenhouse plants—

CONTENTS

Pot-Pourri

From a
Surrey Garden

JANUARY

January 2nd—I am not going to write a gardening book, or a cookery book, or a book on furnishing or education. Plenty of these have been published lately. I merely wish to talk to you on paper about several subjects as they occur to me throughout one year; and if such desultory notes prove to be of any use to you or others, so much the better. One can only teach from personal knowledge; yet how exceedingly limited that is!

The fact that I shall mention gardening every month will give this subject preponderance throughout the book. At the same time I shall in no way attempt to supersede books on gardening, that are much fuller and more complete than anything I could write. For those who care to learn gardening in the way I have learnt, I may mention, before I go further, three books which seem to me absolutely essential—'The

English Flower Garden,' by W. Robinson; 'The Vegetable Garden,' translated from the French, edited by W. Robinson; and Johnson's 'Gardener's Dictionary,' by C. H. Wright and D. Dewar. This last supplies any deficiencies in the other two, and it teaches the cultivation of plants under glass.

The cookery book to which I shall refer is 'Dainty Dishes,' by Lady Harriet Sinclair. It is an old one, and has often been reprinted. I have known it all my married life, and have found no other book on cooking so useful, so clear, or in such good taste. It is the only English cookery book I know that has been translated into German.

I have given you the names of these books, as it is through them I have learnt most of what I know, both in gardening and cooking. It is, however, undeniable that, as the old proverb says, you may drag a horse to the water, but you can't make him drink; and unless, when I name plants or vegetables for the table, you look them up in the books, you will derive very little benefit from these notes.

Just now it seems as if everybody wrote books which nobody reads. This is probably what I am doing myself; but, so far as gardening is concerned, at any rate, I have read and studied very hard, as I began to learn quite late in life. I never buy a plant, or have one given me, without looking it up in the books and providing it with the best treatment in my power. If a plant fails, I always blame myself, and feel sure I have cultivated it wrongly. No day goes by without my studying some of my books or reading one or more of the very excellent gardening newspapers that are published weekly. This is how I also learnt cooking when I was younger, always going to the book when a dish was wrong. In this way one becomes independent of cooks and gardeners, because, if they leave, one can always teach another. Nothing is more unjust than the way a great many people find fault with their gardeners, and, like the Egyptians of old, demand bricks without straw. How can a man who has had little education and no experience be expected to know about plants that come from all parts of the world, and require individual treatment and understanding to make them grow here at all? Or how can a cook be expected to dress vegetables when she has never been taught how to do it? In England her one instruction has usually been to throw a large handful of coarse soda into the water, with a view to making it soft and keeping the colour of the vegetables, whereas, in fact, she by so doing destroys their health-giving properties; and every housekeeper should see that it is not done. Her next idea is to hand over the cooking of the vegetables to a raw girl of a kitchen-maid, if she has one.

I am most anxious that anybody who does not care for old Herbals should pass over those catalogued in March; but, on the other hand, that those who are interested in gardening should look through the November list of books, as they will find many modern ones mentioned there which may be useful to them for practical purposes.

My hope and wish is that my reader will take me by the hand; for I do not reap, and I do not sow. I am merely, like so many other women of the past and present, a patient gleaner in the fields of knowledge, and absolutely dependent on human sympathy in order to do anything at all. I cannot explain too much that the object of my book is to try to make everyone think for him or herself, and at the same time to profit by the instruction which in these days is so easy to get, and is all around us. Women are still behind the other sex in the power of thinking at all, much more so in the power of thinking of several things at once. I hope the coming women may see the great advantage of training their minds early in life to be a practical denial of Swift's cynical assertion that 'mankind are as unfit for flying as for thinking.' Nothing can be done well without thought—certainly not gardening, nor housekeeping, nor managing children. A curious example of this is given in a recently published account of the most famous of modern jugglers. He says that he trained his brain in youth to exert itself in three different ways at the same time. This no doubt is the reason that he is now pre-eminent in his own line.

January 3rd—I will begin by telling you that I was brought up for the most part in the country, in a beautiful, wild, old-fashioned garden. This garden, through circumstances, had remained in the hands of an old gardener for more than thirty years, which carries us back nearly a century. Like so many young people I see about me now, I cared only for the flowers growing, that I might have the pleasure of picking them. Mr. Ruskin says that it is luxurious and pleasure-loving people who like them gathered. Gardening is, I think, essentially the amusement of the middle-aged and old. The lives of the young, as a rule, are too full to give the time and attention required.

Almost all that has remained in my mind of my young days in this garden is how wonderfully the old man kept the place. He succeeded in flowering many things year after year with no one to help him, and with the frost in the valley to contend against in spring. It was difficult, too, for him to get seeds or plants, since the place was held by joint owners, whom he did not like to ask for them. The spot was very sheltered, and that is one of the greatest of all secrets for plant cultivation. An ever-flowing mill-stream ran all round the garden; and the hedges of China-roses, Sweetbriar, Honeysuckle, and white Hawthorn tucked their toes into the soft mud, and throve year after year. The old man was a philosopher in his way, and when on a cold March morning my sisters and I used to rush out after lessons and ask him what the weather was going to be, he would stop his digging, look up at the sky, and say: 'Well, miss, it may be fine and it

may be wet; and if the sun comes out, it will be warmer.'
After this solemn announcement he would wipe his brow
and resume his work, and we went off, quite satisfied, to our
well-known haunts in the Hertfordshire woods, to gather
Violets and Primroses for our mother, who loved them.

All this, you will see, laid a very small foundation for any
knowledge of gardening; and yet, owing to the vivid character
of the impressions of youth, it left a memory that was very
useful to me when I took up gardening later in life. To this
day I can smell the tall white double Rockets that throve so
well in the damp garden, and scented the evening air. They
grew by the side of glorious bunches of Oriental Poppies
and the on-coming spikes of the feathery *Spiræa aruncus*. This
garden had peculiar charms for us, because, though we hardly
realised it, such gardens were already beginning to grow out
of fashion, sacrificed to the new bedding-out system, which
altered the whole gardening of Europe. I shall allude to this
again. I can never think of this old home without my thoughts
recurring to Hood's poem 'I remember! I remember!' too
well known perhaps, even by the young, to justify my quoting
it here.

Equally graven on my memory is a much less familiar little
poem my widowed mother used to say to me as we walked
together up and down the gravel paths, with the primrose
sky behind the tall Beeches of the neighbouring park. For
years I never knew where it came from, nor where she learnt
it in her own sentimental youth. Not long ago I found it in a
book of selections. It was written by John Hamilton
Reynolds, that warm friend of poor Keats, who, as Mr. Sidney
Colvin tells us in his charming Life of the poet, never rose to
any great eminence in either literature or law, and died in
1852, as clerk of the county, at Newport, Isle of Wight. As
Mr. Colvin remarks, it is only in his association with Keats

that his name will live. Yet my mother loved the poem, which is full of the sentiment of our little home:—

Go where the water glideth gently ever,
Glideth through meadows that the greenest be;
Go, listen to our own belovèd river,
And think of me.

Wander in forests where the small flower layeth
Its fairy gem beneath the giant tree;
Listen to the dim brook pining while it playeth,
And think of me.

Watch when the sky is silver pale at even,
And the wind grieveth in the lonely tree;
Go out beneath the solitary heaven,
And think of me.

And when the moon riseth as she were dreaming,
And treadeth with white feet the lullèd sea,
Go, silent as a star beneath her beaming,
And think of me.

But enough of these old woman's recollections, and back to the present, for the sentiment of one generation is very apt to appear as worthless sentimentality to the next.

The garden I have now is a small piece of flat ground surrounding an ordinary suburban house. Kitchen-garden, flower-garden, house and drive can scarcely cover more than two acres. The garden is surrounded by large forest trees, Spanish Chestnuts and Oaks, whose wicked roots walk into all the beds almost as fast as we cut them off. The soil is dry, light and sandy, and ill-adapted to garden purposes. We are only sixteen miles from London, and on unfavourable days, when the wind is in the blighting south-east, the afternoons are darkened by the smoke of the huge city. This is an immense disadvantage to all plant life and very injurious to Roses and many other things. For five or six months in the winter I live away in London. People often envy me this, and say: 'What could you do in the garden in the winter?' But no true gardener would make this remark, as there is much to be done at all times and seasons. Half the interest of a garden is the constant exercise of the imagination. You are always living three, or indeed six, months hence. I believe that people entirely devoid of imagination never can be really good gardeners. To be content with the present, and not striving about the future, is fatal.

Living in London in the winter necessitates crowding the little greenhouse to overflowing with plants and flowers adapted for sending to London—chosen because they will bear the journey well, and live some time in water on their arrival.

January 16th—I can hardly do better to-day than tell you about my dark London room, and what I have in it as regards plant life in this the worst month of the year. I will begin with the dead and dried things that only bear the memory of the summer which is gone. At the door stand two bright-green olive-jars that came from Spain, into which are stuck large bunches of the white seed-vessels of Honesty and some flowers of Everlastings (*Helichrysum bracteatum*). These last are tied in bunches on to Bamboo sticks, to make them stand out. Inside the room, on the end of the piano, is a large dish of yellow, green, and white Gourds. I grow them because they have that peculiar quality, in common with Oranges and autumn leaves, of appearing to give out in the winter the sunlight they have absorbed in the summer. Their cultivation does not always succeed with me, as they want a better, sunnier place than I can sometimes afford to give them. In a very wet summer they fail altogether. The seeds are sold in mixed packets; we sow them at the end of April, grow them on in heat, and plant them out at quite the end of May. In fact, we treat them exactly as you would Vegetable-marrows, only we train them over a fence.

On the backs of my armchairs are thin Liberty silk oblong bags, like miniature saddle-bags, filled with dried Lavender, Sweet Verbena, and Sweet Geranium leaves. This mixture is much more fragrant than the Lavender alone. The visitor who leans back in his chair wonders from where the sweet scent comes.

On the side ledge of two large windows I have pots of the common Ivy of our hedges. We dig it up any time in the spring, and put it into the pots, which are then sunk into the ground under the shade of some wall, and kept well watered. Before bringing it into the room in winter, it is trained up on an iron stake or Bamboo-cane, singly or in bunches, to give variety to its shapes. If kept tolerably clean and watered, this Ivy is practically unkillable, even in London.

Then there are some pots of the long-suffering Aspidistras, the two kinds—variegated and dark green. These also want nothing but plenty of water, and sponging the dust off the leaves twice a week. They make pretty pot-plants if attended to during the summer in the country. They should be well thinned out and every injured leaf cut off, tied together towards the middle, kept growing all the summer in the greenhouse, and encouraged to grow tall; they are then more graceful and satisfactory. They seldom want dividing or re-potting. I have two sorts of India-rubber plants—the large-leaved, straight-growing common *ficus elastica*, and the *Ficus elastica indica*, which is a little more delicate, and the better for more heat in summer; but it has a smaller leaf, and grows in a much more charming way than the other. Keeping the leaves very clean is of paramount importance with both these plants. During the winter they want very little watering, yet should never be allowed to get quite dry, as this would make the leaves droop. If, on the other hand, you see a single yellow spot on the leaves, you may be sure that they are too damp; and, if watering is continued, the leaves will turn yellow, and eventually fall one by one. When they are growing in heat during the summer, they must be watered freely and the leaves well syringed. Both kinds propagate very easily. The top shoots strike in sand and heat; and so do single leaves, if cut out with the eye and stuck round the edge of the pot.

Another plant on the window-sill, *Phalangium liliago variegatum*, is of the same family as St. Bruno's Lily, that lovely early June flower in our gardens. It makes a most excellent pot-plant, young or old, for a room at all times of the year. It has a charming growth, and throws out branches on which young plants grow; these can be left alone, or cut off and potted up in small pots, in which case they root easily in summer, or in a little heat at other times of the year. The flower which comes on the plant in summer is quite insignificant. It is very easy of cultivation, though not quite hardy; and yet, when grown in a little heat, has all the appearance of the foliage of a delicate stove-plant.

In the middle of the room is a *Pandanus veitchii*. This must be sparingly watered. It is a delightful winter pot-plant in all its sizes. The offsets that come round the stems of the old plant root very easily in heat. It does not mind the heat of the fire, but resents frost on the window-pane. *Cocos weddeliana* and its varieties are most useful and well-known drawing-room plants, from South America. To save time, it is best to buy small plants from a nurseryman, and grow them on. They can, however, be grown from seed in a hot-bed in spring, but they are not very quick growers.

I have, wedged in Japanese vases in the Japanese way, which is so highly decorative,[1] two branches of *Physalis Alkekengi* (Winter Cherry) grown from seed. They last much longer in a room, I find, if cut, stuck into clean water, and held up by the wedge, than they do when growing in a pot; cutting the plants well back makes them a better shape, and they flower and fruit more freely the following year.

In a brass Indian vase on a corner of the chimney-piece there are some long branches of the Double Plum (*Prunus spinosa flore pleno*). These branches, with their bright green, bring spring into the room more effectively than anything I know. The little shrub is easy of cultivation, and more than most things repays potting-up and forcing. We plant them out in spring in a half-shady reserve border, and in August we cut with a spade round the roots of those plants which we intend to pot up in October. They do best if allowed to rest alternate years. The charming single *Deutzia gracilis* is treated in exactly the same way.

Never forget, in the arranging of cut flowers, that all shrubby plants and many perennials last much longer in water if the stalks are peeked. The reason is obvious: the thick bark prevents the absorption of enough water. In the case of succulent plants, splitting up the ends of the stalks is often sufficient.

---

[1] For a description of what this means I must refer you to Mr. J. Conder's interesting book (*The Flowers of Japan and the Art of Floral Arrangement*), and to a review of it reprinted at the end of this volume, by kind permission of Mr. W. Robinson, from *The Garden* (37 Southampton Street, Strand) of October 6th, 1894. My allusions to cut-flower decorations all the year round will not be understood without a careful reading of this article.

On a table below the chimney-piece is a small flower-glass filled with a pretty early greenhouse flower, orange and red, called *Chorozemia*, which does well in water. I have made a considerable study of the things that last well in water, as my greenhouse room is very limited, and it has to hold all the plants that are planted out next summer.

The usual *Primula sinensis*, Cinerarias, and many other things die before they get up to London at all. In summer the study is for the sake of my friends, as I send away flowers in large quantities, and I know nothing so disappointing as to receive in London a box of flowers, none of which are capable of reviving when put into water.

On the table, by the side of the glass mentioned above, stands a little saucer with precious, sweet-smelling Geranium leaves. These float on the water, patterning the white surface of the saucer, and supporting the delicious scented flowers, so valuable in January, of the *Chimonanthus fragrans*, with its pretty brown and yellow petals growing, as they do, on the bare branches of the shrub. My plant of *Chimonanthus* is against a wall. It flowers every year with a little care, for it is not very old, but it does not grow in our light soil with the strength and luxuriance it acquires in clay or loam. In Hertfordshire, for instance, quite long branches can be cut from it, which look very beautiful in the Japanese wedges. Our plant gets sufficiently pruned by cutting back the flowering branches. We water it thoroughly with liquid manure when the leaves, are forming in May, and mulch it with rotten manure in October. *Jasminum nudiflorum*, which also flowers well in the winter with us, we treat in the same way, only pruning out whole branches when it has done flowering in spring. No general cutting-back is desirable, as that spoils the growth of the plant for picking next year.

In separate different-sized glasses round the saucer I have a bunch of Neapolitan Violets, some Roman Hyacinths, Ivy-leaved sweet Geraniums, and an excessively pretty light-red *Amaryllis*, from bulbs sent to me this autumn straight from Mauritius, which flower well in the little stove. All these come from a small greenhouse, part of which is divided off so as to allow of its being kept at stove heat. A fortnight ago we had large bunches of *Echeveria retusa*, a most useful, easily managed, winter-flowering plant. It looks very well on the dinner-table, and lasts a long time in water. Dividing and re-potting in April, and keeping it on a sunny shelf through the summer, is almost all the care it requires. Freesias, too, are well worth growing. The success of all Cape flowering bulbs seems to depend on the attention paid to the plant while the leaves are still growing. Many gardeners, when they have cut the flowers, neglect the plants. When the leaves die down, the bulbs want well baking and drying up in full sun, laying the pots on their sides, shaking out the bulbs in June or July, sorting them, taking off the young ones, re-potting, and growing on for early forcing.

On a flower-table by the window are glasses with evergreens. I always cut with discretion my *Magnolia grandiflora*; not a very large plant either, yet I think it does it nothing but good. The clean, shiny, dark-green leaves, with their beautiful rust-red lining, are so effective in a room; and if the stalks are peeled, they last quite a month in water without deterioration. You know, I daresay, the old nursery secret of growing either wheat or canary-seed on wet moss. You fill some shallow pan or small basin with moss, and keep it quite wet. Sow your seed thickly on the moss, and put the pan away in a dark cupboard for nine or ten days. When about two inches high, bring it out and put it in a sunny window, turning it round, so as to make it grow straight. Wheat is white at the base with brave, little sword-blades of green, on which often hangs a drop of clear water. Canary-seed is red, like Rhubarb, at the bottom and green at the top.

I know nothing more charming to grow in dull town rooms or sick rooms than these two seeds. They come to perfection in about three weeks, and last for another five or six. Grown in small saucers, they make a pretty dinner-table winter decoration. Another rather effective change for a dinner-table is the leaves of Bamboos, put all day into water to prevent them curling up. They are then laid on the table-cloth in a Japanese pattern, according to the taste of the decorator, with an occasional flower to give point to the design. Double red Geraniums, late-flowering Chrysanthemums, Primulas, even clumps of Holly or red berries, all do equally well for this purpose.

Growing acorns, either suspended by a thin wire in a bottle, or planted in wet moss—five or six of them together—in flat pans, are pretty. If put into heat in October, they are in full leaf in the middle of January; but if grown in a cool room, the leaves only expand later.

I think it may be desirable for me to say something each month about cooking. Many people neglect to use things which are now so easily got with or without a garden. This foreign way of cooking Potatoes makes a nice variety:—After partially boiling them, cut the Potatoes into slices when cold, and put them into a saucepan. Cover them with milk to finish cooking them, and add fresh butter, Parsley, pepper, and salt.

Salsifys are quite easily grown, and are very good if thrown into vinegar and water, well boiled, cut into small slices, and warmed up with a white sauce in shells, like scalloped oysters. Add a little cheese and breadcrumbs, and brown in the oven.

No one who cares for vegetables and has a garden should fail to refer constantly to 'The Vegetable Garden,' already mentioned. It is an invaluable book, and the number and variety of the vegetables it describes is a revelation to those who have only the ordinary English idea of the vegetables that are worth growing.

Celeriac is an excellent vegetable, not very common in England, and, when carefully cooked, with a good brown sauce, forms a valuable contribution to the winter supply. One of the constant difficulties in the management of a house, whether large or small, where the vegetables are grown and not bought, is that the gardener brings them in, and the cook throws them away into a corner of the scullery or into the pig-tub. Only last summer a gardener from a large place in the neighbourhood said to me while walking round my small garden: 'What! you grow Cardoons? I took in beautiful ones last year, but they were never used; the cook said she didn't know how to cook them.' The following is a good receipt:—The length of time Cardoons require in cooking depends on age and size, and varies from half an hour to three or four hours. Scrape the stalks, and pull off all that is thready outside. Cut them into bits about four or five inches long, or longer if served in a long narrow dish with marrow on toast at each end. As you cut them, throw them into a basin full of water, into which you put a little flour to keep them a good colour. When all are prepared, have ready a large crockery stewpan with boiling water, herbs, a little salt and pepper, and a good-sized piece of raw bacon. The rind of the bacon should be cut in little bits, but not so small as to get mixed with the Cardoons. Boil the whole slowly, and prepare a brown sauce apart with well-flavoured stock. Thicken this with flour (burnt to a light-coffee colour), butter, and a little sherry. Let it simmer for two hours, skimming it well. Strain it half an hour before serving.

The American Cranberries, so generally and so cheaply sold in London, are very pretty and very nice if well stewed in a crockery saucepan with water and sugar; a small pinch of powdered ginger brings out their flavour. They are always eaten in America with turkeys, as we eat apple-sauce with goose. Many people do not know that turkeys are natives of

America, and that the French word *dinde* is merely a shortening of *coq d'Inde* (India being the name given to America for some time after its discovery). It is curious to think that these birds, now so common an article of food at this time of year, were totally unknown to the luxurious Romans. The Cranberries should not be mashed up, but should look like stoned cherries in syrup. They can be eaten with chicken or game, or with roast mutton instead of red-currant jelly. In Norway the small native Cranberry is eaten with any stew, especially with hares and ptarmigan. The custom of eating sweets with meat seems to come to us from Germany and the North; the French hate it.

One of the eternal trials to every housekeeper is the making of coffee. I always use half Mocha and half Plantation. When in the country, I roast the beans at home; and the two kinds must be done separately, as they are not the same size. For breakfast coffee a small quantity of ground Chicory—the best French—is a great improvement, and increases the health-giving properties of coffee and milk; but it should never be used for black coffee. The beans should, in damp weather, be warmed and dried a little before grinding; it freshens them up, as it does biscuits. One of the mysterious reasons for the flat tastelessness of coffee one day and not another is the coffee-grinder not being cleaned out; a tablespoonful of stale ground coffee will spoil the whole. Other reasons are—either the water not boiling, or the water having boiled a long time, or water that has boiled and cooled being warmed up again; this is fatal, as it is with tea. I find the modern crockery percolators a great improvement on the old tin ones, which make very good coffee for a short time; but the lining rubs off, and the tin gets black inside, which will destroy the colour of the best coffee. At Goode's in, Audley Street, or at the Atmospheric Churn Company, in Bond Street, they will sell you any portion of these percolators apart; and the most terrible of breakers can hardly smash everything at once. Many cooks refuse to use Goode's excellent crockery fireproof stewpans, on the plea that they break. But new ones cost no more than the re-tinning of copper stewpans, which has to be done every year. For all stews, and for the cooking of vegetables and fruit, they are invaluable-and in the case of fruit, indispensable.

January 18*th*—One excellent way of arranging flowers in most rooms is to have a table, a kind of altar especially dedicated to them. This does the flowers or plants much more justice than dotting them about the room. If, however, flowers or branches are arranged in vases in the Japanese style, the more they are isolated in prominent places that show them off, the better.

I am now staying with a friend who has no stove, only one greenhouse; and her flower-table, standing in the window, looks charming. At the back are two tall glass vases with Pampas grass in them, feathery and white as we never can keep it in London; a small Eucalyptus-tree in a pot, cut back in summer and well shaped; a fine pot of Arums, just coming into flower; a small fern in front, and a bunch of paper-white Narcissus. These last I fear, must have been grown elsewhere, as they could not be so early here without heat and very careful growing-on.

January 20*th*—I came from London, to pass two or three days in the country and look after my garden as usual. I make lists and decide on the seeds for the year, and look to the mulching of certain plants. Hardly anything grows here to perfection when left alone. Most plants require either chalk, peat, leaf-mould or cow-manure, and half-tender things are now the better for covering up with matting or Bracken-fern. It is seldom of any use to come so early as this; but there has been no cold this year, though one feels it must come. Oh! such days and days of gloom and darkness; but to-day the wind freshened from the northeast, and I could breathe once more. How delightful it is to be out of London again! There is always plenty to do and to enjoy. How the birds sing, as if it were spring! I love the country in winter; one expects nothing, and everything is a joy and a surprise. The Freesias are flowering well; they improve each year as the bulbs get larger. Cyclamens are in the greenhouse, and a large, never-failing, old white Azalea, which forces faithfully and uncomplainingly every year, and from which we cut so many blooms.

The first Aconite! Does any flower in summer give the same pleasure? The blue-green blades of the Daffodils and Jonquils are firmly and strongly pushing through the cold brown earth; nothing in all the year gives such a sense of power and joy. One is grateful, too, for our Surrey soil and climate—to live where it never can rain too much, and where it never accords with Shelley's wonderful description of damp:—

And hour by hour, when the air was still,
The vapours arose which have strength to kill.
At morn they were seen, at noon they were felt,
At night they were darkness no star could melt.

These mild winters have a wonderful effect on plant life. The *Solanum jasminoides* looks as fresh as in November, and as if he meant to stand it out; we shall see. In front of my window, on the ground floor, I have been rigging up a delightful arrangement for feeding Tomtits. I hang half a pound of suet and a cocoanut [coconut] on either end of a piece of thick string. This should be long enough to reach the lower window when suspended from a small iron rod by a ring hanging at the end of it, the rod being nailed to the window-sill above. The string is passed through the top of the cocoanut, of which the bottom is cut off, making a hole large enough for a bird to get in. It greatly adds to the artistic effect to hang the cocoanut about a foot lower than the suet, or *vice versa*. The small birds cling to the string while they peck their food, and so make a continual and beautiful design. To help them to cling, a few little crossbars of wood are knotted into the string and form a sort of rough ladder. In really cold weather, or with snow on the ground, they become wonderfully tame. Another way is to plant a post in the ground with one or two cross-bars nailed to the top, on which are hung similar arrangements to those just described of cocoanut and suet, or an old bone.

This warm winter has suited the Christmas Roses, which are uncommonly good. The great secret in light soils is to mulch them well while they are making their leaves. Water them with liquid manure when their flower-buds are forming, and protect them with lights in the flowering season, especially keeping them from heavy rains or snow. For these reasons grow them in a bed by themselves

In the greenhouse I found a *Choisya ternata*, which I had cut back hard last May, covered all over with its beautiful white flowers. It had been forced in the stove for about ten days. This is a most delightful plant in every way, easy to strike and to layer, quite hardy; though, when growing outside, the flowers are sometimes a little injured by hard late frosts. It is invaluable for cutting to send to London at all times of year, as it lasts for a long time in water, and the shiny dark-green leaves look especially well with any white flowers. The more it is cut, the better the plant flourishes. Every spare piece of wall should have a plant of *Choisya* against it. It is restrained and yet free in its growth, and is therefore even more useful in small gardens than in large ones. It does very well in light soil, but responds to a little feeding. I have some giant Violets which I got from the South of France; here, I believe, they are called 'Princess Beatrice.' They are twice the size of Czars, and very sweet. They are doing well in the frame, but look rather draggled and miserable outside; after all, it is only the end of January.

In mid-winter my heart warms to the common Laurels. In wet winters, especially, they look so flourishing and happy, and they will grow in such bad places. I am sure I shall abuse them so often that I must say, however much they are reduced in a garden, keep some plants in places where few other things would flourish. They will always remain a typical example of Mme. de Stael's good description of evergreens:— 'Le deuil de l'été et l'ornement de l'hiver.' All hardy fruit-trees, like *Jasminum nudiflorum* and *Chimonanthus fragrans*, are better pruned in January than in February, if the weather make it possible.

January 22nd—I take back to London with me today, amongst other things, some *Lachenalia aurea*. All Lachenalias are worth growing. They are little Cape bulbs, which have to be treated like the Freesias, watered as long as the leaves are green, and then dried. They all force well, and *L. aurea* flowers earlier than the other Lachenalias, and is very pretty and effective. This variety has the great merit of being a true yellow by candle-light.

Walking along the streets to-day, I stopped to look at a really beautiful large cross, entirely composed of moss, dotted all over with the lovely little early single Snowdrops. Although I have the strongest objection to the modern use of flowers for the dead, natural and lovable as was the original idea, I had to admire this specimen. Could a more beautiful winter memorial for a young girl be seen, or one which better carries out in these cold days the idea of the French poet Malherbe?

Elle était du monde où les plus belles choses
Ont le pire destin;
Et rose, elle a vécu ce que vivent les roses—
L'espace d'un matin.

The French have carried the abuse of this fashion of funeral wreaths and crosses to an even greater extent than we have here. I shall never forget once in Paris going up to the Père-Lachaise cemetery on a fine morning to visit the grave of a young and much-lamented woman. The wreaths were so numerous that they had to be taken up in a cart the day before. The night had been wet, and the surroundings of the grave were a mass of unapproachable corruption and decay.

Last April, when I was at Kew, the gardener there shook into my pocket-handkerchief a little seed of *Cineraria cruenta*, the type-plant from the Cape, and the origin of all the Cinerarias of our greenhouses. It has a very different and much taller growth than the cultivated ones, and I am most anxious to see if it will do in water, which the ordinary ones do not. It varies in shade from pale to deep lilac, rather like a Michaelmas Daisy. Getting seeds from abroad of type-plants is very interesting gardening. Pelargoniums of all kinds are weeds at the Cape, and, in order to be able to resist the long droughts, they have, in South Africa, tuberous roots like Dahlias. This is well seen in Andrews' 'Botanist's Repository,' which I shall mention among the March books. Pelargoniums, under cultivation and with much watering, no longer require these tubers, and they disappear. Seed was sent to me from some of the wild plants at the Cape, and even the first year, as the plants grew, there were the little tubers, quite marked and distinct.

January 31st—With the high temperature we have had this year, one is apt to forget the horrors of a severe winter, till reminded just lately by two very cold nights. The frosted windows of my bedroom made me think of a charming little poem which appeared last year in the *Pall Mall Gazette* at the time of the very cold weather:—

JOHN FROST

The door was shut, as doors should be,
Before you went to bed last night,
Yet John Frost has got in, you see,
And left your windows silver white.

He must have waited till you slept,
And not a single word he spoke,
But pencill'd o'er the panes and crept
Away again before you woke.

And now you cannot see the trees
Nor fields that stretch beyond the lane;
But there are fairer things than these
His fingers traced on every pane.

Rocks and castles towering high,
Hills and dales, and streams and fields,
And knights in armour riding by
With plumes and spears and shining shields.

And here are little boats, and there
Big ships with sails spread to the breeze
And yonder palm-trees, waving fair
On islands set in silver seas.

And butterflies with gauzy wings,
And birds and bees, and cows and sheep,
And fruit and flowers, and all the things
You see when you are sound asleep.

For, creeping softly underneath
The door when all the lights are out,
John Frost takes every breath you breathe,
And knows the things you think about.

He paints them on the window-pane,
In fairy lines, with frozen steam;
And when you wake, you see again
The wondrous things you saw in dream.

Londoners have the great advantage, in hard frosts, of being able to enjoy these frozen pictures, for nowhere can they be seen to such perfection as on the large window-panes of cold empty shops. Many people must have remarked this last winter.

keen gardeners ought to belong to this society—partly as an encouragement to it, and also because the subscriber of even one guinea a year gets a great many advantages. He can go to these fortnightly exhibitions, as well as to the great show at the Temple Gardens in May, free, before the public is admitted. He has the run of the society's library in Victoria Street; he receives free the yearly publications, which are a series of most interesting lectures (I will give some account of them at the end of the year); and he is annually presented with a certain number of plants. These fortnightly meetings at the Drill Hall are instructive and varied, though they might be much more so. Nevertheless, I think an amateur cannot go to them without learning something, and I am surprised to find how few people take advantage of them. The entrance fee is only a shilling. I went to one of these exhibitions the other day. The great mass of blooms shown consisted of beautifully grown potfuls of Cyclamens in great variety of colour, and of Chinese Primulas; these last, to my mind, are rather uninteresting plants, but they show great improvement in colour as now cultivated. What pleased me most were miniature Irises, grown in flat pans, and some charming spring Snowflakes (*Leucojum vernum*) grown in pots. These are far more satisfactory grown in this way than are the finest Snowdrops in pots, their foliage being so much prettier. The little blue Scillas are extremely effective grown in pans through a carpet of the ordinary mossy Saxifrage.

February 14th—Salads are rather a difficulty during the early spring in English gardens. In seasonless London everything is always to be bought. I wonder why *Mâche* (Corn Salad, or Lamb's Lettuce), so much grown in France, is so little cultivated here? People fairly well up in gardening come back from France in the winter, thinking they have discovered something new. *Mâche* is a little difficult to grow in very light soils, and the safest plan is to make several sowings in July and August. We find it most useful, but, without constant reminding, no English gardener thinks of it at all, though it is in all the seed catalogues. As it is an annual, without sowing you naturally don't get it; and if sown too late, it is bound to fail. In very dry weather we have to water it at first.

If Beetroot is carelessly dug up and the roots broken, they bleed, which causes them to come to the table pale and tasteless. This is the fault of the gardener, not of the cook. Some English cooks boil them in vinegar; this hardens them, and makes them unwholesome. They are much better slowly baked in an oven, and not boiled at all. The poor Beetroot is often considered unwholesome, but if it is served with a little of the water it is boiled in, or if baked with a little warm water poured over it, a squeeze of lemon instead of vinegar, and a little oil added, I think the accusation is unjust. Beetroot served hot and cut in slices, with a white Béchamel sauce (*see* 'Dainty Dishes'), makes a very good winter vegetable. The Old English dish of Beetroot sliced and laid round a soup-plate with pulled Celery, mixed with a Mayonnaise sauce, built up in the middle, is excellent with all roast meats.

At all the best Italian grocers' in London they sell a dried Green Pea from Italy, which makes a pretty purée both as a vegetable and as a soup in winter, especially if coloured with a very little fresh Spinach, not the colouring sold by grocers. The Peas must be soaked all night, then well boiled, rubbed smooth through a sieve, and a little cream and butter added. A nicer winter vegetable cannot be. It is really made exactly like the old pease-pudding served with pork, only not nearly so dry.

Imantophilums are one of the most effective and beautiful of our greenhouse plants at this time of the year, and last very well in water. We kept ours out of doors in an open pit all through last summer. As they threw up several flower-spikes, which we picked off, we feared that they might not do so well this spring; instead of which, I think they have never done better or flowered more freely. A little liquid manure helps them when in flower. Though a Cape plant, the leaves do not die down; and so it must be kept growing, or the foliage is injured.

February 27th—I have lately evolved a good spring vegetable dish. The common green Turnip-tops, which are wholesome, but not palatable if plainly boiled, are delicious when treated like the French puree of Spinach (*see* 'Dainty Dishes'), rubbed through a sieve, and mixed with butter and cream. They are a beautiful bright green. In the country young Nettles done in the same way are very good, but they must be fresh—a state in which they are not to be had in large towns. I have been told how curious it is that nettles never grow in absolutely wild places, but are only to be found in localities more or less haunted by man.

I think Rhubarb, which is so largely grown and eaten in England, both forced and out of doors, is never used on the Continent. I wonder if this is because it does not stand the severe frosts of the mid-Europe winters. We dig up plants and put them into boxes, and force them under the frames of our greenhouse. For later eating, we also cover it in the garden, as everybody does, with pots surrounded by leaves. I do not think that the ordinary English tart is the best way of cooking Rhubarb, unless done in the following manner:— When young and tender, cut it up into pieces the length of a finger, and throw them into cold water, to prevent the ends drying, while a syrup is prepared in an earthenware saucepan with sugar, a few of the rough pieces of the Rhubarb, and a small pinch of ginger. Throw the cold water away from the Rhubarb, strain the syrup, boil it up, and pour it over the pieces. Stew it for a very short time till tender without mashing it up. It looks better if the pieces are slightly arranged in the dish. If anything iron touches the Rhubarb or the syrup, they turn purple and look horrid. Properly cooked, Rhubarb should be of a pretty pink or green colour. Many doctors forbid it. I think it probably may be unwholesome for meat-eating people; this is the case with so many fruits and vegetables.

All my tarts throughout the year are made with the crust baked apart, and the fruit, stewed previously, juicy and cold. Shortly before dinner make the paste called in 'Dainty Dishes' 'crisp paste' for tarts; crumple up kitchen paper into a mound the height you wish your crust to be, place it in the pie-dish—the round-shaped dishes are the prettiest—cover this with a clean sheet of buttered paper, lay your paste over this, bake in the usual way. When done, lift off the crust, take out the paper, pour in the fruit (which can be iced, if desired), put a little raw white of egg round the rim of the pie-dish, and replace the crust. In this way an orange or a strawberry tart can be made without cooking the fruit at all, except in the usual compote way of pouring boiling syrup over it.

Towards the end of February is the best time for making Orange Marmalade (*see* 'Dainty Dishes'), as the Seville oranges in London are then at their best. In all cases when old jam pots, glasses, &c., are used for preserving, it is very desirable to wash them thoroughly in clean water, avoiding all soda or soap, and, when dry, powder them with a little sulphur and wipe clean. If soda is used in anything connected with fruit, it has an injurious chemical action.

The following are the translations of a few careful receipts which were written out by a very excellent French *chef*. They belong to so entirely different a *cuisine* from our ordinary modest and economical receipts, that I think they may be not without interest to some people. It is worth noting how, when a really good French cook wishes to instruct, he is careful to go into the minutest details.

Pot au feu Soup—Proportions: 15 lbs. of beef, 5½ 1bs. of veal, 1 chicken, 2½ gallons of water, 3 fine carrots, 1 big turnip, 1 large onion, a bunch of parsley, half a head of celery, a parsnip, 2 cloves, and some salt.

Remove the fat and tie up the beef and the veal, putting them in a large saucepan; fill the saucepan with cold water to within a little more than an inch from the brim, place the saucepan on the fire with the lid off, add some salt, and let it boil till the scum shows on the surface; remove it with a skimmer. As soon as it seems inclined to boil over, add a few spoonfuls of cold water, so as to make the scum accumulate as much as possible. When at last it boils violently, drop in the vegetables; remove the saucepan to one side of the fire, so that it shall boil only on one side; put on the lid, and let it boil undisturbed, evenly and regularly. After two hours remove the veal. An hour later add the chicken, and, three hours after, strain the soup, without stirring it up, through a strainer on to a napkin stretched over a receptacle large enough to contain the soup. The soup may be skimmed before or after straining.

This stock does for making any kind of soup, Julienne, Brunoise, Croûte au pot, and for all purées of vegetables.

Consommé—Consommé means the foundation of the soup; this foundation ought always to be clear, lightly coloured, and, above all, strong.

Take about 2 lbs. of beef and veal, without fat, chop them up together, and put into a basin. Add half of the white of an egg, work the meats with a wooden spoon and a glass of water, continue to mix with about 1¼ gallon of good strong stock; put the whole into a small saucepan with some carcases of birds (raw or cooked), a branch of celery, and put it to boil on the fire; stir it when there with a wooden spoon, so that the meat shall not stick to the bottom. As soon as it bubbles, remove the saucepan to a very slow, very moderate, well-regulated fire for two hours. The stock, made in this way, ought to become a fine colour, and above all be very clear. Strain it through a napkin that has been previously rinsed in hot water.

Julienne Soup—Ingredients: 3 fine carrots, 2 turnips, 2 small pieces of celery, 2 sprigs of parsley, 1 onion, the quarter of a large Savoy cabbage, the hearts of 2 lettuces, a bunch of sorrel, and a sprig of chervil.

Scrape each of the vegetables according to its requirements. The carrots are cut, in the thickest parts of them, in transverse sections, about two-thirds of an inch thick; shape these into thin, even ribbons by turning the piece round and round till you reach the centre of the carrot, which is not used; then cut these ribbons again into very fine shreds. Cut the turnips into squares; divide them into oblong squares about two-thirds of an inch thick; cut and make them into shreds like the carrots. Gut and shape the celery in the same way. Remove the hard sides of the cabbage, and slice it as fine as possible. Slice in the same way the lettuces, parsley, and onions. The similarity of the vegetables, as much with regard to their thickness as to their length, must be strictly preserved; it is one of the distinguishing characteristics of this soup. Now put a lump of butter into a good saucepan, rather a large one and very thick at the bottom. Add the vegetables, all except the cabbage and the sorrel; these must be scalded in boiling water apart. Place the other vegetables on a slow fire till they turn a fine yellow colour without being burnt; that is the chief characteristic of the soup. As soon as they are done to a turn, add about 2 quarts of good stock or consommé, and a pinch of sugar. When it bubbles, remove to side of fire; add the sorrel and cabbage, after drying them, through a strainer or sieve. The bubbles should only appear on one side. Skim, and, while on the fire, remove the grease as it forms. Let it boil for an hour, if the vegetables are tender; if not, for longer.

Consommé aux Ailerons (*Wing-bone Soup*)—Cut up the whole of 3 or 4 carrots and 2 turnips into slices of about the thickness of a shilling. Cut in rounds of the same thickness, and shaped in the same column-shape, some cabbage leaves—very white ones. This done, wet the carrots first with about 2 pints of stock (consommé). After it has boiled for an hour, add the turnips and cabbage. Let it boil quite gently by the side of the fire for a good hour, till the vegetables are quite cooked.

Separately take 12 or 15 wing-bones of chickens, basted and well trimmed; let them soak during 1 or 2 hours in tepid water, drain and put them into a small saucepan, cover them with stock, and boil up. One hour is enough to cook them. Drain the wings, trim them very neatly, bone them, put them in the soup-tureen, add some fried crusts of bread of the same thickness as the vegetables, also a bunch of chervil and a pinch of sugar, and put all together into the soup-tureen. The boiling of all these vegetables must be done quite slowly, so as to prevent the stock being disturbed.

Gnocchi à la Crème—Make a paste (pâte à choux) as follows:—Ingredients: 4½ oz. of flour, 4½ oz. of butter, 1½ pint of water, 3 whole eggs (4 if small), a pinch of salt and of sugar. Put the water, salt, and sugar in a small saucepan on the fire; when it begins to boil, add the flour all at once. Stir quickly with a wooden spoon, and, when well mixed, put the saucepan on a slower fire; let it dry for a few minutes, and when smooth mix in the eggs, one by one, till smooth and thick, sticking to the saucepan. If the paste seems a little too dry, add a little cream—2 or 3 spoonfuls. Add by degrees 3 or 4 spoonfuls of grated Parmesan cheese. Take a smaller saucepan of water with some salt in it. When the water is boiling, remove it to the edge of the fire. Then take two tablespoons, and fill one with the paste, flattening it with a knife warmed in warm water so as to form the paste into an oval shape; warm the other spoon, and push it under the quenelle to remove it from the first spoon; then drop it into the boiling water. When all the quenelles are shaped in this way and thrown into the saucepan, put it on to the open fire, and let the quenelles poach for some minutes. As soon as they feel firm to the touch, remove the Gnocchi one by one with a strainer, and place them on a cloth till wanted. Make a Béchamel white sauce. Butter a soufflé-dish, place the quenelles round the bottom, in a single row one beside the other, sprinkle this first row with a little grated Parmesan, and add on the top another layer of Gnocchis, laid on alternately to the others. Hide the Gnocchis entirely with the sauce Béchamel, dust them over with a little grated Gruyère, sprinkle them lightly with some melted butter, and put them to bake in a slow oven till well browned without being burnt. Given about forty to forty-five minutes of baking, the Gnocchi should swell to twice their original size. Serve at once.

Béchamel Sauce—Cut into little squares the half of a carrot and a small onion; take a small saucepan, put in a good bit of butter, add the vegetables, fry them lightly without letting them brown. This done, add a good tablespoonful of flour, and let the flour cook quite gently for several minutes on a moderate fire; be especially careful that it does not stick or get coloured, which would quite spoil its quality. This done, let it cool for a moment, then add little by little one pint and a half of boiling milk; work and stir the sauce without ceasing until it boils, remove to side of a slow fire, and let it cook for an hour. Strain the sauce through a flannel or muslin into a bain-marie, with a pinch of salt, and of grated nutmeg very little. Add a good bit of butter while working it with a small egg-whisk. The sauce should be very smooth, creamy, and of a good flavour; if by chance it is too thick, this can be remedied by adding a few spoonfuls of good, thick, and sweet cream.

Pâte à Ravioli—Ingredients for the paste : 9 oz. of flour, the yelks of 4 eggs, a pinch of salt, a little tepid water.

Put the flour on a marble slab, make a hole in the centre, add the yelks of the eggs and the salt, make a paste, not too solid; when it is quite even, let it rest for an hour or two, and cover it with a cloth to prevent it from getting dry.

Preparation for Ravioli—Forcemeat of chicken, or, failing this, one can use veal, if nice and white and tender. Ingredients: 4½ oz. of meat, 2¼ oz. of panade, ¼ oz. of fresh butter, 2 yelks of eggs, salt, and nutmeg.

Remove the sinews and fat carefully from the 4½ oz. of meat. Cut it into little squares, and pound well in a mortar. Add the panade little by little; when mixed, add (only a little at a time) the butter when quite cooled and solid, salt, and nutmeg; mix these ingredients thoroughly, giving to them as much consistency as possible. Now take some boiling salted water in a little saucepan, and test in it a little bit of the forcemeat the size of a walnut; let it poach while well on the fire. If it is rather too firm, one can always add a spoonful of Béchamel or a little thick cream to moisten it.

Parboil in water 1 lb. of spinach, strain it on to a moistened sieve—the sieve must have been well wiped to ensure no water remaining in it. Pass the spinach through a fine wire sieve. This done, add to the forcemeat two or three dessert spoonfuls of spinach, as much grated Parmesan cheese, some salt, pepper, and nutmeg, and a pinch of sugar. Mix all these well together.

Now divide the paste into two equal parts; roll one part out as thin as possible with a roller, keeping it square in shape; slightly moisten the surface with a brush, put some of the forcemeat in a linen jelly-bag with a narrow tin socket at the bottom, and drop little balls of the forcemeat all over the surface, in straight lines about 2 in. to 2½ in. apart from each other. When the whole is covered, roll out the remainder of the paste to exactly the same size and shape, and place it carefully on the top of the other so as to fit exactly; press down round each Ravioli with a small shaping-tin, so as to stick the two layers of paste together; cut each Ravioli into rounds, and arrange them on a small lid of a saucepan floured over so that the paste should not stick to it.

Have ready a sauté-pan with some boiling water and salt in it. Five minutes before serving, drop the Ravioli into the water. As soon as they bubble up, remove to side of fire to finish cooking, strain them onto a sieve, from there into a sauté-pan (fairly large), powder them over with a little grated Parmesan, throw on the Béchamel sauce, which should be very smooth and not too thick; finally, add a good-sized piece of fresh butter and a chip of Paplika. Stir quite gently, so as not to spoil the Ravioli, and serve them in a casserole or in a crust of pastry.

Panade for the Forcemeat—Put about a gill of water in a saucepan, with a bit of butter the size of a walnut. Put the saucepan on the fire; as soon as it boils up, add one tablespoonful and a half of flour; work the mixture at the side of the fire. This paste should be of a good, rather firm, consistency. Put it on to a rather flat dish. Butter the surface lightly, to keep it from drying, and put it to cool.

Mousse de Volaille—Take off the fillets, &c., of three chickens, cut them up into little dice, pound them into a mortar, and reduce them to a paste; this done, pass them first through a wire sieve, and afterwards through a hair sieve or a quenelle sieve. Put this meat into a moderate-sized basin, and stand it in a cool place till wanted. Remove the legs from the carcases of the chickens (these may be used for something else), wash the carcases in cold water, and let them soak for an hour.

Now take 1½ lb. of lean veal, mince it up rather fine, put it in a saucepan which will hold about three quarts of liquid, add the half of one white of egg; mix all together, add two pints of water and nearly a quart of stock, one chopped onion, one carrot, a little celery, and the carcasses; boil up on a quick fire, stirring from time to time with a wooden spoon. As soon as it boils, remove to side of fire, so that it should only boil on one side, and quite slowly, removing the grease from time to time. Let it boil for three hours. Strain the foundation through a well-rinsed cloth. The above is the foundation for the Sauce Supreme.

Sauce Supreme—This sauce requires great care in making. Put in a saucepan 4½ oz. of butter and 3½ oz. of flour. Put the saucepan on a slow fire, and let the flour cook lightly without getting coloured. As soon as the flour is cooked, dilute it with the foundation of chicken, little by little, stirring all the time with a wooden spoon. So as to be able to spread it out without lumps, keep it much lighter than ordinary sauces. Stir it all the time till it boils; when remove it to side of fire so that it should but just boil, and that only on one side. Add two or three raw chopped mushrooms; as the butter and steam rise gently to the surface, remove them, and let it cook for a good hour. Afterwards strain your sauce through a fine cullender into a frying-pan, more wide than deep. Put it on a hot fire, and stir without stopping with a wooden spoon to prevent it sticking; this is an important point. Add one or two gills of good sweet cream. As soon as the sauce sticks to the spoon, that means it is ready. Strain it through a muslin in a little bain-marie; stand the sauce to heat in a saucepan with hot water in it.

Now put the half of a white of raw egg with the chicken, mix them well together, add little by little some good thick fresh cream, and make it blend as much as possible; add three or four spoonfuls of cold Sauce Supreme, and about three gills of thick cream. Test it by dropping a little of the mixture into water. It should be soft, not too solid, and well-flavoured. Always try it before putting in all the cream, or it might become too limp, which would spoil its quality.

Butter the inside of a round cylinder-shaped mould with a hole in the centre of it. Put the mould on the ice for a moment to harden the butter. Fill the mould with the mixture up to about an inch from the rim. Tap the mould gently on a napkin folded several times to equalise the mixture and to heap it together, to prevent the holes which might form themselves inside the sponge.

Put a little boiling water in a saucepan large enough to contain your mould, cover it with a lid, put it in a very slow oven, and let it poach for twenty-five to thirty minutes. See that the water in the saucepan does not boil, for which it is necessary from time to time to add a drop of cold water. Turn out the mould onto an entree-dish; trim with one or two truffles cooked in Madeira. Cover the mould lightly with a little of the Sauce Supreme, and put the rest of the sauce in a sauce-boat.

Mousse de Foies Gras à la Gelée—Take a cylinder-shaped mould with an opening in the centre, put the mould for a second or two onto the ice. This done, pour into it a glassful of meat jelly, cold without being frozen. Turn your mould on the ice so as to line it—that is to say, to make the jelly adhere to the inside of the mould in a thin layer. Replace the mould onto the ice till wanted.

Put into a saucepan or a bain-marie well cleaned out about three gills of good cream, thick and sweet, stand it on the ice for several hours; when about to use it, beat it up with an egg-whisk for seven or eight minutes, without taking it off the ice. It should rise and become firm, like the white of an egg. Put it to strain through a fine strainer.

Pound in a mortar a cooked foie-gras of from 1 lb. 3 oz. to

1 lb. 5 oz. in weight. Pass the foie-gras through a fine hair-sieve. Pound with the foie-gras 4¾ oz. of fresh butter, put it into a basin, and work it with an egg-whisk or wooden spoon, and absorb into it gradually three or four spoonfuls of Sauce Suprême, add a wineglassful of rather firm meat jelly. The jelly should be tepid and added quite gradually, working it in all the time so as to make it quite smooth and soft. Season with salt, pepper, and nutmeg. If it is winter, work it in a warm place to prevent its turning, add the whipped cream quickly, and fill up the mould to the rim. Put the mould into a good, sized jar, and cover it well with pounded ice, and surround the mould with it. Leave it in the ice for two hours or more, according to the season, and especially in summer. When ready to serve, have a basin filled with hot water, dip the mould into it so as to be entirely covered, that it may come away clearly from the mould. Trim with pieces of jelly.

Nouilles Fraîches (*Fresh Nouille Paste*)—The paste for Nouille is made in exactly the same way as for Ravioli, only it must be kept much firmer. Roll it out very thin with a roller, and flour it well, so as not to stick. Cut some strips about 3 in. wide, put several of them one on the top of the other, and slice them with a knife into very narrow strips, 1/10th of an inch wide or less. Spread them out onto a floured plate and cover them with a cloth. When ready to use them, throw them into a saucepan of boiling water with salt in it; after boiling for two or three moments put the saucepan on the side of the fire, stirring a little. Let the paste cook for some minutes, then strain them well, put them back in the same saucepan, add a good bit of fresh butter (about 4½ oz. to 5 oz.), three or four spoonfuls of grated Parmesan, salt, nutmeg, a pinch of sugar, and one of Paplika, a little veal-stock or meat gravy, mix all well together, and serve in a casserole.

Céleris en branches, demi-glacés—Pick and peel very carefully six or eight heads of celery, according to their size.

Bleach them for fifteen or twenty minutes in boiling water, dip them in cold water to cool them, strain them onto a cloth, cut them in two if they are large, fasten them—that is, re-form the Celery by tying it together with a little string at each end. Put them into a saucepan with an onion, one carrot, and a little bunch of herbs—parsley, thyme, bay. Fill up to the brim with half stock and half fat—dripping. Boil it up, then let it cook quite gently by the side of a slow fire or in the oven. They ought to be just done to a turn after three or four hours. Strain them onto a cloth, cut them to equal sizes, remove the outside leaves, if they are hard, serve in a silver casserole, and sauce them over with a good half-glaze or a good veal gravy a little thickened.

Lettuce can be treated in the same way.

MARCH

Slow-growing hardy shrubs—The Swanley Horticultural College—
Gardening as an employment for women—Aucubas berries—Planting
Asparagus—Brussels Sprouts—Sowing annuals—A list of flowering
creepers—'The Poet in the City'—Old illustrated gardening books.

March 2nd—Of all the low-growing quite hardy shrubs,
especially in small gardens, nothing is more useful for picking
and arranging with all kinds of flowers than the common
Box. The kinds vary a little, some being larger-leaved than
others, and the growth of some plants a little more graceful
and branching. The most desirable kinds can quite easily be
propagated by cuttings stuck into the ground in a shady place
in spring. Its depressing characteristic for beginners is that
Box is very slow-growing. Next to this in utility comes the
common Barberry, or *Berberis vulgaris*, as we ought to call it,
which is so well known to everybody now, as it is sold in the
streets of London all through the winter months with its
leaves dyed a dull-red colour. How this is managed I do not
know; I think it spoils the beautiful foliage by making it all

of one tone. With us it turns brown in severe winters, with an occasional red leaf, but in damp soils it gets much redder. Berberis is one of those things much sown about by the birds, for they eat its pretty purple berries in quantities. The young seedlings which come up with us in the beds and shrubberies are easily moved when quite young, and can be put where they are wanted to grow. The best time to move them is wet weather in July or August. They are plants with a perfect growth and exceedingly well adapted to waste places in gardens and the fronts of shrubberies. Spring bulbs will grow through them, and their yellow flowers and dark leaves arrange admirably with the common Daffodil in glass vases. They can also take the place of the picked Arum leaves, which always droop before the flowers when put into water. Out of the little stove, all the winter through, I have long branches of the *Asparagus plumosa*. When cut, it is much more effective if trained up a light branching stick or feathery bamboo. This gives it support, and it is astonishing how long it lasts in water. It is extremely decorative, and will produce a most excellent effect if arranged in the above manner with only one bright flower added at its base.

March 8th—To-day there has come up from the country one of the spring gems of the year, a large bunch of the lilac Daphne, the old *Mezereum*. It is a small shrub, not a quick grower, and most people, especially gardeners, are afraid to cut it. But if this is done bravely at the time of flowering, I think it only grows stronger and flowers better the following year, and you get the benefit of the exceedingly fragrant blossoms. For a few hours the whole of a London house smells sweeter for its presence. Its perfume is peculiar and not quite like anything else I know. The common lilac sort alone seems easy to grow—at least, the white one I have tried has died; but then one must always say in gardening, 'That is probably my fault; I must try again.' No garden, however small, ought to be without this plant. It likes peat and moisture, but is not particular.

Yesterday I paid a visit to the Horticultural College at Swanley, with its branch for women students. It immediately struck me as quite possible that a new employment may be developed for women of small means out of the modern increased taste for gardening. In many of the suburban districts the dullness of the small plots of ground in front of the houses is entirely owing to the want of education in the neighbouring nurserymen, whose first idea is always to plant Laurels or other coarse shrubs. The owners of such villas have little time to attend to the garden themselves. A lady gardener might easily undertake to lay out these plots in endless variety, supplying them throughout the year with flowers and plants suited to the aspect of each garden. The smaller the space, the more necessary the knowledge of what is likely to succeed. Another opening may be found in cases of larger villas, where single ladies might prefer a woman head-gardener, with a man under her, to do the rougher and heavier work. The maintaining of a garden and the tending of a greenhouse is work particularly suited to women of a certain age. A small greenhouse never can be productive of flowers for picking through the dull months without a great deal of thought, care, and knowledge. It seemed to me that the lady pupils at Swanley were too young to profit by the instruction. The parents who sent them there evidently looked upon it as an ordinary school. Surely eighteen or twenty is a better age than sixteen for a woman to know whether she really wishes to learn gardening professionally or not. The employment of women as gardeners is still very much in embryo, although two of the Swanley pupils have been accepted at Kew.

March 10th—The Aucubas fruit well with us, and a branch of their bright shining green leaves and coral berries looks exceedingly well in a Japanese wedge and lasts a long time. We plant the male and female plants close together, but I am not sure that that is necessary.

March 12th—Asparagus should be planted now, and, to save time, it is best to get two-year-old plants from France. I recommend Godfroy le Bœuf, Horticulteur, Argenteuil, près Paris. Dig the ground three spits deep—that is, the depth of three spades—and put in everything you can that is good: well-rotted farm-manure, the emptying of cesspools, butchers' offal, dead animals, anything to enrich the soil for a long time. Cover up, cut out one spit deep in trenches, and plant the Asparagus a good way apart in single crowns. They do best planted in single rows with other crops in between. The goodness of Asparagus depends on the summer top-growth, so, if the weather is dry, they must be watered or liquid-manured, and should never be cut down till late in the autumn.

It is a great mistake, when marking the nurseryman's seed list, to order the vegetable described as 'giant,' 'large,' 'perfection,' etc. Unless your soil is very strong such vegetables do not grow large, and they do grow tough and tasteless. This 'giant' cultivation has been brought about to win prizes at shows. Amongst the delicious vegetables that have been ruined by growing them too large are Brussels Sprouts. I consider those sold in the London shops are not worth eating, they are so coarse; but one can get the seeds of old-fashioned small kinds. These are far sweeter, nicer, and prettier, either for putting into soup, for boiling and frying afterwards in butter, or for boiling quite plainly in the ordinary English way. They are also far more delicate for a purée, which is an excellent way of dressing them. If fried and put on buttered toast, they make a very nice second-course vegetable in winter.

Do other housekeepers ever wonder why we are condemned invariably to eat Whitings with their tails in their mouths and always skinned? One of the reasons is that small Haddocks are constantly sold by fishmongers for the rarer Whiting; and if skinned, they are not so easy to recognise. Try Whitings sometimes as they are eaten in Paris—lay them flat, not curled nor skinned, and cook them in a deep dish with butter or parsley. Squeeze lemon into them, and serve with brown bread and butter. They can also be fried in the usual way, only not curled. I think your male kind will approve of the change.

March 15th—I find that this is the best time for sowing annuals that have to be sown in place. If sown later, they never do so well. Poppies, Love-in-the-Mist, Mignonette, Sweet Sultans, *Bartonia aurea*, etc. This latter is a very effective annual. It must be sown in a large clump and well thinned out, which is the secret of most annuals. Twice a year, about March 15th and September 15th, I sow together broadcast Love-in-the-Mist and *Gypsophila gracilis*. They seem to support each other, and fixing a day for the sowing prevents one from forgetting.

In the old convent gardens Calvary Clover was supposed not to grow unless sown on Good Friday. It is a curious little annual, with a blood-red spot on each leaf, and the seed-pod is surrounded by a case which pulls out, or rather unwinds, into a miniature crown of thorns.

A friend has asked me what she should plant on the front of a lovely old house facing south. It now has on it at one end Ivy and on the other an old Wistaria. My first advice is take away the Ivy; the place is too good for it, and it hides the beautiful old brickwork. An old Wistaria is quite lovely if part or all of it is dragged away from the house and trained over wooden posts, either in front of a window or a door, so as to form a kind of pergola. Until this is done, or it is grown as they do it in Japan—namely, as a standard, with its branches spread and supported all around, and you stand beneath it—you have no idea of the joy that is to be got out of a Wistaria, with its beautiful lilac blooms hanging from the bare and twisted branches above your head and the blue sky behind them. The whole effect is indeed different and very superior to that of seeing the blooms hanging straight and flat from branches nailed close to the wall. Unless it is protected from the north and east, it is of course more liable, in unfavourable springs, to have its 'blooms injured by late frosts. The plant itself, I believe, is absolutely hardy.

The creepers I recommended to plant on a south front are as follows:—

Magnolia grandiflora—the roots must be pulled about, not cut, and manured in the autumn for the first few years after planting, to make it grow quickly; a Yellow Banksia, single if possible, but they are not easy to get; an early yellow Dutch Honeysuckle; a *Pyrus japonica*; *Chimonanthus fragrans*, now called *Calycanthus præcox*; a *Rêve d'Or* Rose; a *La Marque* Rose (no house is perfect without one); a few Clematises, which in non-chalky soils must have chalk and lime or brick-rubbish put to their roots, not manure; *Choisya ternata*, a low-growing shrub, wherever there is room between the other plants; a *Maréchal Niel* Rose. *Forsythia suspensa*, *Jasminum nudiflorum*, *Clematis montana*, and late Dutch Honeysuckle will all do on the east and west sides of a house as well as on the south. Two other things that would grow on the south wall are *Bignonia radicans* and *Garrya elliptica*, a charming evergreen with fascinating catkins, which form in January. The male or pollen-bearing plant is the handsomest.

This list I actually made in the autumn, which is really the best time for planting; but there is often so much to do then that planting is apt to get postponed, and rather than lose a whole year, spring planting is quite worth trying. In damp soils I really believe it answers best. In dry soils, or where a plant is likely to be robbed by the roots of neighbouring shrubs, or by old-established climbers, it is not a bad plan to sink in the ground an old tub or half-cask, or even an old tin footbath with the bottom knocked out. Then fill it with the best soil, and put in your plant; it will benefit more in this way from watering in dry weather. There is nothing so disappointing as to lose a plant in spring, as that means the loss of a whole year.

Having given the above list, which is pretty well as large as any moderate-sized house would hold, I may as well add some further names to choose from, all of which are worth growing. *Magnolia purpurea*, *M. stellata*, and *M. conspicua* may all be grown against walls, or planted in sheltered situations as shrubs. Yellow Jasmine (not *nudiflorum*) in favourable situations does well. *Cratægus pyracantha Iælandi* is the best of the Pyracanthuses—I believe, an invaluable shrub. If well pruned, it berries so brilliantly that where people only inhabit their houses in late autumn it is perhaps one of the most satisfactory plants that can be planted. I know one large red house which is covered all round up to a certain height with this plant, and the effect is very decorative, though to have a house entirely covered with only one species of plant is very dull from a gardener's point of view. Unless carefully cut back and pruned early in the winter, it never flowers and berries well, but forms a dense mass of dark-green leaves.

Cotoneasters, various, are useful much in the same way, and, I think, endure better very dry situations. *Forsythia fortunei* and other varieties. *Pyrus japonica*, now called *Cydonia*, various shades (this is one of the most precious and invaluable of the early flowering shrubs, and deserves the best places to be found on warm walls). *Ceanothus grandiflorus* (*Gloire de*

Versailles) is the largest flowering variety, I believe, and a pretty pale-blue colour, flowering in July, which is always valuable. *C. cæruleus* is a beautiful dark-blue colour; it flowers earlier, and is not so hardy. *Cercis*, or common Judas Tree, and *Buddleia globosa* both look well on walls where there is room. *Vitis coignetiæ* is a very handsome rapid grower, and covers quickly a barn, a roof, or a dead tree. The claret-coloured Vine, with its little bunches of black grapes, is very effective. The grapes are used in France and Germany for darkening the colour of wine. *Abelia rupestris*, a lovely little, rather tender shrub, would grow admirably against low greenhouse walls. Why are such spots generally left quite empty by gardeners in large places? The single white McCartney Rose would do well in a similar situation, and for those who are in the country in June it is well worth a place. *Aimée Vibert*, *Gloire des Rosemaines*, and *Fallenberg* are delightful Roses for house or pergola. Sweet Verbena (*Aloysia citriodora*)—Why, oh! why, is this little shrub, which everyone is so fond of, grown so little out of doors? Practically, with a little care, its roots are quite hardy, as in the very severe winter of two years ago only one of mine, out of five or six plants, was killed. It requires nothing but planting out late in May, watering, and not picking at first, as the growth of the shoots makes the roots grow. It may be picked in early autumn as much as you like, but the summer growth should not be cut down to the ground till the following spring. It is the easiest plant possible to strike in spring, and there should be plants of it planted in greenhouses, others grown in pots, and brought on in stoves in spring; but nearly all gardeners are satisfied with one little plant of it in a pot, unless they are urged to increase it. Mock Orange (*Philadelphus grandiflorus*) looks very well against a warm wall in July, but should not be nailed in too tight. *Piptanthus nepalensis* on a warm wall is admirable, but rare; I have only seen it once. *Schizophragma hydrangeoides* is a good wall-plant. For those who can get it to do on a half-shaded wall, is there any greater joy to the south country gardener than the *Tropælum speciosum?* There is an illustration of it in the 'English Flower Garden' (Flame Nasturtium), where it is depicted growing up strings. I think, however, it looks better if grown over some light creeper, Jasmine especially. It wants peat and moisture, and, above all, it must be in a place the spade or fork never reaches, as its thin little creeping white roots are easily disturbed, and even mistaken for a weed and thrown away.

March 22nd—Such a lovely spring day, in spite of its cold wind; it makes me long to be sixteen miles away in my little garden. Even here in London great pure white stately clouds are sailing over the blue. How lucky I am to be going away so soon! I wish it gave half as much pleasure to the rest of the family as it does to me; but one of the few advantages of old age is that we may be innocently selfish. A day like this makes me think of a little poem that appeared in the *Spectator* twenty years ago. It was written by a young clergyman's wife, who worked hard amidst the sordid blackness of a manufacturing town on the banks of the Tyne. My young friends will say, 'How morbid are Aunt T.'s quotations!' It is perhaps true; but all bright, lovable, sympathetic souls had a touch of morbidness in the days that are gone, and these 'Notes' have no meaning at all unless I try to give out in them the impressions received during forty years.

THE POET IN THE CITY

The poet stood in the sombre town,
And spoke to his heart and said:
'O weary prison, devised by man!
O seasonless place and dead!'
His heart was sad, for afar he heard
The sound of the spring's light tread.

POT-POURRI FROM A SURREY GARDEN

He thought he saw in the pearly East
The pale March sun arise;
The happy housewife beneath the thatch,
With hand above her eyes,
Look out to the cawing rooks, that built
So near to the quiet skies.

Out of the smoke and noise and sin
The heart of the poet cried:
'O God! but to be Thy labourer there,
On the gentle hill's green side—
To leave the struggle of want and wealth,
And the battle of lust and pride!'

He bent his ear, and he heard afar
The growing of tender things,
And his heart broke forth with the travailing earth
And shook with tremulous wings
Of sweet brown birds that had never known
The dirge of the city's sins.

And later, when all the earth was green
As the garden of the Lord—
Primroses opening their innocent faces,
Cowslips scattered abroad,
Blue-bells mimicking summer skies,
And the song of the thrush out-poured—

The changeless days were so sad to him
That the poet's heart beat strong,
And he struggled as some poor caged lark,
And he cried, 'How long—how long?
I have missed a spring I can never see,
And the singing of birds is gone.'

> But when the time of the roses came
> And the nightingale hushed her lay,
> The poet, still in the dusty town,
> Went quietly on his way—
> A poorer poet by just one spring,
> And a richer man by one suffering.

I must begin to tell you about my old garden books, and how I first came to know about them, and then to collect them. Until lately I was absolutely ignorant of their existence, and had never seen an illustrated flower book of the last century. About fifteen years ago I was living in London, with apparently small prospect of ever living in the country again, or of ever possessing a garden of my own. When 'A Year in a Lancashire Garden,' by Henry A. Bright, was published in 1879, the book charmed me, and I thought it simple, unaffected, and original. I had not then seen Dr. Forbes Watson's delightful little book, 'Flowers and Gardens,' alluded to by Henry Bright. 'A Year in a Lancashire Garden' has been much imitated, but, to my mind, none of the imitations possess the charm of the original. It is a fascinating chat about a garden to read in a town and dream over as I did. It revived in me, almost to longing, the old wish to have a garden, and I resolved, if it were ever realised, that every plant named by Henry Bright I would get and try to grow. This I literally carried out when I came to live in Surrey. His joys have been my joys, and his failures have sometimes been mine too. In the 'Lancashire Garden' I was delighted to find a sentence which exactly expresses an opinion I had long held, but never met with in words before. As I agree with it even more strongly now than I did then, it is well I should quote it here, for the evil it denounces exists still, not only in England, but even more in several countries I have visited abroad: 'For the ordinary bedding-out of ordinary gardens I have a real contempt. It is at once gaudy and monotonous. A garden is left bare for eight months in the year, that for the four hottest months there shall be a blaze of the hottest colours. The same combination of the same flowers appear wherever you go—Calceolarias, Verbenas, and Zonal Pelargoniums, with a border of Pyrethrums or Cerastiums; and that is about all. There is no thought and no imagination.' Yet twenty years ago this sort of garden was like Tory politics, or Church and State, and seemed to represent all that was considered respectable and desirable. I shall never forget the bombshell I seemed to fling into a family circle when I injudiciously and vehemently said that I hated parks and bedded-out gardens.

In Mr. Bright's book I first saw the mention of Curtis's 'Botanical Magazine,' and afterwards came across a few stray illustrations out of it. Many of these old gardening books were, I fear, cut up and sold for screens and scrap-books when there was no sale for the complete works. I was much struck with the beauty and delicacy of these hand-coloured flower plates, and so began my first interest in old flower books, which has led by degrees to my present collection. At one time I thought of giving some account of the Herbals and botanical works at the library of the South Kensington Natural History Museum, where there is a very fine collection, which begins with the early Herbals and includes botany and gardening books. This, however, proved to be too ambitious a work; but a short account of my own books may be of some interest, for these, though far from being a large collection, extend over nearly three hundred years. The knowledge of the very existence of these beautifully illustrated Herbals and old gardening books is even now limited, though they are within reach of everybody at the Natural History Museum. Probably the reason why these books so suddenly fell out of all knowledge is owing to the letterpress, which is often in Latin, having, for one reason or another, become obsolete. No one now consults Herbals medically, or goes to old books for botanical instruction.

I will arrange the account of my books in chronological order, according to the date of their publication:—

1614. 'Hortus Floridus, by Rembertus Dodonæus and Carolus Clusius.' This is the earliest gardening book I possess. It was printed in Amsterdam, and is a real representation of cultivated garden flowers, not a Herbal in any sense. It has a frontispiece with the portraits of the two authors, which was common enough in the old Dutch books of the seventeenth and eighteenth centuries. Jupiter and Diana are represented on either side of the page, with wreaths of flowers hung along the top, and plants growing in pots placed at the bottom. The title of the book is in the centre. The plates are not coloured, but the flowers are very well drawn. There are two charming pictures of Dutch gardens surrounded by an arched wall with creepers, straight paths, and beds edged with box. In one a woman is gathering Tulips, dressed in the quaint fashion of the period, and a man is leaning over a wooden or stone railing looking at her. The number and variety of exotic flowers figured in the book is surprising. Besides all the ordinary spring bulbs which are now grown, there are Sunflowers, called Indian Golden Suns (Helianthuses, of course, all came from America), Cannas, Marvels of Peru (called *Merveille d'lnde à diverses couleurs*), Nicotiana, etc. Insects are introduced on several of the plates, and in one or two instances mice are feeding on the bulbs which lie on the ground. The African *Agapanthus* is called *Narcissus marinus exoticus*. Both the Hellebores are here, and all the flowers are so well drawn as to be perfectly recognisable. The book is an oblong shape, bound in unstiffened white parchment. It is well preserved, though some Philistine lady of the last century has, with patient industry, pricked some of the flowers and insects all round for the purpose of taking the outlines for needlework. The book historically is certainly interesting. The text is in Latin, but even the unlearned reader is able to realise how horticulturally perfect may have been the gardens of Europe where Louis XIII. of France played as a child, and the number and richness of the flowers which our Prince Charles of Wales (his future brother-in-law) may have gazed at from his palace windows or enjoyed when gathered. This, perhaps, helped to nourish the great taste for art which Charles I., more than all our other kings, developed later in life.

1629. I have both the Parkinsons. The first published of the two has the following curious descriptive inscription written on a shield at the bottom of the title-page:—

PARADISI IN SOLE
PARADISUS TERRESTRIS.

A GARDEN OF ALL SORTS OF PLEASANT FLOWERS WHICH OUR
ENGLISH AYRE WILL PERMITT TO BE NOURSED UP:
WITH
A KITCHEN GABDEN OF ALL MANNER OF HERBES, RAVIES, AND
FRUITES
FOR MEATE OR SAUSE USED WITH US,
AND
AN ORCHARD OF ALL SORTS OF FRUIT-BEARING TREES
AND SHRUBBS FIT FOR OUR LAND,
TOGETHER
WITH THE RIGHT ORDERINGE, PLANTING, AND PRESARVING
OF THEM, AND THEIR USES AND VERTUES.
COLLECTED BY JOHN PARKINSON,
APOTHECARY OF LONDON

The picture on the title-page portrays the Garden of Eden with Adam and Eve tending the flowers. The outward edge is rimmed with spikes representing the sun's rays. At the top is the eye of Providence, and on each side a cherub symbolising the winds. In the centre of the garden is the famous Vegetable Lamb, supposed to be half animal and half plant. This curious myth of the Middle Ages lingered on, and was actually discussed as a matter of faith by scientific men towards the end of the eighteenth century. The Borametz, or Scythian Lamb, or Vegetable Lamb of Tartary, as described by travellers, appears in both the frontispieces of Parkinson's books. When studying the flower books at the South Kensington Museum, I felt curious about this tradition, which the Church of the Middle Ages took up, making it a matter of faith that the Vegetable Lamb grew in Paradise and was in some mysterious way typical of the Christian Lamb. My brain was soon cleared by finding at the Museum a book written by Mr. Henry Lee, and published as late as 1887, giving an excellent account of the whole tradition. This book, called 'The Vegetable Lamb of Tartary,' contains several pictures, reproduced from old books, of the lamb. Some represent it growing, as Parkinson has it, on a stem, from which it was supposed to eat the grass as far as it could reach and then die. Another picture is of a tree with large cocoons, which burst open and display a lamb. The belief seems to have been that the lamb was at the same time both a true animal and a living plant. Mr. Lee carefully goes through the whole tradition, quoting all the known sources from which it arose. According to him, about the middle of the seventeenth century very little belief in the story of the Scythian Lamb remained among men of letters, although it continued to be a subject of discussion and research for at least a hundred and fifty years later. He sums up his explanation with the following sentence:—'Tracing the growth and transition of this story of the lamb-plant from a truthful rumour of a curious fact into a detailed history of an absurd fiction, I have no doubt whatever that it originated in early descriptions of the cotton plant, and the introduction of cotton from India into Western Asia and the adjoining parts of Eastern Europe.' All this seems so simple as explained by Mr. Lee, how the early travellers came back and said, 'In the far East there is a tree on which grows the most beautiful fine wool, and the natives weave their garments of it.' The Western mind could conceive of no wool except that of a lamb; in this way the fiction grew, and was passed on from one writer to another. In a poem by Erasmus Darwin, published in 1781, of which more hereafter, it is alluded to as a plant that grew on the steppes of the Volga in the following terms:—

> E'en round the Pole the flames of love aspire
> And icy bosoms feel the sacred fire.
> Cradled in snow and fanned by Arctic air,
> Shines, gentle Borametz, thy golden hair;
> Rooted in earth, each cloven foot descends,
> And round and round her flexile neck she bends,
> Crops the grey coral moss and hoary thyme
> Or laps with rosy tongue the melting rime;
> Eyes with mute tenderness her distant dam
> And seems to bleat—a 'vegetable lamb.'

Curiously enough, when in Norway last year, I came across an old wooden chair, and the back was carved in a way that seems to me conclusively to represent this old tradition. The design is a lamb enclosed in a circular cocoon, surrounded by branches and leaves. This chair I have now.

In the 'Nineteenth Century' of January 1880, there appeared a very interesting article on Parkinson's 'Paradisi in Sole,' called 'Old-fashioned Gardening,' by Mrs. Kegan Paul. She describes the title-page, and says, 'The tree of knowledge, its fruit still unplucked by Adam, appears in the centre of the plate.' I thought we were told that Adam never did pick it, but received it from the hand of Eve? But this is a trifling criticism on a useful and original article. Mrs. Paul makes a great many delightful quotations from Parkinson, and says that he is 'not content to deny that single flowers can be transformed into double "by the observation of the change of the Moone, the constellations or conjunctions of Planets or some other Starres or celestial bodies."' Parkinson holds that such transformation could not be effected by the art of man. In her condemnation of bedding-out and in her admiration of the old-fashioned English garden, read by the light of these sixteen years, Mrs. Paul's article is almost prophetic. The 'Paradisi in Sole' is essentially a book describing a garden of 'pleasant flowers' and with many interesting details about their cultivation. There is no allusion to medical matter at all, though, as usual, the botanist was a doctor. The woodcuts are rather coarser and rougher than in the Dutch book before described, but they are fairly drawn and generally like Nature. In a little book by Mrs. Ewing, called 'Mary's Meadow,' the author speaks a good deal of this book of Parkinson's, and in a footnote she alludes to the fact that the title is an absurd play upon words, after the fashion of Parkinson's day. Paradise is originally an Eastern word, meaning a park or pleasure ground. *Paradisi in sole Paradisus terrestris* means Park-in-son's Earthly Paradise!

1640. We now come to Parkinson's second book, 'The Theatre of Plants, or an Universal and Complete Herbal. Composed by John Parkinson, Apothecary of London and the King's Herbarist'—('the King' being Charles I., at the time just preceding his execution). The frontispiece is quite as curious in its way as the one in the 'Paradisi in Sole.' It has a portrait of old Parkinson in a skull-cap, looking very wise and holding a flower that looks like a Gaillardia. In the middle of the page is the title, with Adam on one side, dressed in the skin of a beast and holding a very fine spade, like the spades used in France to this day. This, I imagine, represents Toil, while Wisdom is personified on the other side by Solomon. He is clad in the conventional dress of the kings of the Middle Ages—a long cloak, a cape of ermine, a spiked crown, a sceptre, bare legs, and a pair of Roman sandals. At the top of the page is the eye of God with a Hebrew word written below it. At the four corners are four female figures representing Europe, Asia, Africa, and America. Europe, only, is in a chariot drawn by a pair of horses. Asia, riding a rhinoceros, wears a very short skirt and curious, pointed, curled shoes, not unlike the slippers still worn in Turkey, and a stiff headdress that resembles those used by women in the thirteenth century. Africa has no clothes, only a hat, and rides a zebra. America has a bow and arrow, and rides, also without clothes, a curious long-eared sheep. These ladies are surrounded by the vegetation supposed to be typical of each country. Among other plants, Asia has again the Vegetable Lamb before described, and Asia, not America, has the Indian Corn (Maize), which, I believe, is supposed to be as exclusively indigenous to America as Tobacco is. It appears to have been entirely unknown to the Old World, and has never been found with other corn in any of the old tombs, or alluded to in the classics. Its cultivation must have spread very quickly, and it is known all over the South of Europe as *Blé de Turquie* to this day. *Turquie* was the term used in the Middle Ages for describing anything foreign. When the early discoverers of Canada went up the St. Lawrence and reached the rapids, which still bear the name of *La Chine* rapids, they thought they had reached the China seas and joined the continent of Asia. It is, therefore, curious to note that Parkinson figures an American plant amongst the vegetation of Asia. The old Red Indian natives of North America used to sow the Maize with a fish on either side of the seed to propitiate their gods. No wonder it grew luxuriantly. Africa has in the foreground what appears to be a Stapelia, Aloes, and Date-palms. America has Cactuses, Pineapples, and the large Sunflower, being the vegetation rather of South than North America. As representing the geographical knowledge and art notions of the day, it is decidedly an interesting title-page. The woodcuts throughout the book are of the whole plant, root and all; but they are without much character, all about the same size, and less well-drawn than the flowers in the 'Paradisi.' The medical properties of the plants are described at length and with much detail, and are really curious. I wonder if our complicated prescriptions and remedies will some day sink to the level which the science of herbs has reached to-day. It would not be so very surprising if this should happen, considering how much the faith put in the modern drugs resembles the belief in cures as described in these old Herbals. At the Museum there is a great collection of Herbals of all nationalities, especially German. They are all much of the same kind, and illustrated in the same way as this one of Parkinson's, leading one to conjecture that the medical science throughout Europe at this time was about on a level.

1633. 'The Herbal or General Historie of Plants gathered by John Gerarde, of London, Master in Chirurgerie.' This edition of Gerarde's Herbal appeared between the publication of Parkinson's two books just described, but it is a reprint of an earlier edition, very much enlarged, and amended by Thomas Johnson, citizen and apothecary. The frontispiece is stately and serious. The title is on a shield in the middle, with a column on each side dividing it from two draped figures, Theophrastus on the left and Dioscorides on the right. Above these two figures, but divided from them by a line, are Ceres and Pomona, both fully draped. Ceres has a sheaf of wheat in her arms, and behind her grows the Indian corn. A ploughed field is spread out in the distance on her left. In the middle, between these figures, are growing plants and flowers and an orchard. At the bottom of the page is a fine portrait of Gerarde, holding a flower I do not recognise. He is dressed in the correct costume and ruffle of Charles I. On each side of him the spaces are filled by two vases of different shape and design, in which are various flowers arranged in a stiff and formal manner, typical of flower arrangements in that time and long after, as we see depicted by art in this and other countries. Nowhere on the page does there appear any representation of the Vegetable Lamb, nor can I find any reference to it in the text. On the other hand, however, there is an elaborate allusion to what Mr. Lee describes in his book on the Vegetable Lamb, before mentioned, as the companion superstition of the Barnacle Geese. Gerarde gives a most interesting and detailed account—too long, alas! for me to quote—of having seen the barnacles and watched their development into tree-geese. He corroborates his own observation by quoting the like experience of others. He also states in all gravity that 'the shells wherein is bred the barnacle are taken up in a small island adjoining to Lancashire, half a mile from the mainland, called the Pile of Foulders.' Mr. Lee says:—'The growth and development of the story of "the Scythian Lamb" from the similarity of appearance of two really different objects may be best explained by comparing it with another natural-history myth which ran curiously parallel to it. I allude to the fable that Sir John Mandeville tells us he related to his Tartar acquaintances, viz., that of the "Barnacle Geese," which has never been surpassed as a specimen of ignorant credulity and persistent error.

'From the twelfth to the end of the seventeenth century it was implicitly and almost universally believed that in the western islands of Scotland certain geese, of which the nesting-places were never found, instead of being hatched from eggs, like other birds, were bred from "shell-fish" which grew on trees. Upon the shores where these geese abounded, pieces of timber and old trunks of trees covered with barnacles were often seen, which had been stranded by the sea. From between the partly opened shells of the barnacles protruded their plumose cirrhi, which in some degree resemble the feathers of a bird. Hence arose the belief that they contained real birds. The fishermen persuaded themselves that these birds within the shells were the geese whose origin they had been previously unable to discover, and that they were thus bred, instead of being hatched, like other birds, from eggs.' Mr. Lee states that the old botanist Gerarde had, in 1597, the audacity to assert that he had witnessed the transformation of the shell-fish into geese. What Gerarde states, as I read it, is that something like a bird fell out of the shell into the sea, 'where it gathereth feathers, and groweth to a fowle bigger than a mallard and lesser than a goose.' He distinctly says that if it fell on the ground it died.

The drawing of the plants throughout Gerarde's book is more delicate and finished than in Parkinson's.

1691. I have a little gardener's almanack of this date. My copy is the '8th edition, and has many useful additions.' This book is without illustrations except for a frontispiece of a young man and young woman admiring a garden through a doorway. The woman is attended by a page, who is holding a modern-looking sun-shade. This is curious, as umbrellas did not, I believe, come into general use till very much later.

1693. Evelyn publishes his translation of 'The Compleat Gard'ner, written by the famous Monsieur de la Quintinye, Chief Director of all the Gardens of the French King.' They must have been wonderful gardens, those of Louis XIV.; and one of the most beautiful hand-coloured flower books in the library of the museum at South Kensington was executed by order of the king for Madame de Montespan. This translation of Evelyn's has some interesting little illustrations of gardens, plans of beds, fruit-trees, pruning, &c. The frontispiece is a portrait of Evelyn in a hideous wig of the day.

1710. I have an English Herbal by William Salmon, doctor to Queen Anne. It contains a most fulsome dedication to the queen. The type of man who even in that century was capable of publishing such an effusion would be very likely, I think, to have caused the death of all Queen Anne's children, while quite convinced all the time that they died solely by the will of Almighty God. What a curious person that Queen Anne must have been, who allowed the great category of persecuting laws against the Catholics in Ireland to be framed in her reign, and whom Horace Walpole called 'Goody Anne, the wet-nurse of the Church'! The book is purely medical, and is supposed to be principally written for the use of doctors, but it describes flowering garden plants as well as the wild ones. It has a large, coarsely executed frontispiece, mostly torn out in my copy. The drawings of the plants show no artistic improvement over Parkinson's, but are much in the same style.

1739. 'New Improvements of Planting and Gardening, both Phylosophical and Practical, by Richard Bradley.' This is a small book with rather good copper-plates, and interesting as showing the researches and ideas of an intelligent man just previous to the illuminating of botany through the works of Linnæus, who in 1739 was only thirty-two. He knew that earthworms were hermaphrodites, but from a text of Scripture he was convinced that plants have their seeds in themselves, and that every plant contained in itself male and female powers. The common Aucuba, so long a puzzle to botanists, only received its green-leaved pollen-bearing mate from Japan towards the middle of this century. Before that it was only propagated by cuttings, and never bore any red berries. The gardening books of the last century are full of useful hints, as gardening was then practised and written about by men of the highest education; and very often this was done solely for botanical and what they called 'philosophical' reasons. Sometimes the childish earnestness of their ignorance concerning facts now known to every schoolchild accentuates the extraordinary advance and increased popularising of knowledge since that day.

1732. 'Hortus Elthamensis, à Johanne Jacobo Dillenio, M.D.' Two folio volumes published in London, and interesting as showing the general development of the improved power of illustrating. The plates are coloured by hand, and contain many figures of Cape Aloes, Geraniums, and other African plants, either depicted with their roots or as growing out of the ground. The text is in Latin.

1771. 'Uitgezochte Planten, by Christ. Jacob Trew, Georgius Dionysius Ehret, Joh. Jacob Haid.' The characteristic of this large folio is that it begins with very fine separate portraits of the three authors. One seems to have been the botanist, one the artist, and one the engraver. It was brought out at Amsterdam by subscription, as was so common with handsome books in those days. The book begins with a long list of subscribers. The flower-plates are extremely fine, very strongly coloured, and as fresh and bright as the day they were painted, each page being covered with a sheet of dark-grey thick hand-made paper, such as Turner loved to sketch upon. One of the things figured is the Japanese plant, *Bocconia cordata* ('Plumed Poppy,' Robinson calls it), which we have been in the habit of thinking a new plant in our gardens. Many of the plates are interesting and a few remarkable, and the botanical details of the flowers beautifully drawn, some natural size and some magnified.

1771. 'The Flora Londinensis, by William Curtis.' The first number was brought out by subscription on the above date. I have the two volumes of the first edition. It is the handsomest the most artistic, and the best drawn of any English illustrated botanical books I have seen. I do not know who was the artist, but I imagine not Curtis himself. These plates have some of the qualities of Jacquin's drawings, of which more hereafter. How much they were in communication, a not uncommon custom of the time, I do not know. Curtis's first book was a translation of Linnæus's, with the title of 'An Introduction to the Knowledge of Insects.'

In 1773 Curtis was appointed lecturer of the Chelsea Garden. The plates of 'The Flora Londinensis' are lovely large folio, and most delicately drawn and tinted. The text is in English, and is descriptive of the wild flowers and plants growing round London. No doubt the book was suggested to Curtis by Vaillant's 'Catalogue of Plants in the Environs of Paris.' It retains strongly the Herbal character, and the medical details of diseases are weird and extraordinary. The decision and particularity of the assurance that every disease to which flesh is heir will be relieved by the use of certain plants are quite surprising. The place where the innocent little wild plants are picked is always named, and it is pathetic to think of the growth of the city, and how the places mentioned are now densely covered with buildings and streets.

The second edition, in five or six volumes, finished by Dr. Hooker, is far the more valuable and complete. Curtis began his 'Botanical Magazine, or Flower Garden Displayed' in 1778. I have the first sixty-seven volumes of this lovely and best known of all the Old English gardening publications. It is purely horticultural. Every alternate page is an illustration, with the letterpress on the opposite side describing the nature of the plant, the country from which it comes, and its cultivation here. With the same truthful accuracy with which he tells the home of the wild plant, he names the nurseryman or amateur who has flowered the exotic. The best drawings by far are in the early numbers, and were executed by Sowerby. The two who succeeded him were Sydenham Edwards and Dr. Hooker. Spode, the man who perfected the process of mixing bone-dust into the paste used for china in the early part of this century, used these illustrations a good deal for his pretty china dinner and dessert services, with the names of the flowers or plants marked at the back of the dishes.

1791. 'The Loves of the Plants, in two parts: The Botanic Garden and the Economy of Vegetation. A Poem by Erasmus Darwin,' seems to me one of the real curiosities of literature. It is unique, so far as I know, in its sincere desire to clothe the latest science in the garb of the Muse. The frontispiece, by Fuseli, is a drawing most characteristic of that artist and full of all his affectations. *Flora*, attired by the elements, is a striking example of the fashion and bad taste of the day, and yet it is full of ingenuity and skill in drawing. This frontispiece is well worth, by itself, the price I gave for the whole volume. Another print in the book, by the same artist, is called 'The Fertilisation of Egypt,' meaning, of course, the rising of the Nile. A huge unclothed man with a dog's head is praying to the star Sirius. A note explains this by saying 'the Abbé La Pluche observes that as Sirius, or the Dog-star, rose at the time of the commencement of the flood, its rising was watched by the Astronomers and notice given of the approach of the inundation by hanging the figure of Anubis, which was that of a man with a dog's head, in all the Egyptian temples.' Erasmus Darwin's mind was evidently fascinated, as was common with all the scientific men of the day, by the fertilisation of plants. In one of his notes he says, 'The vegetable passion of love is agreeably seen in the flower of the *Parnassia* (Grass of Parnassus), in which the males alternately approach and recede from the female' (a practice not wholly unknown to many beside the innocent *Parnassia*), 'and in the flower of Nigella.' We call it now Love-in-the-Mist, 'in which the tall females bend down to their dwarf husbands' (a picture sometimes seen in modern drawing-rooms). Darwin goes on to say, 'I was surprised this morning to observe, amongst Sir Brooke Boothby's valuable collection of plants at Ashbourne, the manifest adultery of several females of the plant *Collinsonia*, who had bent themselves into contact with the males of the same plant in their vicinity neglectful of their own.' The plate and note of *Gloriosa superba* I have mentioned elsewhere. As an outcome of the extraordinary effect of Linnæus's work on thinking minds at the end of the last century, the book is of great interest, though we should not call it poetry in the modern sense. Erasmus Darwin was the grandfather of our great Darwin, who did for the middle of this century so much more than even Linnæus did for the end of the last.

1778. 'Miscellanea Austriaca, by Nicolai Josephi Jacquin.' This is the earliest Jacquin book that I have. It is in two small volumes of note-books, with all the illustrations at the end. The text is in Latin; but this is of no consequence, as Jacquin's books are all botanical, not horticultural, and their botany is obsolete. This remarkable man, Nicholas Joseph Jacquin, whose industry must have been untiring, was born at Leyden in 1727, and educated there at the University for the medical profession. This meant in those days the highest botanical education which could be obtained. He went to Vienna, at the suggestion of a friend, to practise medicine, but when there his great botanical knowledge brought him to the notice of Francis I. This emperor seems to have been a great patron of botany and gardening, the fashionable combination of the day. He sent Jacquin to the West Indies for six years to collect plants for the Schönbrunn Gardens, paying his expenses. Jacquin did not die till 1817, leaving an unfinished work, 'Eclogæ Plantarum Rariorum,' the only one of Jacquin's books that has a German as well as a Latin text. The second volume was not published till 1844, by Edouardus Fenzl, long after Jacquin's death. The colour and painting are very inferior to Jacquin's work. Towards the end of the last century, in the midst of wars and revolutions, the crumbling of old methods of government and the change of social customs, an extraordinary band of able men all over Europe were quietly working in concert and with constant communication. Their object was to increase the knowledge of the science of botany by reproducing, with the greatest botanical exactness of detail, the plants imported from all parts of the world as they flowered in Europe for the first time in the various greenhouses and stoves. It is remarkable that the books of this period, even of different countries, very rarely illustrate the same plants. The botanical curiosity, the feeling of something new, rare, and not fully understood, which is such an incentive to the human mind, has gone for ever as far as this kind of simple botany is concerned. Of these highly gifted men, who worked on lines which can no more be repeated than the missals of the sixteenth century in Italy, Jacquin, no doubt, was the most artistically interesting. No one who has not seen his works can realise the beauty, the delicacy, the truth, the detail to which flower-painting can be brought. None of the other flower-painters that I know show anything like the same talent of throwing the flower on to the paper with endless variety, and of adapting the design to the size and growth of the particular plant. This result seems produced by his botanical exactness, and not, apparently, by any intention to make a beautiful picture. No two pages are ever filled in the same way. This does away entirely with the ordinary wearisome monotony of turning over drawings one after the other, with the flower right in the middle of the page. His books fetch a considerable price, and are difficult to procure. The one I sometimes see in English catalogues is in my possession, five volumes of 'Collectanea ad Botanicam Chemiam et Historiam naturalem, 1786.' My copy was a surplus one at the British Museum, of which it bears the stamp and date of sale, 1831. The plates maintain their usual excellence and are nearly all coloured, with a brilliancy that has not suffered at all from time. Some are of wild flowers, mosses, Lycopodiums, insects, and serpents. All Jacquin's drawings stand out wonderfully on the paper, but there is no shading, except that the modelling is indicated by a stronger tone of the same colour; and the relief and value, without any tinting of the background, are most effective. In the case of the bushy little Alpines the plant is spread out like seaweed and the root drawn, which gives the whole growth and proportion of the plant.

1793. 'Oxalis Monographia' is an exquisite study of about a hundred Oxalises. Nearly all the plates are coloured. Most of these delicate little plants with their bulbous roots come from the Cape of Good Hope. Jacquin seems to have had a peculiar affection for them, as, besides this monograph, he constantly figures them in his miscellaneous works. I have often tried to procure his book on Stapelias, also a large family of Cape plants rather like small Cactuses, but have never been able to do so and have only seen it at the Museum.

1797-1804. 'Plantarum Rariorum Horti Cæsarei Schoenbrunnensis.' These four superb folios, containing five hundred spotless plates by Jacquin, represent some of his very finest work. The plates are all coloured, in a much stronger and more finished way than in his other books. Some of the plates are folded and larger than the book, and others extend across the whole width of the book. As an example of the richness of the plates I will describe one taken at random, which he calls *Vitis vulpina*. The shoot of the vine starts from a short piece of stronger branch at the very top of the page, and curves to the bottom, turning up at the end with young leaves and tendrils. This young shoot has two bunches of the flower as it appears in spring. Quite at the top, on the right, is a detached autumn leaf turning red, and drawn from the back with every vein showing. Half-way down, on the left, is a bunch of ripe purple grapes; with one pip, drawn life-size, at the side. Below this is a single flower, highly magnified, with a drawing apart showing pistil and stamen. There are ten life-sized leaves on the branch, and the whole is contained on an unfolded plate. A short botanical description of each plant is added in Latin. The hand-made paper on which these plates are printed puts to shame all that we now produce. Many of the plants are named differently from what they are now. To those who have never seen Jacquin's works these volumes are an absolute revelation. At the same time his genius will always appeal more to the artistic than to the scientific mind, although in the biographical notices of him that I have seen he is only mentioned as a doctor and a botanist. At the Natural History Museum is a large and much-valued collection of his letters and original drawings.

1794. 'Thirty-eight Plates with explanations, intended to illustrate Linnæus' system of vegetables, and particularly adapted to the letters on the elements of Botany. By Thomas Martin, Regius Professor of Botany in the University of Cambridge. 'These plates are beautifully drawn, and exemplify very well the careful draughtsmanship of a botanist of the day. They are most faithfully hand coloured, and are only inferior to the best from a little want of gradation.

1794. I have the 'Life of Sir Charles Linnæus, by D. H.

Stoever, translated from the original German by Joseph Trapp.' It is, I believe, the only biography of him ever written. To this is added a copious list of his works and a biographical sketch of his son, whose life is an interesting example of talents shared by a father and son. The son, who died unmarried at the early age of forty-one, seems to have been a brilliant and much-loved individual. Trapp dedicates his translation to the Linnæan Society of London. It contains a portrait of the elder Linnæus, a cheerful, bright, up-looking profile, with the curly wig of the day, and a large branch stuck in his buttonhole, as was not uncommon in the portraits of botanists. He was born in 1707, was the son of a Swedish minister, and the grandson of a peasant. His industry and energy must have been exceptional, and he chose truth as his guide. His first book was the 'Flora of Lapland,' which was perhaps the reason why that little Northern flower, *Linnea borealis*, is the plant that has received his great name. He married at twenty-seven, and his father-in-law seems to have put small faith in his botany, and advised him to apply himself more exclusively to the theoretical and practical study of physic. After his marriage he made money as a doctor in Stockholm, and it is not otherwise than interesting to know that when attacked with very severe gout at forty-three, and the doctors who attended him began to despair of his recovery, he cured himself by eating nothing but Strawberries for a time. Afterwards he kept the gout entirely in check by taking a Strawberry cure every summer. In several ways the book gives an interesting picture of life in the last century. Linnæus's books are characterised by religious sentiment, nevertheless they had the misfortune of being considered at Rome as heretical and materialistic productions. In 1758 they were inserted in the catalogue of forbidden books; no one durst either print or sell them under pain of having every copy confiscated or publicly burnt. This proceeding was implicitly condemned during the papacy of the excellent and truly enlightened Ganganelli, Pope Clement XIV. Linnæus himself mentions this occurrence in a letter to the Chevalier Thunberg in the following terms:—'The Pope, who fifteen years ago ordered those of my works that should be imported into his dominions to be burnt, has dismissed the Professor of Botany who did not understand my system, and put another in his place, who is to give public lectures according to my method and theory.'

1797. 'The Botanist's Repository, by H. Andrews.' This is a rare book, I believe, and ought to be in ten quarto volumes. I have only the first eight. It contains coloured engravings only of new and rare plants, many of which cannot, I think, have flowered in England, as there are several Proteas, which are exceedingly difficult of cultivation under glass. Andrews' great fondness for plants from the Cape of Good Hope makes one almost think he must have been there—Gladioli, Ixias, and curious Cape Pelargoniums, which are the parents of all our greenhouse varieties. On the bottom of the title-page is a charming little drawing of that humble plant the *Linnea borealis* ('Twin Flower,' Mr. Robinson calls it), which I have never yet been lucky enough to flower. The design represents two little flowering branches raised on either side like two arms. I feel much drawn to the man Andrews, who so skilfully placed it there, just a hundred years ago, to do honour to his great master. Andrews' other book is 'The Heathery, or a Monograph of the Genus Erica.' Again I have only the small edition published in 1804. The folio one is very scarce. This is a pretty, interesting book, with moderately well-drawn plates, coloured by hand. The Heaths are such a large family, and nearly all apparently come from the Cape of Good Hope. I cannot understand why people who have several greenhouses should not grow more of these charming plants. They require a certain amount of special treatment, a very cool house and plenty of air. It seems such a pity that private gardeners only care to grow the few plants which they can exhibit for competition—markedly, just now, Orchids and Chrysanthemums. These Cape Heaths look lovely picked and wedged, or growing in the greenhouse, and, I should imagine, would do especially well in houses by the sea. On the frontispiece of his book Andrews has a quaint picture of a greenhouse for growing his Heaths.

Towards the end of the year I will tell you about those of my books which belong to this century.

APRIL

Whims of the weather—Spring flowers—The herbaceous nursery—Love for the garden—A light sprayer—Homely French receipts—French gardening—The late frosts.

April 2nd—We came down to our little Surrey garden, only sixteen miles from London, for good yesterday; and though the wind be ever so cold and the skies ever so grey, I yet feel that that which makes going to London worth while is the joy of coming back again. The ceaseless interest of a garden of this sort is in the variety, not only of the plants, but in the actual growth caused by the different seasons. This year the winter has been very mild, and dry too, which is unusual— and then came a very wet March, such as I do not remember since we have lived in Surrey, these fourteen years. It is really amusing to watch all that happens consequent on these whims of the weather; the early and late, the wet and the dry, all making immense difference in the plants. Some are successful one year, and some another.

Nothing is more charming just now than the Forsythias. They are absolutely hardy, but they flower best on walls, even a north one, as the birds are extremely fond of the buds and can get at them much better when the plant is grown as a bush. The birds always seem to be extraordinarily destructive in this garden; but I see that most gardeners, in their books, make the same complaint, and rather apologise to the common-sense of their readers for cherishing and feeding instead of destroying them. In my garden I hang up on the trees, the pump, or shaded railings, little boxes with part of one side cut out for the birds to build in, and with lids that lift up for me to have the pleasure of looking at them. The fact is, birds do quite as much good as harm, though the harm is the more apparent; and who would have a garden without song?

The Crown Imperials are in full flower. They, like many other bulbs in this light soil, reproduce themselves so quickly that they want to be constantly lifted, the small bulbs taken away and put in a nursery (if you wish to increase your stock), and the large ones replaced, in a good bed of manure, where you want them to flower the following year. It is best, if possible, to do this in June, when the leaves have died down, but not quite disappeared so that the place is lost; one can, however, always find them in the autumn by their strong smell when the earth is moved beside them.

The orange Crown Imperials do best here, so, of course, I feel proudest of the pale yellow. Both colours are unusually good this year. In my youth they were rather sniffed at and called a cottage plant. I wonder if anyone who thought them vulgar ever took the trouble to pick off one of the down-hanging bells and turn it up to see the six drops of clear water in the six white cups with black rims? I know nothing prettier or more curious amongst flowers than this. I have not got the white one, but must try and get it; I am told it is very pretty, and so it must be, I should think. The lovely little *Omphalodes verna* ('Blue-eyed Mary,' Mr. Robinson calls it) is in flower under my trees. The soil is too dry for it to flourish very successfully, and yet it is always worth growing everywhere. Next year I shall try lifting it in March and putting it into pots. The great thing is to remember that it divides and propagates much better in early spring than in autumn. The graceful, pale grey anemone *Robinsoniana* is doing better this year. Now that it has taken hold, I hope it may spread.

All the early tulips and some of the later are out; what delicious things they are! None are better than *Gesneriana greigi* and *sylvestris*. The beautiful Parrot Tulips will come later. *Ornithogalum nutans* is a weed most people dread to get into their borders, and not unnaturally; but if put in a place where spreading does no harm, or planted in grass, where it does not flourish very much it is a bulb well worth growing. It blooms better if divided every two or three years. The flowers are very lovely when cut, and, like all their tribe, they last well in water, looking most refined and uncommon, and are especially good to send to London. I do not make many remarks here on the lovely family of spring bulbs-Tulips Scillas, Hyacinths, Daffodils, and Narcisses-for the same reason that I passed casually over the forced ones in February. We can all grow these easily enough by marking the catalogue and paying the bill. Anybody who does not understand their cultivation will find every detail on the subject in the older gardening books, as I have stated before. Of all the Dutch nurserymen from whom have bought bulbs, J. J. Thoolen at Overveen, near Haarlem is the cheapest, though I do not say that he is better or worse than any other. In my experience, all the finer kinds of bulbs are better for taking up in June or

July well dried in the sun, and planted again in September. When they are planted in grass they must, of course, be left alone to take their chance. Nothing can be more delightful than the spring bulbs. I grow them in every way I can—in pots, in beds, in borders, and in the grass.

Besides the Bulbs, the Arums, and the Azaleas, I have in the little greenhouse next the drawing-room several very pretty *Primula sieboldii*: they remain in the frames in pots during the summer, to die down entirely and are re-potted in the autumn. They are hardy, and will grow out of doors, but the blooms do not then reach to such perfection. There is a large box filled with the last of the Neapolitan Violets and a pan of *Saxifraga wallacei*, one of the most effective of the smaller Saxifrages. I never succeeded with it out of doors till I divided it in June, planting it in the shade, and in October I replaced it in the sunny bed for spring flowering. In that way it can be increased to any amount. This treatment I pursue with many plants:—*Heuchera sanguinea*, one of the most precious of the Canadian flowers, and the best worth cultivating, especially in small gardens. The pretty *Saxifraga granulata flore pleno* disappeared year after year till treated more or less in this way. In June, when the leaves die down, the little bulblets are taken up and planted in groups in a shady place. They make their leaves in October, when it is easy to move them back into the border or onto the rockery where they are to flower. The double flower is of a very pure white, and its long stalk adapts it well for glass vases and table decoration. The large sweet-smelling double white Rocket, which I mentioned before as growing so well in the damp Hertfordshire garden, defeated me altogether for some years; it made a fair growth of leaves, but never flowered. Now it succeeds perfectly. After flowering, we break it up, put it into a shady place, and replant it in the borders in the autumn. All this sounds very troublesome, but it is really not so at all, as it is so quickly done. The only trouble is remembering when to do the things; but that soon comes with practice, and the time of year always recalls what was done the year before to the true gardener. Everybody recognises this treatment as necessary for violets, double and single—which, indeed, do not flower well without it. The invaluable Imantophyllums, which began to flower in the warm greenhouse in January, are doing so still: so are the Arums, which people insist on calling 'Lilies.' They are not lilies at all, but belong to the same family as the 'Lords and Ladies' and 'Cuckoo Pint' of our hedges. The large greenhouse Arums come from the Cape, where they are an absolute weed, appearing wherever the ground is disturbed or turned up. They are there called Pig Lilies, perhaps because they feed the pigs on the roots. In the damp places, I am told, they are magnificent, growing finer and larger than they ever do in pots in England; at the same time, when they come up in dry and heathy places, they are perfect miniature plants with delicate little flowers like shells. Arums in pots require lots of water while growing and flowering, and are better for a saucer to hold it.

A beautiful crimson Amaryllis, which I brought back from Guernsey some years ago, is in flower. It has never flowered before; but we understand so much better than we did the drying and ripening in the sun of all the Cape bulbs, and this makes the whole difference to their flowering.

April 3rd—This is the time of year when we make up our nursery, which I consider one of the most important gardening acts of the whole year, and one most fruitful in results. We take up, from wherever they happen to have been left last autumn, herbaceous Phloxes, early outdoor Chrysanthemums, and Michaelmas Daisies. These are broken up into small pieces, according to the number of plants that are likely to be wanted in the borders or to give away, and planted in rows in a half-shady corner of the kitchen garden. Here they are left to grow and increase till some wet day in July, when they are planted in bold masses where they are to flower. They really move better in dry weather than in wet, and I say a wet day merely because it reduces the trouble of watering, which is all the attention they require. They fill up bare places and holes in the borders, and flower as they never did with us in the old days when they were left alone. This treatment especially suits the Phloxes, which is curious, as they are moved when just coming into flower. The rows in the spring must be labelled with the names and colours, as the different hues of the flowers war with each other if promiscuously massed. The Michaelmas Daisies flower earlier in this way than when left to starve in a dry border or shrubbery, but one can always leave some in unfavourable places to flower late.

April 4th—All the Linums and Linarias (*see* Mr. Robinson's book) are useful for house and table decoration, and are very suitable for small gardens. The common blue Flax is a lovely thing; so is the white French Willow-weed (*Epilobium*), which is most useful, and flowers earlier in the year than the common lilac one.

As a single plant, for beauty of growth and foliage there are few things as lovely as the common Hemp plant (*Cannabis sativa*). It is an annual, easily grown in April in a pot or box, and planted out.

In gardening, as in most things, it is thought that is really required, and that wonderful thing which is called 'a blind god'—love. But blind love is mere passion. Real love in every form, even towards animals and plants, is watchful and ever seeing, never missing for a moment what is for the good and the advantage of the beloved. In walking round and round the garden, with a practised eye one soon sees when a plant is getting on well or the contrary. When a plant is doing badly, it means the conditions are unfavourable, and it is then our duty to find out why. In my garden the usual cause of failure is dryness, and many and many a plant has been saved, since I understood this, by a timely mulching or a good can of water. When things are coming into flower, especially early Alpines, Gentians, etc., it is quite safe to water, even in cold weather, early in the year. Do they not flourish where the ice-water drips upon them from the first melting of the snows under the spring sun? Early spring plants do badly in our soil; but were I there, to watch and to water just at the right time, I feel sure they would look more flourishing.

A most beautiful light sprayer for watering small plants is easily made in the following way:—Take a piece of sheet zinc five or six inches long and four or five inches wide. Cut a piece half an inch wide on each side of the zinc to within an inch of the middle, so making a little band attached to the main piece, and fold this tightly round the spout of the watering-pot; bend the zinc sprayer upwards in the middle in a way to enable the water from the pot to flow over it in a continuous sheet.

Sorrel is a vegetable seldom grown in English gardens, and still seldomer properly dressed by English cooks, and yet it is excellent, either cut up in the white soup called 'Bonne femme,' dressed like Spinach, or puree'd as thin as a thick sauce. With veal, cooked in all ways, it is especially good. When the summer gets on and it is old, it is desirable to add a little Lettuce with it to soften it, as it gets too sour. It is one of those vegetables never quite so good in towns, as it is best freshly picked, and if faded should be revived in water before cooking. The receipts for cooking it in 'Dainty Dishes' are quite right.

For those who keep cows, or who can have plenty of good fresh cream, the following, I think, will be found a really excellent pudding:—

Crème Brûlée—Boil one pint of cream for one minute, pour it on the yelks of four very fresh eggs well beaten, then put it again on the fire and let it just come to the boil. Pour it into the dish in which it is to be served, and let it get cold. Strew a thick crust of powdered sugar over it, put it in a slow oven for ten minutes, then brown it with a salamander, and serve it cold.

April 5th—We started to-day to spend a week in a French country house, sleeping one night on our way at beautiful Chartres, which, as I am not writing a guidebook, I shall not describe. The weather was bitterly cold; and when we humbly asked at the hotel for some hot water, the answer we got was 'On n'échauffe plus.' The French submit more meekly than we do to this kind of regulation, which is curious, as they are so much more sensible, as a rule, than we are in most of the details of life. I was interested to see in the small court of the hotel a quantity of most flourishing Hepaticas. These flowers, Mr. Bright tells us, defeated all his efforts in his Lancashire garden. I have tried them in various aspects, but they make a sorry show with me in Surrey. In this little back-yard they shone in the sunshine, pink and blue, double and single. I suppose the secret is that they do not mind cold, but they want sun. I wonder if anyone is very successful with them in England? How I remember them, in the days of my youth, pushing through the dead leaves in the little oak woods in the valleys up the country behind Nice, then, as now, 'Le pays du Soleil,' but probably long since all changed into villas and gardens instead of woods and fields.

A French country house! How different it all is! In some ways we manage best, in others they do. This was rather a cosmopolitan than a typically French house, and yet in a country how traditions linger and customs cling! We saw and did many interesting things, thanks to the cordial hospitality and kindness of our host and hostess. I, however, will only allude to certain domestic details which I learnt during my stay, and which may instruct you as they did me.

What interested me much from a housekeeping point of view was, not only the excellence of the cooking, as that now can be seen elsewhere, but the management of the kitchen. It seems a small thing to state as an example, but I was told that no French housekeeper who at all respects herself would ever allow lard to come into her house. Everything is fried in what they call *graisse*, and we call suet. Five or six pounds are bought from the butcher—anywhere in England they will let you have it at sixpence a pound. This is boiled for two or three hours, skimmed and strained, and poured into jars ready for use, taking the place of lard when butter or oil are not used. Since I came home I have never had any lard in my house. Many people here do not know that dripping can be cleared by frying some pieces of raw potato in it till they turn brown; this will clarify it nicely.

All chickens, game, birds of any kind, are roasted far more slowly than with us, and at wood fires. The livers, gizzards, &c., are chopped up and put inside the bird. It is always basted with butter, which is poured round the bird when sent to table. This is a very great improvement with all birds, especially fowls, on the pale watery gravy or the thick tasteless sauce as served in England. Our method of sticking the liver and gizzard into the wing is a useless waste, for they shrivel into a hardened mass before our fierce coal fires. The French, if they do not think the livers, etc., necessary for improving the gravy in the roasting often make them the foundation of a pie or side-dish. This cutting up the liver and basting with butter is a hint well worth remembering, and should be universally applied in the roasting of all birds. I noticed that all roast meat was basted with fat or butter, and the gravy served just as it was, without straining or clarifying, with all the goodness of the meat in it.

This we have practised ever since at home, with great approval. Many people would object to this as greasy. I only say, 'Try it.'

A very good, easily made French soup is as follows:—

Potage Paysanne—Cut one large onion into dice, put them into a stewpan with two ounces of butter, and fry a nice golden colour. Then take a half-inch-thick slice of bread toasted to the same colour; break it into small pieces, and put them into the stewpan with a pint of good stock. Simmer gently for thirty-five minutes, then serve. Quantity for four persons.

The following receipt for a tame duck I can thoroughly recommend; if you follow it exactly, it cannot go wrong:—

Caneton à l'Orange—Take a good fat duck, clean it out, and put the liver apart. Singe the duck, and clean it very carefully. Then mince the liver with a little onion and some grated bacon or ham, add salt and pepper. Put the stuffing inside the duck. Now close the opening of the duck; leave the skin of the neck long, and bring it round under the duck to close the tail. Spread on the table a clean pudding-cloth, and roll the duck in this rather tightly, to preserve the shape. Tie up the two ends of the cloth with string. Put into a stewpan, with boiling salted water. Continue to boil it quietly for one hour for an ordinary duck, one hour and ten minutes if large; it will then be cooked, and ought to be a good pink colour. (Chickens boiled in the same way are excellent.) Take three oranges, peel them with a spoon, cut the peel in quarters, taking out *all* the white; shred the peel as if for Julienne soup; put it into water for seven or eight minutes, drain on a cloth. Take the rest of the orange, removing all the white; put the pulp into a good *reduced* stock half glazed. Add Spanish sauce (*see* 'Dainty Dishes'), two or three spoonfuls, and a little red wine—port is best. Pass through a sieve, and then add the chips of orange-peel. Unpack the duck, serve on a dish, surround it with pieces of orange; put a little sauce over the duck and the rest in a sauce-boat.

Another good and useful receipt is the following:—

French Pie—Cut up 2 lbs. of lean veal, 2 lbs. of bacon, and 2 lbs. of lean pork, in very thin slices. Place them in layers in a fireproof pie-dish. Moisten with stock, and chop up a little herb and very little onion, and put it between the slices of meat. Cover with a sham crust of flour and water. Take all the cuttings, parings, bones, &c.; cook these in water or weak stock, and reduce to a large teacupful.

When the pie has baked some time slowly, take it out, take off the crust and pour in the teacupful of stock. When it has cooled, it improves the appearance of the dish to put some well-made aspic jelly (*see* 'Dainty Dishes') on the top.

As it was the end of Lent, I had the chance of seeing several *maigre* dishes. All the good cooking which hung about monasteries and convents was swept out of England by the Reformation. It has returned only in my lifetime, for gastronomic or health reasons rather than for religious mortification. The old object was to make tasty and palatable what the rules of the Church allowed. The French have a real talent for making good dishes out of nothing, and this they share with no other nation in the world. Ox-tails are not used to make soup in France, or were not; but when the French refugees came over here, they found ox-tails were thrown away and were very cheap. They immediately utilised them, and made the excellent ox-tail soup which we use in England to this day. The black cooks of America, I am told, never spoil good materials, and they cook good things excellently. The English have a peculiar gift for taking the taste out of the best materials that are to be found in the world. A few terrible tricks of the trade are answerable for a good deal of this—iron pots and spoons; soda thrown into many things; water poured over roasted meat for gravy; soups cleared with the white of eggs. This will spoil the best soup in the world, not only taking away all flavour of meat and vegetables, but supplying a taste that is not unlike the smell of a dirty cloth. Of late, in the effort to keep pace with foreign cooking, things in England have grown too messy, and I sometimes regret the real Old English dishes of my childhood. The system of trying to make one thing look like another is very objectionable, I think, and wanting in good taste. But I must return to my *maigre* receipts. The details can be found in 'Dainty Dishes.'

Vol-au-vent au Maigre—Make a high Vol-au-vent crust. Prepare some quenelles made of fish—any white fish would do (lemon-soles, whiting, haddock, gurnet, &c.); some white bottled mushrooms preserved in salt, not vinegar (this is most important); some small pieces of boiled fish. Mix these together in a white sauce made of butter, flour (slightly cooked first, but not coloured); then add the milk, warm the whole together, and pour it into the crust.

A rather nice cake for luncheon can be made as follows:— Take three eggs, put them into the scale and weigh against them three equal parts of flour, sugar, and butter. Then break the eggs and put the yelks into a basin, melt the butter, add the flour and sugar, and mix the whole. At the last moment add the whites of the eggs, beat slightly, and put it into the oven in a round flat tin with a thin rim. Serve it on a large round plate. Fresh-water fish, so rare now in England, though the traces of tanks and ponds are always to be found in the neighbourhood of old abbeys and monasteries, are still much eaten in the country in France. Pike and carp marinaded are constantly seen at table. Marinading is far too little done in England; it is most useful for many things—hares, venison, beef, and grouse—and it preserves the meat for some time, if that is what is wanted. It is described in 'Dainty Dishes,' but I give you also the following receipt:—

German Receipt for Roast Hare—Take a bottle of common white wine (or any remnants of already opened bottles); cut up onions, carrots, herbs, bay-leaf, a clove or two; and pour the whole over the raw hare in a shallow baking-pan basting it well every few hours in a cool place for two or three days. Then prepare the hare. Take off the head, lard it well, and put it into the roasting-pan with a little dripping and more onions, carrots, herbs, salt, and pepper. When roasted, take it out of the oven, pour off all the grease, and replace it by half a breakfast-cupful of thick sour cream, which is to be mixed with the gravy at the bottom of the pan. Replace it in the oven, baste well with the mixture, and serve just as it is, pouring the sauce over the hare.

Chervil is always used in France for spring decoration of fish, cold meat, &c. It is much hardier and more easily grown than Parsley, and lives through the coldest weather if covered up with sticks and fern. In severe winters Parsley sometimes fails in English gardens.

The life in the little French town near which we were was like a page out of a volume of Balzac's 'Vie de Province,' so full of character, and, in a sense, so far away and old-fashioned.

I had the privilege of visiting and hearing the story of one of that charming type, the French old maid. I sat in her kitchen whilst her *bonne* prepared the Sunday dinner for herself, an adopted child, and the inevitable male friend, be he doctor, notary, or priest. The soup was *maigre* and economical:—One large onion cut up and fried in butter in a saucepan over a very slow fire till a nice yellow-brown. Then the saucepan filled up with boiling water from a kettle, and allowed to cook half an hour. Then strained, and a sufficient quantity of Vermicelli added. Cook for fifteen or twenty minutes more, and serve. A chicken, prepared as before described, was roasted for an hour and a half before a slow wood fire, basted with butter all the time, and served with the butter round it as gravy. The salad was carefully picked young Watercress (never used by itself for salads in England), with oil and vinegar, and a hard-boiled egg cut into small quarters laid on the top. (Few know that Watercress can be grown in ordinary garden soil, in half-shade, if sown every spring.) The wine was good, and the sweets came from the pastry-cook.

During our short stay in France I saw several gardens, but nothing at all interesting. As we drove through the villages I noticed specimens of a white variety of *Iberis gibraltarica* (Candytuft) grown in pots, carefully pruned and cared for, standing in the windows of the cottages. Managed in this way, it made a very charming spring pot-plant. I have never seen it so treated in England. It is not quite hardy. I brought home cuttings, but they all died. I have now several plants which I have grown from seed. From their appearance I do not think they will flower well till they are two or three years old; they will want hard cutting back directly after flowering.

It was early in the year, and no sort of spring gardening was aimed at in the large bare beds cut in rather coarse grass. I think turf is overdone in England; but why it should be attempted at all where it grows badly, and is rarely successful, I cannot imagine. How infinitely prettier it would be to have earth planted with shrubs and low-growing, creeping plants, with grass paths! The shrubs that I saw in France seemed to me as much over-pruned—indeed stiffly cut back in spring— as they are under-pruned in England.

April 16th—We returned home last night. At this time of year how a week or ten days changes the growth in one's garden! I must confess that sometimes, coming home after dark, I have taken a hand-candle to inspect some special favourite.

Buddleia globosa is well worth growing, even in a small garden. It has many merits besides its golden balls, which so charmed Mr. Bright, and which here, at any rate, I think rather disappointing. The growth is lovely; and the tone of the green unusual, mixing well with many summer flowers. It lasts a long time in water in the hottest weather. The more you cut it, the better it seems to do. It was killed to the ground in the cold winter of '94-95, but broke up from the roots as strong as ever. Some plants do this; others never recover. The shrubby Veronicas never do break up from the roots here. My large Arbutus, killed the same winter, threw up a few shoots, but never did any good, and died the next year. I think the shrubby Veronicas so well worth growing that I have five or six varieties; and as they are not quite hardy, I keep pots of cuttings every winter. This we do also with three or four nominally hardy Cistuses, though they are a little more difficult to strike. Helianthemums or Rock-roses are well worth growing from seed in a sunny dry situation. I know nothing more charming than these delicate bright-flowered little plants blazing and blinking in the sunshine. I have a double-flowered scarlet Rock-rose, not figured in any of my books and which I have rarely seen in gardens. It flowers persistently for many months.

April 17th—We have had lately a severely cold week—Blackthorn winter indeed. How the poor garden shrivels and shrinks, and seems to lose all its colour!

Many years ago, in a volume of Tennyson given me by Owen Meredith, he wrote on the fly-leaf the following little poem, full of sympathy for the gardener:—

POT-POURRI FROM A SURREY GARDEN

In Nature can aught be unnatural?
If so, it is surely the frost,
That cometh by night and spreadeth death's pall
On the promise of summer which spring hath lost.
In a clear spring night
Such a frost pass'd light
Over the budding earth, like a ghost.

But the flowers that perish'd
Were those alone
Which, in haste to be cherish'd
And loved and known,
Had too soon to the sun all their beauty shown.
Lightly vested,
Amorous-breasted
Blossom of almond, blossom of peach—
Impatient children, with hearts unsteady,
So young, and yet more precocious each
Than the leaves of the summer, and blushing already
These perished because too soon they lived;
But the oak-flower, self-restrained, survived;
'If the sun would win me,' she thought, 'he must
Wait for me, wooing me warmly the while;
For a flower's a fool, if a flower would trust
Her whole sweet being to one first smile.

MAY

Vegetable growing—Autumn annuals—Spring seeds—Description of my own garden—Weeding—Houses facing west—Flowering shrubs—May flowers—Sundials—Roses and Creepers—History of the Tulip—Salads—Plant shelters—Sweet Verbena—Blue Anemones—Packing out flowers—A few simple receipts—Plants in pots.

May 1st—I have not mentioned during these spring months the cultivation of the kitchen garden. I leave that entirely to my gardener, only helping throughout the year by looking up in Vilmorin's book (mentioned in January) any special vegetables which are not generally cultivated in England, and noting any deficiency in quantity or quality. No one can expect everything to be equally successful every season, as an unfortunate sowing, a dry fortnight, a late frost, or a cold wind are answerable for a good deal in any garden. It is always some consolation if one finds one's failures are shared by one's neighbours, because then it is more likely to be from some atmospheric cause than from one's own bad cultivation. All the same, the best gardeners have the fewest failures.

We do not sow Sunflowers and many autumn-flowering annuals before the first week in May. For out-of-the-way hardy and half-hardy seeds I find no one is more to be relied on than Mr. Thompson of Ipswich. His packets of seed are not so large nor so expensive as those of some other first-class nurserymen, a great advantage for amateurs. His catalogue is one of the best—simple, concise, and clear, and giving all the information really wanted, except perhaps by beginners. These, however, are equally depressed and bewildered by every catalogue and every gardening book.

Nothing is so delightful as the first warm days, which come sometimes at the beginning, sometimes later in May. By this time all the March seeds are well up, the whole garden teems with life, and all Nature seems full of joy. The following little poem, which was in a May *Pall Mall* two years ago, expresses so charmingly the joyousness of spring that I copied it out:—

BABY SEED SONG

Little brown seed, oh! little brown brother,
Are you awake in the dark?
Here we lie cosily, close to each other;
Hark to the song of the lark—
'Waken!' the lark says, 'waken and dress you;
Put on your green coats and gay.
Blue sky will shine on you, sunshine caress you—
Waken! 'tis morning—'tis May!'

Little brown seed, oh! little brown brother,
What kind of flower will you be?
I'll be a poppy—all white, like my mother;
Do be a poppy, like me.
What! you're a sunflower? How I shall miss you
When you're grown golden and high!
But I shall send all the bees up to kiss you;
Little brown brother, good-bye.

May 3rd—It seems almost useless to describe my garden. Though I myself am so very fond of it, there is no reason anyone else should understand why I love it; and when I read the description of the gardens that other people love, I wonder I can bear with it at all. It is surrounded, as I said before, with large forest trees; and that most objectionable of conifers, a Wellingtonia, grows almost in the middle of the garden. I cannot cut it down, as this would deprive the lawn-tennis ground of the only shade it has. How I long to turn that lawn-tennis ground into a sunk Dutch garden, with its low red wall all round it! Yet I know I should miss them very much if I no longer heard the cries of the lawn-tennis game or the more recent click of the croquet-balls.

The top of the low wall, in front of the south side of the house, is a long bed of Tea Roses. Mr. Robinson names all the best sorts, so I need not do so. They do not flourish very well with us, I confess, and yet certainly better than any other Roses. It is their first flowering in June that is not very good. From August to October they are a great delight, flowering at intervals during all that time, and sending up long lovely shoots of brown leaves, that one can gather without scruple, as they are sure to be injured by the winter frosts; and the more the blooms are cut, the more they flower. At the other side of the lawn-tennis ground I have a little rockery, the system of which I can recommend to anyone who wants room and various aspects for plants without blocking out the rest of the garden or the distance beyond. We dug a large deep hole in the ground, carrying up gradually a small irregular path to the level of the ground on each side, roughly placing pieces of flat stone on each side of the path (to form steps) and all round the hole at the bottom. We kept the earth from falling by facing it with a wall of stones, stuck flatly and irregularly into the earth; this makes an excellent cool and deep root-bed for many Alpine and other plants. When it rains, there is a natural tendency for the water to drain down in all directions into the hole at the bottom. This hole had been dug deeper in the middle, and puddled with a little clay, not cement; and large stones were laid in the bottom, to retain the water longer than it naturally would remain in our sand. For really dry weather some pipes are laid on undergound to a tap in another part of the garden, from which the water runs into a tub at the top of the rockery for watering, and the overflow falls into the hole. In this way our tiny water-bed is kept moist in the dryest weather.

We grow in the water one of the most beautiful of our river plants, the *Ranunculus lingua,* or Water Buttercup. It has a noble growth and large, shining, yellow flowers, which bloom for a long time. Its only fault is that, if given the position it likes, it grows and increases with weed-like rapidity, and in a small space must be ruthlessly thinned out when it begins to grow in spring, and often later as well. We have in the hole Japanese Primulas and Japanese Iris (*Kempferi*), though they do not flower as well as in the dry bed above, which is the hottest, dryest, most sunny place in the garden; and the only attention they get, after being planted in good leaf mould, is some copious waterings when the flower-buds are formed. They have the largest, finest flowers I have ever seen in England. I must not forget our native Forget-me-nots, which, Tennyson says, 'grow for happy lovers.' It is a much more persistent flowerer than the garden kind.

In his 'Lancashire Garden' Mr. Bright praises very much the *Primula japonica,* and nothing can be more charming and unusual than the whorled growth of its flower-stems. He calls the blossoms crimson; I call them dark magenta—at any rate, they have that purple tinge which spoils so many reds. Where they really look well is in a moist ditch or on the damp half-shaded edge of a wood. If the ground is prepared for them, and the white kind planted too, they sow themselves in endless variety of tone from dark to light; but they are not especially suited for beds or mixing with other plants, and from their colour are not worth growing in pots.

All round the top of the hole described above is a raised bed, left irregular in places from the throwing-up of the earth that was dug out. The whole thing is on a very small scale in my garden, but it partakes slightly of the nature of the rockeries at Kew, which anyone interested in this kind of gardening can see, and by seeing learn. The great point of making a rockery is to have large mounds of good earth, and then lay stones on them, making terraces and little flat beds, stoned over to retain the moisture and prevent the earth being washed away. The old idea was to have stumps of trees or mounds of stones and brick, and then fill in the interstices with earth. This is no good at all; the plants have no depth of earth, and perish. The trouble of such gardening consists only in the constant hand-weeding that it requires. This must be done by someone more or less experienced, as very often the most precious plant looks like a small weed, while in other cases many planted things are no better than weeds if left alone, and quickly choke and destroy all their less vigorous neighbours.

Weeding! What it means to us all! The worry of seeing the weeds, the labour of taking them up, the way they flourish at busy times, and the dangers that come from zeal without knowledge! When we first went to live in the country, an affectionate member of the family, who hates weeds and untidiness of all kinds, set to work to tear up ruthlessly every annual that had been sown, and with pride said, 'At any rate, I have cleared that bit of ground.' Weeding, if tiring, is also a fascinating employment; and so is spudding. The first is best done in dry weather, the second in moist. I am all for reducing lawns and turf, except for paths, in small gardens; but what there is of grass should be well kept, and free from weeds. A quantity of daisies showing up their white faces, though pretty in theory, are in fact very unbecoming to the borders on a sunshiny summer's day.

The longest side of the house faces west. How I love it because of this! To my mind, every country house is dull that does not face west, and have its principal view that way. Modern civilisation forbids us to enjoy the sunrise, but the varied effects of the sunset sky glorify everything—the most commonplace gable or the ugliest chimney-stack, a Scotch fir or an open field, which assumes a green under an evening primrose sky that it never has at any other time. The sky is like the sea for its ever-changefulness. You may watch sunsets most carefully every day in the year, and never will you see twice exactly the same effect. How we all know, and notice after midsummer, that marching south of the sun at setting-time! The old fellow in June sets right away to the north, over the Common, changing groups of trees and a little distant hill to purple and blue. At the autumn equinox he looks straight in at the windows as he goes down between the stems of the two tall fir-trees. Who, when forced to come in to dinner on a summer's evening, does not appreciate a west dining-room with tall panes of glass which give the power to measure the gradations of the sky, from the deep grey-blue of night's garments at the top, to the bright gold, streaked with purple and crimson, at the base—the earth growing mysteriously dark all the while, and the evening star shining brighter every minute? Architects tell you, and men say, they prefer that a house should face south-east. I do not at all agree with them; the effects of evening to me are too much to give up for any other advantage in the world, real or imaginary. It is far easier to make some other room into a breakfast-room, to catch the morning sun in winter, than to change your dining-room in the summer for the sake of the sunsets.

To the west, then, I have my fountain, level with the turf, and with only the ornament of some special plants. To the right of the fountain is a large bed of carnations, slightly raised and terraced with stones, to give good depth of rich soil, unrobbed of moisture from the strong-growing shrubs behind, that are especially necessary for protection from the north and east. I strongly advise that on first coming to a new place you should never cut down much till you have given all the consideration possible to that matter of protection. I cannot repeat too often that wind-swept gardens can never be really satisfactory to the gardener.

On the left of the fountain, cut in the grass, are the two long borders, far the most difficult part of the garden to keep as I should wish them to be. They should be always gay and bright, the highest plants planted down the middle; and even they should be unequal in height. All plants that grow forward into the grass must be kept for other beds edged with stone or gravel. Borders cut in grass must be luxuriant and not untidy, and filled principally with plants which in their non-flowering season are not unsightly. It is for such borders that the seed beds and the reserve garden are so indispensable.

On the left of these borders are a few specimen plants cut in the grass:—A *Polygonum cuspidatum*, which is a joy from the first starting of its marvellous quick spring growth to its flowering-time, and to the day when its yellow autumn leaves leave the bare red-brown branches standing alone after the first frosts of October; a Siberian Crab, beautiful with blossom in spring and with fruit in autumn; also that lovely autumn-flowering shrub *Desmodium penduliflorum*, which has to be cut down every year, and which is never seen to advantage in a border because of its feathery and spreading growth.

Behind these again, and facing due north and shaded from the south, is a large bed of the old Moss-Rose, which in this position does exceedingly well. The large branches are partly pegged down, and they are not pruned back very hard. Behind the fountain, away from the house, are bamboos, Japanese grasses, and low-growing, shrubby Spiræas; the smallest gardens should not be without some of these, more especially *S. thunbergi*, so precious for its miniature early flowers and its lovely decorative foliage, and very useful for picking and sending away. *Clethra* (Sweet Pepper Bush) is also a useful little shrub, as it flowers in July, when watering helps it to bloom well. But I have only to refer you again and again to the 'English Flower Garden.' If you study this, you will never lack variety or plenty, whatever your soil, or your situation, or your aspect—no, nor even your nearness to that deadly enemy of plant life, a smoky town.

A lovely spring-flowering shrub is *Exochorda grandiflora*. I can most conscientiously say, 'Get it.' It is perfectly hardy; the flowers, full-blown and in bud, are of an exquisitely pure white, and the foliage is light-green, delicate, and refined.

One of the most precious of May flowers, and one not nearly enough grown, is the early Dutch Honeysuckle. It is nearly white, though it dies off yellow. I have named it in the lists, but it deserves, if only for picking, a place in every garden. Being an early bloomer, it requires a warm place, and would do admirably against the low wall of any greenhouse. Those precious frontages to greenhouses, in large places and in what I call 'gardeners' gardens,' are so often left unused, neat, empty, and bare. On these wasted places many lovely things would grow, and none better than this beautiful Dutch Honeysuckle, with its double circles of blooms, its excellent travelling qualities, and its powerful sweet scent, unsurpassed by anything. It is, I suppose, like many things, better for good feeding. It wants nothing but cutting back hard as soon as it has made its summer growth, after flowering, to keep it well in its place. It flowers profusely year after year, and it is easily increased by summer layering.

Old Man or Southernwood (*Artemisia abrotanum*) ought never to be forgotten. It grows easily from cuttings stuck into the ground in any of the early summer months. I am told that it is an especial favourite with the London poor. Perhaps its strong smell brings back any chance association with the country and the cottage garden. It reminds one of the old story of the poor Irishman, when the Lady Bountiful of the place had transformed his cabin into the graceful neatness of an English cottage. He gazed half-indignantly and half-gratefully on the change. 'It is all very kind,' said he, 'but the good lady does not know how dear to a poor man is everything that reminds him of the time when he played, instead of working. These great folks do not understand us.' But, after all, are we not all like that? Does not sweet Nature herself throw a veil over the storms of middle-life and soften memories, which become sharp, vivid, and clear only concerning our young days and the time when 'we played,' full of buoyant hope for all that lay before us?

I have always wished for a sundial in the middle of my grass walks where they widen into a circle. Even in an unpretending modern garden I do not think a sundial is affected—or, at any rate, not very—and I long to write round the top of it my favourite among the old Italian mottoes:—'I only mark the bright hours.' To the left of my long borders are four large, most useful, square beds, divided by narrow green paths. These are planted and sown, and renewed three or four times a year; and I always wonder how anyone gets on without such kinds of beds. The Love-in-the-Mist and *Gypsophila gracilis* are sown broadcast here together twice a year, in March and in September. I always save my own seed of Love-in-the-Mist; but in doing that, you must be careful to mark the best, largest, and bluest flowers. Then what you keep is far better than what you can buy; but, unless you take this trouble, seeds grown in one place degenerate. To the right of the long borders are two large Rose beds with Roses—old-fashioned rather than very large ones. The Hybrid Perpetuals do so badly in the light soil; but here are *Gloria Mundi*, Cottage-maid, the dear little pink *Rose de Meaux*, the large white Cabbage, and so on.

Beyond the Rose beds is a covered walk, made with stems of small fir-trees bound together with wire—an attempt at a pergola, but not by any means as solid as I should like. On this grow vines, hardy climbing Roses, Honeysuckles, and a dark claret-coloured Vine (which looks well), *Aristolochia*, Clematis (various), and, to make a little brightness in spring, two Kerrias. The single one, which is the original Japanese plant, is very uncommon, and yet so pretty—much better for wedging than the double kind, the old Jews-mallow of cottage gardens.

All these plants want constant watching, pruning, manuring, chalking, mulching. One ought always to be on the watch to see if things do not look well, and why they do not. The great thing to remember is, that if a plant is worth growing at all it is worth growing healthily. A Daisy or a Dandelion, fine, healthy, and robust, as they hold up their heads in the spring sunshine, give more pleasure and are better worth looking at than the finest flower one knows that looks starved, drooping and perishing at the flowering-time. With many plants here, if not watered at the flowering-time, the buds droop and the flowers never expand at all.

We have been eating lately, as Spinach, and found it quite delicious, the leaves of the Chicory, which Sutton calls 'Christmas Salad.' It is a first-rate plant all through the winter, an excellent salad, and now so good, useful, and wholesome to eat cooked. It should be dressed as recommended for Spinach in 'Dainty Dishes.'

This is the time to make Rhubarb jam; if carefully made, and a little ginger added, it is very good indeed.

To my mind, few flowers please the eye as the Tulip does.

T. gesneriana, with its handsome long stem and brilliant flower, gives me especial delight. The Tulip is a member of the Lily family, and has an interesting history, which I read one day in a newspaper. It is a native of Asia Minor, and was brought from Constantinople in 1557. It was first flowered in England in 1559 by the wife of an apothecary. She had procured the first bulb from a grateful sailor who had brought it home in return for attentions during sickness, by which his life was saved. It was all he had, like the widow's mite, but it was a source of great profit to the wife of the apothecary, who tenderly cultivated it, and sold the bulbs for a guinea each after she had, by good care, procured a sufficient stock of them.

May 5th—The garden looks dull just now; but four weeks of no rain always produce that effect on this soil. When the showers do come, everything revives in the most extraordinary way, partly from the earth being so warm and dry. The only rather showy things in the garden are some early red Rhododendrons, and they look droopy; a Siberian Crab, which has been one mass of snowy-white blossoms for a fortnight; and a most desirable little shrub called *Deutzia elegans*, quite hardy, totally unaffected by our coldest winters, flowering every year, and wanting no attention except the cutting-back every year after flowering. Berberises I do not find quite so hardy as one expects them to be, but this very likely is because they do not grow very robust, owing to the dryness of the soil. *B. Darwinii* was nearly killed by the severe winter, but is now flowering profusely, and is a lovely and desirable shrub. The whole charm of flowering shrubs, to my mind, depends on their being given lots of room, and sufficient care being taken of them to make them individually healthy plants. The dear little pink *Daphne Cneorum* is doing well, but I have myself often given it a canful of water during the last fortnight. It is very, much strengthened if, after the flowering, you layer a certain number of the branches, covering them with a little peat; this enables you to increase your stock of plants, and improves the size of your specimen plant.

All this last month we have been eating the thinnings of seedling Lettuces as salad, and they are most delicious. All kinds of Lettuces seem to eat equally well; they are grown in boxes in a frame. I first thought of eating them from seeing that they were thrown away to give room for those that were going to be planted out. I now purposely grow them in extra quantities, and in succession, so that my salads may never fall short. Even out of doors, in the summer, we sometimes grow them if our large Lettuces run to seed. They make infinitely better salad than the tough little brown Cos Lettuces, grown with such care in frames all through the winter. All the year round I always mix the salad on the table myself, using nothing but oil, vinegar, salt, and pepper; and I always have brought to table, on a separate little plate, some herbs, Tarragon, Chervil, and some very young Onions; these I cut up over the Lettuces before I mix in the oil and vinegar. If you have no young Onions, Chive-tops do very well. These herbs are an immense addition to any salad, but are far from universally used in England, though they are quite easy to grow, for anyone who has a kitchen garden, even a small one. The Tarragon, however, and the Onions have to be grown in the conservatory in the winter. Many young gardeners do not know that the secret of young Potatoes being good, and not watery, is to take them out of the ground several days before you boil them. A little Mint chopped on to young

Potatoes instead of Parsley makes a pleasant change; but then we English like Mint, and it is very different here from the Mint grown in dry countries, which is just like Peppermint. The French have a way of boiling Asparagus which is especially good for the thin green Asparagus so common in our English gardens:—You tie them into a bundle, and put them, stalk downwards, into a fairly deep saucepan. In this way the heads are only cooked by the steam, and do not become soppy.

May 10th—I have a friend who to-day writes she is having iron rings driven into an old stone house round the windows so as to hold pots of Carnations and Geraniums, to hang down as they do in Tyrol and Switzerland. This will look pretty, no doubt, if it answers; but in our cold and windy summers I am sure they would do better if one pot were sunk inside another with some moss between, so that the evaporation caused by the wind, which freezes the roots, should not be so great. Abroad the pots are frequently glazed either all the way down or part of the way down; this stops evaporation. So many greenhouse plants, when they are 'stood out,' as the gardeners say, get injured by the cold winds on the pots, which does far more harm than the wind on the leaves. One of the best and simplest remedies is to dig moderately deep trenches with a raised border round them of turf or boards, and stand the pots in these, instead of on the open ground. Sheets of corrugated iron cut to convenient sizes make excellent movable shelters for plants from the north-east wind. Shelter in all forms, without taking too much 'out of the soil, as trees and shrubs do, is the great secret of success in all kinds of gardening. I should spend my life in inventing shelters if I lived on the East Coast; but I confess that temporary protections are not very pretty. Another good method of obtaining shelter is to use common hurdles of iron or wood, or flat laths with Gorse or Bracken twisted into them. When all your hand-lights are in use in Spring, a good deal of protection from frost may be given to the seed beds by sheets of newspaper held down by a stone or two; muslin sewn over a zinc wire-coop will keep out six or seven degrees of frost. Dried Bracken spread over frames is even better for keeping out frost than matting, and is nearly as easily removed.

May 11th—Epimediums are charming little plants with lovely, graceful foliage, and are well worth growing if you have a moist and shady corner. *E. pinnatum* is perhaps the best, and has long clusters of small yellow flowers; the leaves are very pretty, and mix well with any flowers.

Aloysia citriodora (Sweet Verbena) is a plant that is a universal favourite. I have never known anyone, not even those who dislike strongly scented flowers, not be delighted with the delicious refreshing smell of its leaves, which they retain long after they are dried. Yet you go to house after house, and find no plants growing out of doors. Their cultivation is simple, and they require but little care to make them quite hardy; out of five or six plants which I have out of doors, only one died in the hard winter two years ago. If you have any small plants in your greenhouse (if not, buy them at sixpence apiece), put them out at the end of May, after hardening off, in a warm sunny place, either close to a wall or under the shelter of a wall. Water them, if the weather is dry; and do not pick them much the first year, as their roots correspond to the top growth. Cut off the flowers as they appear. When injured by the frost, never cut the branches down till quite late in the following year. It is this cutting-back that causes the death of so many plants; the larger stems are hollow, and the water in them either rots or freezes the roots. In November cover the roots of the Verbena with a heap of dry ashes; this is all the care they require, and they will break up stronger and finer each year. I have kept plants in this way year after year, even in an open border. I believe they would grow in London gardens as long as they have plenty of sun; and if the plant is weak when they begin to grow in the spring, it would be well to pick off some of the shoots. The cuttings strike quite easily all through the summer in sand in a greenhouse or under a bell-glass.

May 14th—I suppose it is the same with everything in life that one really cares about, and you must not, any of you, be surprised if you have moments in your gardening life of such profound depression and disappointment that you will almost wish you had been content to leave everything alone and have no garden at all. This is especially the case in a district affected by smoke or wind, or in a very light sandy soil. Five weeks without a drop of rain, and everything bursts into flower and as quickly goes off. Two or three days ago the lilacs were quite beautiful, having responded well to last year's pruning; now they are faded and scentless, and almost ugly. The German Irises, too, were blooming well, with long healthy stalks. I find that what helps them here is to grow the small pieces one buys from the nurseryman for two or three years in rich garden soil, where they grow quickly, making roots and leaves. After that I move them into some dry border facing east or south, and I find that they then flower as well as one can possibly desire. The beautiful pale-blue *Anemone apennina* is now nodding its little blue heads under my big trees. In the far-away days of my childhood— it must have been in the 'Forties—a really typical man-of-the-world presented my mother with four well-bound volumes of Mrs. Hemans' poems. Imagine any man giving such a present now! And yet she wrote some pretty things, of which the following is a specimen, and certainly it is quite as good as many modern flower-poems:—

TO THE BLUE ANEMONE

Flower of starry clearness bright,
Quivering urn of coloured light,
Hast thou drawn thy cup's rich dye
From the intenseness of the sky?
From a long, long fervent gaze
Through the year's first golden days
Up that blue and silent deep
Where, like things of sculptured sleep.
Alabaster clouds repose
With the sunshine on their snows?
Thither was thy heart's love turning,
Like a censer ever burning,
Till the purple heavens in thee
Set their smile, anemone?

Or can those warm tints be caught
Each from some quick glow of thought?
So much of bright soul there seems
In thy bendings and thy gleams,
So much thy sweet life resembles
That which feels and weeps and trembles,
I could deem thee spirit-filled
As a reed by music thrilled
When thy being I behold
In each loving breath unfold,
Or, like woman's willowy form,
Shrink before the gathering storm,
I could ask a voice from thee,
Delicate anemone.

Flower, thou seem'st not born to die,
With thy radiant purity,
But to melt in air away,
Mingling with the soft spring day.
When the crystal heavens are still,
And faint azure veils each hill,
And the lime-leaf does not move,
Save to songs that stir the grove,
And earth all glorified is seen,
As imaged in some lake serene—
Then thy vanishing should be,
Pure and meek anemone.

Flower, the laurel still may shed
Brightness round the victor's head,
And the rose in beauty's hair
Still its festal glory wear,
And the willow leaves droop o'er
Brows which love sustains no more
But thy living rays refined,
Thou, the trembler of the wind,
Thou, the spiritual flower,
Sentient of each breeze and shower,
Thou, rejoicing in the skies,
And transpierced with all their dyes,
Breathing vase, with light o'erflowing,
Gem-like to thy centre glowing—
Thou the poet's type shall be,
Flower of soul, anemone.

May 16th—None of the small cheap bulbs are better worth growing than the Alliums, white and yellow. They increase themselves rapidly, and are quite hardy, though the white ones force well and are useful. People object to them because the stalks smell of garlic at the time of picking, but it goes off as soon as they are put into water; and the flowers are lovely, delicate, and useful, and have the great merit I mention so often of remaining a long time fresh in water. We leave some of the bulbs in the ground, and take up others. Those that are taken up and dried in the sun flower best the following year; and the finest bulbs can be planted together, the yellow making a fine splotch of colour just as the yellow Alyssum is over. The smaller the garden, the more essential it is to get a succession in colour. Avoid many white flowers in small gardens; in roomy gardens with shady corners nothing looks better than the common single white and purple Rocket, raised from seed and planted in bold groups. It will grow in very dry places, but it soon gets untidy, and has to be cut back, which it does not seem to mind at all.

Tiarella cordifolia ('Foam-flower,' Mr. Robinson calls it) is a little Canadian plant which ought never to be left out of any garden.

May 19th—This is the first day of one of the great gardening interests and treats in the year—the Royal Horticultural Show in the Temple Gardens. I go every year now, and should be sorry to miss it. How odd it seems, that for years and years I never went to a flower show, or knew anything about them, and now they have become one of the interests of my life! The great attraction this year is the revival of what are called old-fashioned late single Tulips—Breeders, Flames, &c. Those who like to buy the bulbs, ordering them carefully by the catalogue, may have their gardens gay with Tulips for over two months, certainly the whole of April and May. The quantity of Apples, for so late in the season, was what struck me as almost the most remarkable thing at the show. One of the great growers told me that he had tried every conceivable plan for keeping Apples, but that nothing answered so well as laying them simply on open, well-aired shelves in a fruit-house that was kept free from frost.

Tradescantia virginica (Spiderworts) are plants that do admirably in light soils, and flower two or three times in the summer, wanting nothing beyond thinning-out and transplanting, and dividing in the autumn. The pale-blue and the white are even more beautiful than the dark-blue and the red-purple; but they are all worth having, with their quaint-shaped flowers, so unlike other things. Every year, towards the end of May, I put in cuttings of Lavender and Rosemary. If the weather is dry, they are what gardeners call 'puddled-in,' which means that the ground is very much wetted first. In this way I have a constant supply of young plants. Rosemary is only really hardy with us if planted under the protection of large shrubs; the keen winds of March cut them off in the open. Many other plants can be increased in the same way—early flowering shrubs such as *Ribes sanguinum,* the Forsythias, &c. Last spring, in Suffolk, I saw a charming little garden-hedge made of *Ribes sanguinum,* all one brilliant mass of its flowers. This is quite worth trying; its success would depend on its being sharply pruned back the moment after flowering and before its seeds ripen. If your cuttings take, you can make your hedge in October. It is rather a repetition of the well-known and often-seen Sweetbriar hedge, which is all the better in a light soil for cutting back the young growths in July as well as for the spring pruning. It is a very good plan this month to take off some of the shoots—apt to be too numerous—that sprout on the pruned-back creepers, such as White Jasmine, Vines of all kinds, and *Bignonia radicans,* which handsome old garden favourite buds so late that the flowers do not expand unless treated in this way.

May 22nd—Not the smallest and dryest garden should be without *Stachys lanata,* a white woolly leaved plant, called Rabbit's Ears by cottage children, and particularly attractive to some people, who through life retain the love of a child for something woolly and soft. Certain characteristics are always reminding us, especially in some women, even when old, that they were once children. These leaves were formerly used as edgings to beds in a very objectionable way; but when grown in large clumps, they are most useful for picking. When cut, they go on growing in water, as Buttercups and Forget-me-nots do, and mix very well with many flowers, especially with *Narcissus poeticus,* any of the German Irises, and the lovely white *Scilla campanulata,* a cheap bulb, of which we can hardly have too many. There is a blue and a pink kind, but the white is the most lovely; and, in my opinion, all three are better worth growing than the usual Hyacinths, double or single. I think the people who live in the country in spring would find it more satisfactory to grow their greenhouse bulbs in large, open pans, several together, and covered with some of the mossy Saxifrages, than the usual two or three in a pot that gardeners are so fond of. If the pan has no hole at the bottom for drainage, you must put in lots of crocks, and be careful not to over-water; but bulbs like their roots moist.

I made a curious experiment with the little double *Prunus.* One moved last autumn, and one moved last spring out of the nursery into a sunny, sheltered border, are both covered with bloom, and lovely objects. Another plant, which was left in a sunny border for a year, has no bloom on it at all, though it is quite healthy. This is one more proof of how much is to be done with reserve gardens and moving in this light dry soil. Next month I shall choose a wet day, and move them all back again into the nursery. The white Dog-tooth Violet and the various Fritillarias are very satisfactory things. They like shade and a certain amount of moisture, but it is not necessary for their cultivation; they will grow anywhere. The common *Saxifraga,* London Pride, is a most desirable, useful plant; it is the better for dividing every two years. It travels well picked, and is so pretty and decorative in water; it looks well with large red Oriental Poppies, with no green at all. *Silene,* too, looks well with it in small glasses, for a change.

Deutzia crenata is a charming shrub, and flowering well this year. Unless the garden is very small, anyone who lives in the country in spring ought to have it. There is so little room for shrubs in a very small plot of ground, and no garden can be beautiful except when the lie of the ground and the surrounding circumstances are beautiful. The only ambition that can be indulged in with a small flat ground is to grow the greatest number of healthy plants possible in the least amount of space, and so secure continuous and varied flowers for nine months of the year.

The planning and laying-out of a small garden without great natural advantages ought to be as practical and simple as possible, a mere improvement on the cottage garden:—A small, straight path of brick or paving-stone, or grass or gravel, though that is the least desirable of all to my mind. Let beds be on either side. If you have shrubs round the edge of the garden to hide the paling, have a grass path in front of the shrubs, and then square or long beds in the middle. Never have a small lawn with beds cut in that; nothing gives so much labour and so little satisfaction as beds cut out of grass, and what makes them uglier still is bordering them again with some plant. The flowers are much better out in the open, away from the moisture-devouring shrubs. In gardening, as in many things in life, let your wits improve on what is rather below you; never look at the squire's big garden in your neighbourhood, and then try and imitate it in small. Nothing makes a more charming edging for beds, if you have gravel paths, than large flat stones; it boil as fast as possible, with the lid off. Keep damming it all the time. When done (which means that it is soft, but with a little hardness left in the middle), strain it off onto a sieve, and then let cold water run on it till it becomes quite cold. Put it back into the saucepan without water, to get hot enough for table. It should take 1 hour to get hot; it will be a bad colour if hurried.

Curry Of Ham Toast—This receipt is useful to finish up an old ham:—8 oz. of lean ham chopped very fine, 1 teaspoonful of Harvey and 1 of Worcester sauce, 1 teaspoonful of curry paste, a small piece of butter, a good tablespoonful of white sauce, and 2 tablespoonfuls of thick cream. All these should be mixed together and heated. Cut some rounds of toast, and serve very hot.

The following receipt for bottling green Gooseberries I think you will find useful. The great point is to pick them just at the right moment, when neither too large nor too small. And much depends on waxing the corks well; so I add the receipt for that.

Bottled Green Gooseberries—Pick off noses and stalks, but be careful not to burst the berries. Then fill some wide-mouthed bottles quite full, tie over the mouths paper with pricked holes, stand the bottles in boiling water, and just let the fruit turn colour (no sugar or anything with the fruit). Take the bottles out, and cork and seal them. The old way was to bury them head downwards in a garden border; but if well sealed, to keep out all air, I do not believe that is necessary. Green Currants are excellent done the same way, and Morella Cherries, small Plums, and Damsons; only these must be ripe.

Wax for Bottles—2 parts of beeswax, 1 part of resin, 1 part powdered colour (Venetian red). Melt the beeswax and resin in an old iron saucepan. (Only melt, do not boil.) Then stir in the colour and let it cool a little, both to avoid the pungent vapours and to thicken slightly. Dip the corked tops of the bottles while holding them horizontally over the pot, and turn them round, so as to run the extra stuff into the joint; they are the better for a second dip. Leave the remains of the wax to harden in the pot, which should be used for this purpose only. It can be melted again at any time, and more added as wanted.

May 30th—A good deal of real gardening pleasure and satisfactory ornamental effect is to be had from growing plants in pots and tubs, vases and vessels of all kinds, both in small and big gardens. I use large Sea-kale pots, when they are no longer wanted for the Sea-kale, by turning them upside down, putting two bits of slate in the bottom of the pot, some drainage and a few lumps of turf, and filling it up with really good soil. As a variety a Rhubarb-pot is useful. If you live near a pottery, they will turn you out pots to any shape you fancy. Flat ones, like those used by house-painters, make a pleasant change, especially for small bulbs; also petroleum casks cut in two, burnt inside, then tarred and painted. It must never, of course, be in any case forgotten to have holes large enough to make good drainage. I use butter casks treated in the same way, and have some little oak tubs in which bullion came from America. These are very strong; and some water-loving plants do much better in wood, since the evaporation in summer is not nearly so rapid as from the earthenware. That is an important thing to remember, both as regards sun and wind. If the plants are at all delicate, and brought out of a greenhouse, the pots, when standing out, ought to be either quite sunk into the earth or shaded. This cannot, of course, be done in the case of pots placed on a wall or terrace, or on a stand; constant care about watering is, therefore, essential. Even in wet weather they often want more water if the sun comes out, as the rain wets the leaves, but hardly affects the soil at all.

On the Continent, where all kinds of pot-cultivation have been longer practised than in England, flowerpots are often glazed outside, which keeps the plants much moister, and makes less necessity for frequent watering. The French, especially, understand much better than we do the potting-on of plants. They begin by putting seeds into pots no bigger than a thimble, and sinking them in boxes with cocoanut fibre; the little plants are then potted-on very gradually, never injuring the roots at all. The merciless way in which gardeners often tear off the roots collected at the bottom of a pot is most injurious to the plant. The large red jars that still bring oil from Italy, covered with their delightful coarse wicker-work, are useful ornaments in some gardens. They are glazed inside, and boring a hole in the bottom of them is not very easy work. They have to be more than half filled with drainage; and plants do not do well in them for more than one season, as the surface of earth exposed at the top is so small. In old days the oil merchants in the suburbs of London used to cut them in two vertically, and stick them against their houses above their shops, as an advertisement or ornament. Enthusiastic amateurs will find that they get two very nice pots by sawing them in half horizontally, just below the sham handles. The top part, when reversed, requires the same treatment as was recommended for the Sea-kale pots. Many different things may be grown for standing out of doors in the large pots and tubs above described, and one plant may succeed another. The first rule, I think, is to grow in them those plants which do not grow especially well in your own local soil. To put into a pot what is flourishing much better in a bed a few yards off is, to my mind, a mistake.

I grow in pots large old plants of Geraniums—Henry Jacoby is especially good. They are kept on in the greenhouse from year to year, their roots tied up in moss and crowded into a pot or box with no earth and very little water through the winter; early in April they are potted-up and protected by mats in a pit, as we have no room for them in the greenhouse. This causes them to be somewhat pot-bound, and they flower brilliantly during the latter part of the summer. French Marguerites (the yellow and the white) with large leaves are good pot-plants early in the year—far prettier than the narrow-leaved kinds. A double Pomegranate I have had for many years in a pot; and if pruned out in the summer, it flowers well. The large, old-fashioned, oak-leaved, sticky Cape Sweet Geranium, which has a handsomer flower than the other kinds, makes a very good outdoor pot-plant. In potting-up strong, growing plants that are to remain in the pots for some time, it is useful to put some broken-up bones with the crocks at the bottom of the pots for the roots to cling to them.

Fuchsias, especially the old-fashioned *fulgens,* are satisfactory. Carnations—Raby Castle, Countess of Paris, and Mrs. Reynolds Hole—I grow in pots, and they do extremely well; they must be layered early in July, and answer best if potted up in September and just protected from severe frosts. This year we took up a large clump of Montbretias out of a dry sunny bed of Cape bulbs in the kitchen garden, just as they were coming through the ground, and dropped them into a large Sea-kale pot. They flowered exceedingly well, and in September we put them back in the dry border to die down. In fine summers Myrtles and Oleanders flower well with us in tubs, not in the open ground. We treat Oleanders as they do in Germany—cut them back moderately in October, and dry them off, keeping them in a coach-house, warm shed, or wherever severe frosts will not reach them. When quite dry, they stand a moderate amount of frost. Then in March they are brought out, the ground is stirred and mulched, and they are taken into a greenhouse and brought on a bit. In May they are thickly covered with good strong horse-manure and copiously watered. At the end of the month they are stood out in the open on a low wall. During May, June, and July they cannot have too much water; after that they want much less, or the leaves turn yellow and drop off. *Campanula pyramidalis* (*see* 'English Flower Garden'), a biennial, does well in pots, if shaded—blue and white both in one pot, or apart. The seedlings have to be potted up in autumn (plants a year old); as with the Canterbury Bells, if you cut off the fading flowers the flowering season is much prolonged. Canterbury Bells (*Campanula medium*) make charming pot-plants for large rooms or corridors in May or June. They are annuals, and the seed can be sown out of doors in March or April, keeping the seedlings well thinned, transplanting in the autumn, and potting-up the following spring (*see* 'English Flower Garden'). If strong crowns of *Campanula persicifolia* are potted up in autumn, they force beautifully in a moderate greenhouse in spring, and are most satisfactory for picking or otherwise.

Some years I grow *Solanum jasminoides* over bent wires in pots; they are rather pretty. *Clethra* (Sweet Pepper Bush), a small North American shrub, we lifted from the reserve garden in June and put into a pot, and it flowered very well. The variety of plants which can be experimented upon for growing in pots out of doors in summer is almost endless. Love-lies-bleeding (*Amaranthus caudatus*) is an annual; but if sown in January, and very well grown-on as a fine single specimen plant, it looks handsome and uncommon in a green glazed pot or small tub. Nothing we grow in pots is more satisfactory than the old-fashioned *Calceolaria amplexicaulis*. It does not grow to any perfection in the beds, the soil being too dry; but, potted, it makes a splendid show through the late summer and autumn months. A red-brown kind, little grown now, which I brought from Ireland, and which I cannot name, also succeeds very well. They both want potting-up in good soil in April. The shrubby Veronicas (*Speciosa rubra, Imperialis,* and the variegated *Andersoni*) I grow in pots because they flower beautifully in the autumn; and the drowsy bumblebees love to lie on them, in the sunshine, when the *Sedum spectabile* is passing away. They are not quite hardy with us, as they cannot withstand the long, dry, cold springs. This in itself justifies the growing them in pots; in mild, damp districts they are large shrubs. The small bushy Michaelmas Daisies we put into pots at the end of July, and they fill up blank spaces on the wall late in the year.

The blue Cape *Agapanthus* everybody grows in tubs. They have to be rather pot-bound and kept dry in the winter, to flower well; as the flower-buds form, they want to be well watered and a weekly dose of liquid manure. Hydrangeas I find difficult to grow when planted out. The common kinds do exceedingly well in tubs, in half-shady places, if they get a good deal of water. A variegated half-hardy shrub called *Procosma variegata* makes a showy and yet restrained pot-plant. Large standard Myrtles I have had covered with blooms in August in tubs. My large old plant, which I had had many years, was killed this spring by being turned out of the room it had wintered in too early, because we came from London sooner than usual. The great difficulty in small places is housing these large plants in winter. They do not want much protection, but they must have some; and the death of large old plants is grievous. We have just built a new greenhouse, which we are going to try with no heating beyond a lamp-stove in very cold weather. If I lived in the country in the winter, I should grow small Evergreens in pots and try various experiments, which are of no use to me, as I live in London. In many cases the plants would not get injured by frost if one pot were sunk inside another.

JUNE

Hands and fingers after weeding—Shrub-pruning—Boxes for birds—
Robins in greenhouse—'Burning Bush'—Two Polygonums—
Strawberries—Geraniums and cuttings—Cactuses—Freesia bulbs —
Gloriosa superba—Luncheon dishes—Cucumbers.

June 2nd—It must be admitted that one of the great drawbacks
to gardening and weeding is the state into which the hands
and fingers get. Unfortunately, one's hands belong not only
to oneself, but to the family, who do not scruple to tell the
gardening amateur that her appearance is 'revolting.'
Constant washing and always keeping them smooth and soft
by a never-failing use of vaseline—or, still better, a mixture
of glycerine and starch, kept ready on the washstand to use
after washing and before drying the hands—are the best
remedies I know. Old dog-skin or old kid gloves are better
for weeding than the so-called gardening gloves; and for
many purposes the wash-leather housemaid's glove, sold at
any village shop, is invaluable.

Good gardeners tell you never to cut flowers except with a sharp knife. This is good advice for shrubs or pot-plants, the clean cut being better for the plants; but I advise that the knife should be on a steel chain a foot or so long, with a good pair of garden hook-shaped scissors at the other end— for the cutting of annuals or lately planted plants with a knife, in light soil, is very much to be avoided. The smallest pull loosens, the roots, and immediate death, in hot weather, is the result. Another advantage of knife and scissors together on the chain is that they are more easy to find when mislaid, or lost in the warm and bushy heart of some plant.

June 4th—Now, and even a little earlier, is the great pruning-time of the year for all spring-flowering shrubs. No doubt this cutting-out may be especially important in a, light soil such as ours, where things flower themselves to death, like pot-bound plants. It is rather tiresome work; it requires one person to cut out the old wood and slightly cut back the topmost branches with a long-handled nipper, and another to stand at a little distance and give directions. Without this precaution, the tree or shrub would often become lop-sided and unsightly. It is impossible for the man who is cutting to see what should be taken out. *Choisya ternata* must be gone over and cut back severely, in spite of all one may have gathered from it while in flower. Also with Lilacs, Laburnums, Weigelias, Crab-apples, Double Cherries, Viburnum, and *Pyrus japonica,* this pruning—at any rate, in light soils—must never be neglected or forgotten. Very often only a little cutting-out is required. If it is done too late, it does more harm than good, and injures next year's bloom. *Clematis montana* succeeds much better if the young growth is cut off every year, which prevents it from getting tangled and matted, and all going to leaf instead of blossom. It is the same with Honeysuckles and Brooms. We sow the Brooms— white, yellow, and red and yellow—every year. They can always be transplanted when quite young to where they are to flower, and a good supply of young plants is so useful.

The bird-boxes this spring have been well used by my little couples. Fly-catchers and Wrens never fail; but this year we have had rather an uncommon bird, a Red-start, and in the nest are seven eggs, though Bewick asserts that they only lay four or five. The eggs are pretty in colour, like the Hedge-sparrow's. The Red-start's eggs are a little longer and narrower in shape than the Hedge-sparrow's. A pair of Robins have hatched out three families this year in my greenhouse—fourteen young Robins! They began early in March, and built on a top-shelf; when the little ones were hatched, the old birds were so tame that they did not mind at all our putting the nest into a deep pot and placing it near the window for them to feed their young more conveniently. We also thought that in the pot it would attract less the attention of a terrible bird-killing old cat we have. He stays near a nest, scratching, till the parent birds are in such a frenzy of agitation and fear that they kick the young ones out of the nest; he then devours them at his leisure.

To those who have room I recommend the Venetian Sumach (*Rhus cotinus*), but it is not worth growing if it is crowded up. The most perfect way to grow it is to put the young plant in a well and richly made hole in the lawn, or at the edge of a shrubbery, the formality of which you wish to break. As it grows, cut away the turf from under it, and mulch it every winter; this makes it grow quickly. When it gets into a good big plant, leave off mulching, and dress it with chalk, which will make it flower and bear its lovely feathery seeds in July. In a good sunny situation it will turn a flaming red colour, which is the reason for its English name of the 'Burning Bush.' It does better in moderately damp soils than with us, but a little care will make it grow anywhere. It is well adapted for picking and putting into water, as the leaves have a faint aromatic smell; but it is not suited to very small gardens, for it spreads and takes up too much room. Crowding spoils its great characteristic of rooting into the ground all round.

The finer sorts of Clematis (*see* 'English Flower Garden') only do fairly well in our soil; and till I gave them plenty of chalk they often died. All the large *Jackmani* tribe (*see* nurserymen's catalogues) want cutting back to the ground very early in the year, before they begin to break in the spring; but they are worth all care and trouble. Many gardeners do not agree with me, but I am very fond of specimen plants grown in holes cut in grass, if they are planted with care, to group with shrubs behind them, and so as not to present a dotted-about appearance. In large gardens there are places enough—in shrubberies, by the side of water, or elsewhere—where these single specimens can grow healthily. In really small gardens they take too much room. In medium-sized gardens they become a feature and an interest. Several plants, besides the Venetian Sumach before mentioned, are such fine growers that they are well worth an individual place to show them off:—

Polygonum cuspidatum and P. *sacchalinense* are very effective, and grow splendidly in dry soils if the outside suckers are pulled out every spring; they want no other care. *Bocconia cordata* (Plume Poppy), a Japanese plant, also wants no other treatment; and in this way the old shoots grow up finer and stronger each year. They are herbaceous, like the Polygonums, and it is best not to cut down their hollow stems till the spring. *Leycesteria formosa* has a good growth; its uncommon brown flowers come late in the summer. (*Kerria japonica,* especially the single one mentioned before; the Privets, the golden one and the Alexandrian are the best.) Tamarisks, so seldom grown away from the sea, which are very pretty, especially the one with tiny pink flowers that come out in the spring (*T. parviflora,* I believe it is called); and many hardy Bamboos can all be grown separately as specimen plants; as also the two Eulalias, *japonica* and *zebrina,* the tall Japanese grasses. The *Arundo donax* is the lovely tall cane that grows in the ditches in Italy. But beware how you move it, if once you get it to grow; it does not at all like being disturbed. *Acanthus* in full sun is very handsome, and grows large in rather a moist place; so does the Giant Parsnip, but it is only a biennial.

June 9th—The Strawberry season is beginning. For many years this fruit was poison to me; now it gives me pleasure to think that I live almost entirely upon it for some weeks in the summer, eating it three times a day, and very little else, according to the practice of Linnæus, as quoted in March. It is of great importance that anyone who has room to grow Strawberries at all should grow several varieties—early, medium, or late (*see* catalogues). For ices, creams, jams, &c., I greatly recommend some of the high-flavoured, old-fashioned Hautboys; they are not very easy to get. The fruit grown on heavy soils round London for the market is often very tasteless; but one must work away with books and experience to get good Strawberries and a fairly long succession of them. In growing Strawberries, everything depends on making some new rows every year; layering the runners early, too, makes a great difference in the young plants the next year. 'Dainty Dishes' has some instructive old-fashioned receipts for Strawberry jam. Strawberries make an excellent compote if boiling syrup is poured over them. Raspberries are much better treated in this way. Currants require stewing. It improves all summer compotes to ice them well before serving.

I do not at all despise planting out the old-fashioned scarlet and crimson Geraniums—Pelargoniums, they ought to be called. Old plants are very much better than the small cuttings; but I have a few of these as well, and pots full of cuttings of the sweet-leaved kinds, of which there are so many varieties, and which are planted out the first week in June. Among red Geraniums, nothing is so fine and satisfactory as Henry Jacoby; it is a very steady bloomer, and has a fine rich colour. When you are planting out your Geraniums and cuttings, do not forget that some must be kept back in their pots and given constant care and attention all through the summer for late autumn and winter flowering in the greenhouse. We keep our plants for winter in a cold frame through the summer, and carefully pick off the flower-buds. Raspail is an excellent double variety for winter picking. One the nurserymen call 'Raspail Improved' is perhaps what it professes to be, though I do not see very much difference. It is because I live in London in the winter that I so much recommend double Geraniums, as the flowers of the single kind require to be gummed before they are packed. If not, they arrive only a little heap of scarlet petals in the paper, beautiful and lovely, but quite useless for putting into water.

My old books taught me to take an interest in Cactuses, which in the early part of the century were much grown. They are very easy of cultivation, and well worth growing for those who spend June and July in their gardens. A succession must be aimed at, as the drawback is that the blooms only last a short time. The old *Cereus speciosissimus* surpasses in beauty and splendour any garden plant I know, with its brilliant scarlet petals shot with the richest purple and its handsome white tassel of stamens. Another beautiful flower is the large white night-flowering *Cereus;* and if brought, when just about to bloom, into the hall or sitting-room, its delicious perfume pervades the whole house for twenty-four hours, if not for longer. Although Cactuses are very easy to cultivate, yet what they require they must have, or they do not flower at all, and then gardeners throw them away. Wholesome neglect is better than too much misdirected care; they want to be kept very dry, and not too warm all through the winter, but quite free from frost. In April they are re-potted, if they seem to require it; but that is seldom. Once started into growth, they want heat, light, sun, a little nourishment, and plenty of watering and syringing, with rain-water if possible; hard chalky water is bad for them. When they have done flowering, I plant them out in a good warm border till the middle of August. This does them a lot of good, and helps them very much to make new growth; they should be well syringed overhead while growing. Anyone really interested in Cactuses will learn all they want to know in a little book called 'Cactus Culture for Amateurs,' by W. Watson. The old and long-neglected taste for growing Cactuses is certainly reviving, and some of the finest kinds can be grown with very little trouble or expense. Mr. Watson is Assistant Curator of the Royal Botanic Gardens at Kew, where there is a large collection of Cactuses. He writes as one who knows, and the book is full of practical instructions.

I have a great many Stapelias, South African plants rather resembling miniature Cactuses in their growth, and requiring the same treatment. They are very curious, and are described in a modern book translated from the German, called the 'Natural History of Plants,' as belonging to a group of plants called 'indoloid.' Sometimes the scent of these South African Stapelias resembles that of decomposing mammalian flesh, sometimes of rotten fish, &c. This, of course, attracts insects. Flowers provided with indoloid scents resemble animal corpses in their colouring, having usually livid spots, violet streaks, and red-brown veins on a greenish or a fawn-coloured background. All the same, the flowers are to me curious and rather beautiful, so entirely unlike anything else. This month is the time to sort out the Freesia bulbs that have been drying in the sun, in their pots, laid on one side on the shelf of the greenhouse. The largest bulbs are re-potted now or in July in good strong loamy soil, but hardly watered at all till they begin to show through the earth. The next-sized bulbs are potted a month later. When the quite small ones are put into a box to grow on for next year they are too small to flower. Early potting-up of Freesias is very important if they are to flower early.

June 20th—For anyone with a small stove or warm greenhouse I can thoroughly recommend the growing of the *Gloriosa superba* or Creeping Lily. It is a lovely and curious flower; it lasts very long in water, and flowers continuously for two or three months. Its cultivation is simple enough: buy the bulbs in April, pot them up in good Lily soil (*see* Johnson's 'Gardener's Dictionary' for this and all other greenhouse and stove cultivation of plants), start them in heat, and grow them up wires or thin branching sticks, or anything that gives them support; water them well while growing; and as they begin to go off after flowering, and the leaves turn yellow, dry them gradually till they have quite died down. Then lay the pots on their sides, and keep them quite dry, but in a warm temperature, till you re-pot them the following spring. The flowers are lovely—crimson and yellow, with crinkled, turned-back petals, and they wedge so well in small flat vases.

In the last century the disciples of Linnæus took great pleasure botanically in this plant, as the pistil bends at nearly right angles in a most curious way, to insert its stigma amongst the stamens; and it is a good illustration of the sex of plants. It is figured in that old book I alluded to in March of Erasmus Darwin's, called the 'Botanic Garden,' and in the poem named 'The Loves of the Plants' it is thus spoken of:—

Proud Gloriosa led three chosen swains,
The blushing captives of her virgin chains,
When Time's rude hand a bark of wrinkles spread
Round her weak limbs, and silver'd o'er her head;
Three other youths her riper years engage,
The flatter'd victims of her wily age.

I must acknowledge that I have watched attentively a great many blooms of 'proud Gloriosa,' and have admired her immensely, but I never could see the difference in the length of the stamens, or that first one set of three and then the other set of three came to maturity.

I consider it quite as essential for amateurs who really care about their gardens to grow out-of-the-way plants in the greenhouse and conservatory as in the garden. Why should only just a few easily grown and eternally repeated plants, everywhere the same, be alone chosen from the wonderful and beautiful and abundant supply that Nature provides us with, while many rarer sorts, with a little care and knowledge, are quite suitable for growing under glass? A study of Veitch's or Cannell's catalogues, and looking up the names in Johnson's 'Gardener's Dictionary,' makes a selection quite easy, even if you cannot visit any of the first-class excellent nurseries in summer, or if you do not possess any of the old illustrated books.

June 27th—For those who live in the country, or those who spend the early summer months in towns and have their flowers sent up, no family of plants are more useful than the Campanulas (all described in the 'English Mower Garden'). Perhaps the one we could least do without is the beautiful *C. persicifolia*. It takes little room, is a true perennial, and divides well in the autumn. In light soils it flowers better if treated as a biennial and sown in a seed bed annually, so as to have a good supply of young plants every year. The seed sown in June or July can be planted out in October and potted up the autumn of the second year for flowering in pots in the early spring in a greenhouse. They are then good strong plants, and several can be put in one fairly large pot. *C. grandis* is a stronger and coarser plant. It is far more beautiful for picking if grown in a poor soil and under the shade of bushes or trees. But it is hardly worth growing in a small garden, though it is what I call a friend among plants; it gives a good deal, and requires so little, and looks cool and beautiful when picked and placed by itself in a large glass bowl filled with water. Its tiny rosette-like leaf-growth is also useful, attractive, and ornamental, especially in the autumn. It travels as well as the other Campanulas, only it must be picked in bud. The flowers expand well in water; so do those of the common Canterbury Bell.

As a summer luncheon dish this Mayonnaise soufflé of crab is rather out of the common:—Slightly butter the lining of a soufflé-case, pin a buttered band of paper round rather high, and season the eatable part of a crab with pepper, salt, oil, and vinegar; whip some nice aspic jelly, and put a little in the bottom of the lining. Make a bed of Mayonnaise sauce on the top of the aspic, put in the crab, then some more chopped aspic; it should be about three inches above the tin lining. Stand it in the ice-box till wanted. Put the lining in the case, sprinkle with fried breadcrumbs, and serve with a plate of chopped aspic jelly apart.

A less complicated luncheon dish is as follows:— Take some ripe tomatoes, equal-sized; cut a round hole and scoop out a portion of the middle, fill in with cold minced chicken and Mayonnaise sauce, put some aspic in the dish, and serve the tomatoes, on round pieces of fried bread, cold.

The following fresh chutney is good with any roast or cold meat:—Equal parts of cucumber, onion, and sultanas chopped very fine, some salt and cayenne. Moisten with vinegar, and press for two hours. It will keep some time: when wanted for use, warm in a little gravy and let it get cold.

A very much prettier way than the usual English one of serving cauliflower is to break it up in pieces large enough for one helping; boil them very lightly, so that they should be quite firm and dry, almost crisp. It quite spoils them if they are soft and sodden. Serve apart, in a good-sized boat, some white creamy sauce into which you grate a little Parmesan cheese.

Small pieces of cauliflower put into clear soup, and Parmesan cheese handed apart, is a good way of using up cauliflowers that are just beginning to run to seed.

Young onions boiled in clear soup give it an unusual and gelatinous consistency.

Raw sliced cucumber is quite a different dish if cut very thin and soaked in salt and water for two or three hours before it is wanted. It is then drained and pressed, and served with oil, vinegar, and pepper, in the usual way.

There are several ways of cooking cucumbers; I suggest the following:—Peel and cut up a cucumber into pieces about two inches long, and divide each piece into two. Soak them for two or three hours in brown sugar and vinegar. Stew them in a little stock, and serve them as a vegetable.

Another way is to stew these pieces in a little butter. Make the sauce apart by boiling the peel in a little milk and butter, rub it through a fine sieve, mix in a little yelk of egg and pour over the pieces.

A third way is to take a large old cucumber, peel it, cut off the two ends, and boil it very lightly. When done, make an incision down the middle, not quite to the two ends. Scoop out the seeds, and fill in the hollow with a light stuffing of suet, herbs, breadcrumbs, and egg. Serve it whole, like a rolly-poly pudding, with a yellow Dutch sauce round it.

I find, all through the year, that a compote is a much more popular way of cooking fruit than in a tart. The great secret of making compotes is to stew some fruits, and only to pour boiling syrup over others. For instance, Red Currants are not good unless stewed for some time in an earthenware dish in the oven. Raspberries are quite spoilt by this treatment.

JULY

The Welsh Poppy—Astrantias—Old Green Peas—Red Currants—
The Madonna Lily, *L'épée de la Vierge*—The value of the reserve
garden—An English summer's day—Light soils and dry summers —
Other people's gardens—Notebooks—Sunny lawns—Dutch
gardens—Fountains and water-tanks—*Lobelia cardinalis*—Watering out
of doors—Two hardy shrubs.

July 6th—One of the prettiest weeds that we have in our
modern gardens, and which alternates between being our
greatest joy and our greatest torment, is the Welsh Poppy. It
succeeds so well in this dry soil that it sows itself everywhere;
but when it stands up, with its profusion of yellow flowers
well above its bed of bright green leaves, in some fortunate
situation where it can not only be spared, but encouraged
and admired, it is a real pleasure. It is not a Poppy at all, but
a *Meconopsis*. It is quite easy to distinguish between the two,
once having grasped the fact that the seed-vessels of the entire
Poppy tribe are flat on the top, whereas the seed-vessels of
the *Meconopsis* are pointed. There are several varieties of
Meconopsis, all very desirable, and to be found, as usual, well
described in the 'English Flower Garden.'

Their cultivation is a little more difficult than that of the ordinary annual and biennial, so one hardly ever sees them anywhere, but they are well worth the little extra trouble. Among the many small plants of easy cultivation and persistent flowering, Astrantias are very useful, especially in light soils, where things flower and are over so quickly. There are several shades; I have a pink and a green. They have a most refined beauty of their own, and last well in water. They are best grown from seed, and are well worth every care. Any soil will suit them, and they will grow in half-shade or full sun.

Some dry summers Green Peas do very badly with us; they dry up so quickly. We all know the hesitating remark to the cook: 'The Peas were not so good last night.' 'No, m'm, they are getting old.' When they do get old, the following is an original French receipt for stewed Peas, which is very good indeed:—Put the Peas into a saucepan with a good-sized Cabbage Lettuce cut up, a white Onion, a sprig of Parsley, four ounces of butter kneaded with flour; put the butter in small lumps on the Peas, also a very little salt and a piece of white sugar. Cover the saucepan, and let it simmer slowly for about three-quarters of an hour.

Currants ripen very early with us. It is a good plan, in order to keep them for eating when other fruit is not so plentiful, to tie the whole bush up in coarse muslin just as the Currants are getting ripe. This protects them from birds and from insects, and they hang well on into September, and are perfectly good. Black Currants will not stand the same treatment.

The following is a good receipt for Red Currant jelly, one of the preserves best worth making at home:—Gather the Currants on a dry day. Strip them off their stalks, and squeeze the juice through a cloth. Leave the juice to stand in the cellar for twenty-four hours; then pour it into another cloth, carefully leaving the thick sediment behind. For each pound of juice allow one pound of powdered white sugar (not bought ready pounded, but done at home). Put the juice on the fire in the preserving-pan, and keep stirring it from the first with a silver spoon, adding the sugar, which should be standing close by, in spoonfuls. When the sugar is all added and dissolved, it will be necessary to take off the rising scum with a flat sieve-spoon, very well scalded and cleaned previously; and by placing a little jelly on a saucer it will be seen by the consistency when it has jellied. As soon as there is a sign of this take the pan off the fire, let it stand five or ten minutes, and fill the jelly glasses, which should previously have been well sulphured, and be standing ready face downwards. Next day they should be covered with rounds of paper soaked in brandy. Half a teaspoonful of brandy should be sprinkled over each glass, and then they should be tied or gummed up in the usual way.

July 8th—I consider no trouble too great, whether the garden be large or small, to grow the beautiful stately Madonna Lily (*Lilium candidum*). It requires very different treatment from other Lilies, and flourishes in rich, heavy soils in full sun, where many Lilies would fail. Gardening books often tell you it is fatal to move these Lilies, but I think this has arisen from gardeners moving or disturbing them when they have 'done' their orders in October or November, and when the Lilies have made an autumn growth; moving them then is fatal. When I used to leave them alone, they made an excellent top growth in spring, but dried up and died down without flowering. What I now do when they begin to die down some time this month, whether they have flowered or not, is to dig them up carefully with a fork, remove all offsets, re-make and manure the ground well, mixing with it some brick rubbish or chalk, and then replace the large bulbs, planting them rather deep, and not too close together. In this way every bulb flowers. A little liquid manure helps them to open well when they are in bud the following June. The small offsets are pot into a nursery apart, and many of them will flower the following year in a way that does admirably for picking.

A few years ago I brought from Paris some bulbs of *Ornithogalum pyramidale,* the flower-spikes of which are gold at the end of June in the Paris flower market under the name of *L'épée de la Vierge.* I have never seen the plant grown anywhere in England as I have grown it, and yet in every way it is quite one of the most satisfactory flowers for picking that I know. If you gather it just as one flower is coming out, the whole of the long spike grows and flowers in water up to the very top, bending and curling about, and assuming the most graceful curves. No one can grow a better flower plant to send to London. It has one fault in the garden—the leaves droop and turn rather spotty and yellow before the flower comes quite to its prime; but this defect can indeed be forgiven for the sake of its many merits. I cultivate it nearly as I do the above-mentioned Lilies; only, when the bulbs are dug up, we place the small ones at once in a nursery, but the large ones are well dried in the sun and not replanted till October. A mulching when they begin to show through in the spring does them good. Mr. Barr sells the bulbs, but I cannot say if his are as fine as those I brought from Paris six or seven years ago. I know no summer-flowering shrub so beautiful as the *Hydrangea paniculata grandiflora.* I have tried over and over again to grow it, but it does badly and then dies. It is not the soil only, for I once saw a magnificent specimen growing under a wall at Ascot, where the soil is the same as ours. I suppose it never has had quite a good enough place. It should be cut back hard every spring, and, when growing freely, wants much watering; I am told that constant applications of soot-water do it good. I dare say I shall succeed in time.

July 10th—This is about the time we move our things from the reserve garden, spoken of before, and from the late-sown seed beds, and plant into the borders and square beds those amiable autumn annuals that do not seem to mind moving at all, such as French Marigolds, Tagetes, Everlastings, Scabious, &c. The Phloxes Michaelmas Daisies, and early low-growing Chrysanthemums, grown in the reserve garden, move just as well in warm, dry weather as in wet, only, of course, they must be well and continuously watered till the weather changes and they have taken hold. The large *Sedum spectabile*, so loved by the bees in September, also moves perfectly in the same way, and, in a large mass, makes a very handsome autumn plant. I am sure that the system of reserve garden and moving plants and seedlings in July can be extended and experimented upon to almost any extent. Next year I must try it with the *Veronica spicata*—white, blue, and pink. They are very pretty things when flowering well and healthily and they come into bloom at a time of year when herbaceous plants are scarce. *Campanula turbinata*, blue and white are useful for the same reason.'

Alstrœmerias do very well on dry, light soil; they want mulching in spring, but are no trouble at all when once established. *A. aurantiaca* is the easiest to grow but *A. chilensis* is the most beautiful. The seeds of the best flowers are worth keeping and sowing, to improve the colour and size of the flowers. The white one I have not yet succeeded in making grow from seeds, but I saw it at the Horticultural Show, and it was most beautiful and delicate. I find that buying the bulbous rootlets dried is no use at all, they do not grow. They do not mind moving in August after flowering, and they are best increased as Lilies of the Valley are—by digging out square pieces, filling in with good soil and dropping in the pieces cut out where they are wanted somewhere else without disturbing the earth that clings to them. If you ever try to force your own Lilies of the Valley, pick out the best crowns, but never put them into the greenhouse till frost has been on them, and never mulch outdoor Lilies of the Valley before March, and then only with leaf mould. As Lilies are an early spring flower, you will find they do better under a wall facing east than anywhere else.

July 14th—How beautiful are the really hot, lovely English summer's days. They come sometimes, and they are exquisite; nothing beats them. Why, oh! why, can I never enjoy such things without that tinge of sadness which moderns call morbidness? It does no good, but I think of someone who is ill, or of those masses and masses of people in that dreary great city so close. As I enjoy my garden alone, with the beauty and the flowers, the flood of summer light and the intense pleasure of it, I long to do something, and longing generally resolves itself into picking flowers for somebody. This little poem by Paul Verlaine seems to give the colour of it all, and the pain:—

LA VIE

Le ciel est par-dessus le toit,
Si bleu, si calme!
Un arbre par-dessus le toit
Berce sa palme.

La cloche dans le ciel qu'on voit
Doucement tinte,
Un oiseau sur l'arbre qu'on voit
Chante sa plainte.

Mon Dieu, mon Dieu, la vie est là
Simple et tranquille;
Ce paisible rumeur-la
Vient de la ville.

Qu'as-tu fait, O toi que voilà,
Pleurant sans cesse—
Dis, qu'as-tu fait, toi que voilà,
De ta jeunesse?

July 15th—July is a very busy month in all gardens. The borders must be cleared and replanted, the seeds of perennials have to be gathered and sown, and many other things require attention. The Delphiniums may bravely be cut down after flowering; it does them no harm, and they often break again and have stray flowering sprays in the autumn. Some of the best seed should be sown every year. The same with the Verbascums; if cut down, they flower again, in rather a different way, but very charmingly, in the autumn. July is also the great time for sowing perennials, or perennials that are treated as biennials; and when you have fine flowers or good colours, it is quite worth while to mark the flowers by tying a piece of bass or coloured wool round the stalk. These little white ties are recognised and respected by the gardeners while clearing the borders, a work which it is essential to do in July. I sow a great many things every year, and find them most useful—Gaillardias, *Coreopsis lanceolata,* Snapdragons (Antirrhinums). Oh, how useful and beautiful are the tall yellow and the tall white Snapdragons! They can be played with in so many ways: potted up in the autumn, grown and flowered in a greenhouse, cut back and planted out in the spring to flower again, admirable to send away; in fact, they have endless merits, and in a large clump in front of some dark corner or shrub they look very handsome indeed. They are lovely picked and on the dinner-table, especially the yellow Snapdragons, but, like many other things, they just want a little care and cultivation, which they often do not get; and they ought to be sown every April, and again in July. The smaller the garden, the more essential are these plants for people who like having flowers to pick; but I warn everyone against those terrible inventions of seedsmen, the Dwarf Antirrhinums; they have all the attributes of a dwarf, and are impish and ugly. The flower is far too large for the stalk, and they are, to my mind, entirely without merit. July is the time I take up both the English and the Spanish Irises, which makes them do ever so much better. The English Irises are best planted again at once, only taking off the small bulbs. The Spanish Irises are best dried in the sun and replanted in September. In both cases the small bulbs are planted in rows in the kitchen garden; they take up little room, and in this way the stock is increased. In our soil, unless treated in this way, they dwindle, cease flowering, and ultimately disappear. I lost many from not knowing this in my early gardening days, when I was certainly green in judgment. The Spanish Iris likes a dry place in full sun; the English Iris does best in half-shade, and likes moisture if it can get it, but flowers well without; the leaves are what suffer most from dryness— long, succulent, moisture-loving things that they are.

July 17th—We have had a most unusually hot dry summer, and to go into the garden is absolute pain to me, for all the trouble and labour of the year seem more or less wasted. Plants are miserably forced into bloom, to go off almost immediately; and it is little consolation to know a week's rain will make many plants beautiful again, for the especial beauty of early summer is over. July and August are always trying months here. The soil is so very light, and one must pay the penalty; even the heavy soils, I am told, are suffering much this year.

One ought, too, to study with great interest and take note of what survives, and even does better in these very dry years. That handsome, rather coarse-growing perennial, *Buphthalmum cordifolium,* now called *Telekia speciosa*—as if one such name were not enough for a stout-growing composite—

looked shrivelled and unhappy last month, but it has flowered better than usual, and it is a handsome plant. The pretty feathery *Gypsophila paniculata* never suffers from dryness, it has such a splendid big tap-root. The Gaillardias, moved from the seed bed in spring, have done very well in full sun.

The *Coreopsis grandiflora* blazes in the sunlight. I save a little seed from the largest flowers of both of these, and sow them every year, so as to have a continual supply of young plants. It is not to avoid buying fresh seeds that I mark the best flowers of some, but because by this means, and by saving only from the best flowers, I get really better plants.

My Carnations are much less good than usual this year, but I cannot blame the weather for this. I stupidly followed the advice in some of the gardening papers last year of leaving the layers on the old plants till April. I shall never do so again; here it does not answer at all; but I shall layer them as early as possible, take them off in October, and make up the bed then. It is a very good plan to plant a row of young Carnation plants in the kitchen garden, some distance apart, so that they may be layered earlier than in the beds.

July 25th—Not the least delightful part, in my opinion, of the growing knowledge of gardening is the appreciative visiting of the gardens of others. On first going into a garden one knows by instinct, as a hound scents the fox, if it is going to be interesting or not. One's eyes are sharp, and a joyful glow of satisfaction comes over one on seeing something not by any means necessarily new, but unknown to oneself. When looking through old books or modern catalogues, one feels one has nothing in one's garden, but I must confess that visiting other people's gardens very often makes me feel I really have a very fair collection. A notebook is a most important companion on gardening expeditions. I use metallic paper, to ensure a permanent record, and an ordinary pencil. I write the date and name of the place, then jot down the names of plants and general observations. I have also kept a kind of gardening journal for many years, making notes three or four times in the month, and on the opposite page I keep lists of any plants I buy or bring home from friends, with the date; noting the deaths the following year is instructive. I have lately had a rain-gauge given me. This is a great interest and amusement, especially where rain-water is always in demand and often running short. I did not know the importance of rain-water when first we came to live here; and though we have lots of roofing, we are not sufficiently provided with underground tanks. Our small ones are supplemented now as much as possible by petroleum barrels sunk into the ground, and the water-shoot from the roof allowed to pour into them. You can connect this first barrel with others by a little piece of lead piping, and so increase the storage.

For those who have not got very good memories for the names of plants, I strongly recommend them, if they can draw, to make a little coloured sketch, however small, on the page of a gardening book next the name of the plant. This will be found a great help to the memory; I began gardening so late in life that I had to get all the help I could. I have lately been visiting what I call intelligent gardens, and will make a few remarks about them. In one place where Roses grow well I saw a beautiful specimen of La Marque Rose—one of the most satisfactory Roses for a wall. Everyone ought to try and grow it who has room and a fairly good Rose soil. The long flowering branches were cut a yard or more in length. At the end of each branch was a beautiful bunch of pure, cream-white Roses, seven or eight in number, with buds in between, and pale, healthy, green leaves down the stem. Two such branches in a narrow-necked vase, bronze or blue or dark green, are an ornament to which nothing can be added for any room, be it in a cottage or a palace. As a decoration for a large dinner-table, nothing can be better than these Roses when they are in their prime, which, unfortunately, is but for a very short time.

In the old days of bedding-out, lawns used to be cut up into beds and patterns. Now the fashion has changed, and bedding-out has become so generally condemned that most people have levelled and turfed-over the rounds, stars, crescents, and oblongs that used to enliven their lawns for a short time, at any rate, every autumn. As a result of this reaction, there are now an immense number of large, dull lawns, which as a rule slope slightly away from the house, and often to the south. They are wet in rain, and dry and brown in hot weather. They have their weekly shave with the mowing-machine, and lie baking in the sunshine. The poor plants, which would flower and do well in the open, are planted at the edges of the shrubberies, where—in a light soil, at any rate— they are robbed and starved into ugliness and failure by their stronger neighbours.

There are several ways of breaking up lawns. One is by turning the lawns into grass paths, along which the machine runs easily, and making all the rest into open, informally shaped beds. These can be planted in every kind of way—in bold masses of one thing alone, or at most in mixtures of two, such as Roses and Violas; Azaleas and Lilies; Carnations and more Violas, or mossy Saxifrages; Campanulas in succession, tall and low-growing; a bold group of Bamboos and *Bocconia cordata*; or simply with a selection of a few low-growing shrubs; and so on *ad infinitum*. Another way, and one that finds small favour with gardeners, and with considerable reason, because of the trouble of turning the mowing-machine round the plants, is to break up the lawn with sunshine-loving specimen plants—Mulberries, Savins, Sumachs, clumps of creeping Ayrshire Roses and Honeysuckles, poles covered with claret-coloured Vines,

Clematis, &c. Yet another way is to have a double pergola running all round the lawn in a square, or only down both sides, with a grass path, broad and stately, underneath the pergola. This can be made of stone or brick, oak-trees or fir-poles; or, if wanted very light, of Japanese large Bamboos—to be got now in London, I believe. These Bamboos look best if two, three, or five are blocked together unequally, with different-sized openings in between, and used as supports for fruit-trees and flowering shrubs of all kinds. As these plants grow, bamboos and wires have to be put across the top to support the creepers. In the middle is a large square of grass; the openings are left turfed, but where the supports are put into the ground a narrow bed must be made for the plants. This enables them to be manured, chalked, watered, and generally cared for. I now come to what is, in my idea, by far the most enchanting plan for breaking up a lawn, which is to sink a small Dutch garden in the middle of it.

The size of the Dutch garden must, of course, be in proportion to that of the lawn. If the proportion cannot be kept, it would be better to leave it alone. It should have a redbrick wall all round it, and be oblong or square, as suits the situation. The entrances to it are by brick steps, one in the middle of each of the four sides. The height of the wall is about three feet from the ground on the outside, and five feet on the inside. Along these walls, on the inside, are rather wide beds, bordered by paths made of rows of large, square red tiles, laid flat and not quite joining, so that tiny alpines and mosses may grow in between them at their own sweet will. If preferred, this narrow path can be made of bricks or broken paving-stones. The object of this path, besides the convenience of standing dry to pick the flowers or weed the beds, is that the front of the bed can be planted in groups, not in rows, with all sorts of low-growing things:—Alyssums, Aubrietias, Forget-me-nots, Pinks of all kinds, Saxifrages, and mosses. On the side shaded by the wall and facing north small ferns, Campanulas, and shade-loving plants are the only ones that will do well. Primroses, Auriculas, and the spring-flowering bulbs and Irises do best on the side facing east; and the summer and autumn plants like to face west and north, as they weary of the hot sun all the summer through.

All the year round this little garden can be kept a pleasure and a joy by a little management, and by planting and replanting from the greenhouse, the seed-beds, or the reserve garden. The wall looks best if entirely planted with Tea-roses. As they grow, they send up long waving branches, which beautifully break the hard line of the wall. The middle of the walled garden is grass, and the mowing machine can never cut or injure the plants, feather forward as they will on to the tiled path between the beds and the grass. In the centre there can be a sundial on a square base; or, if you have water laid on, a small square or oblong cement tank let into the ground, quite level with the grass, as a fountain and to be handy for watering. All day long the water in the tank is warmed by the sunshine. This kind of fountain is an enormous improvement, I think, to small suburban gardens, and it is prettier oblong than square. The fountain must be made of cement and six or eight feet deep. If the garden slopes at all, the overflow from the fountain can be guided by small watercourses on to different beds. I have pockets of cement made at irregular intervals at the edges of the fountain to hold water-plants and such things, which then appear reflected on the surface of the water, not as they grow against a dark shrub or a group of Italian Canes of Bamboos, but against the blue sky above them—an endless pleasure to those who notice such things. A piece of water, however small, and the sound of water falling from a small fountain, or even from a raised tap if the tank is near a wall, is such an added enjoyment to life on a hot summer's day, not to mention the infinite superiority for watering of having water that has been exposed to the sun and air. If not artificially fed, gold-fish live and breed healthily in these tanks.

Water-plants, such as the Sweet-smelling Rush, the flowering Rush *Butomus umbellatus,* the Water-lily, the Cape pond-weed *Aponogeton*, can all be grown in tanks if the plants are planted in baskets or hampers, not pots, and let down to the bottom. They give food for the fish, and keep them healthy; a tank also serves as a dip for swallows on the wing, and as a breeding-place for the beautiful blue dragon-fly.

To go back to the Dutch garden. I think at the corners of, or on each side of, the entrances there may be pots with plants in them, or balls of stone, or anything else in character with the rest of the stone or brick work, which should be formal and slightly constrained in design, as I consider all brickwork in a garden close to a house ought to be. If planted as I described, no two such gardens would ever be the least alike; no law could bind them, and no wind destroy them.

One of the most perfect ways of laying out a long flat piece of ground I have ever seen was in a garden in Salisbury. One long, very long, broad grass path, right down the middle; wide herbaceous borders on each side, with low plants in front and tall ones behind; and at the back of these again, on each side, was the kitchen garden—Gooseberries, Currants, and Raspberries, and in between all the usual kitchen-garden vegetables; beyond that was a small cinder-path, and then a wall on either side, shutting off the neighbours. One wall faced nearly north and the other nearly south. The long garden, stretching from the house eastward and westward, was ended by the river; the tall spires of the cathedral towered behind the house. I have often thought that the same disposition of an oblong piece of ground would turn a depressing laurel-planted suburban garden into a thing of joy and beauty, even without the cathedral towers and the swift, clear, running river.

One of the most beautiful of late summer plants—I see my friends often fail with it—is the *Lobelia cardinalis* and *L. fulgens*, Queen Victoria. It is generally injured by kindness, sown in the early spring, drawn up in greenhouses, and planted out weak and straggling, when it does nothing. It is a North American bog-plant, where it lies frost-bound for months, so it is not cold that kills it; but it likes a long rest. I generally take up my old plants and keep them very dry in a box in a frame, planting them out at the end of March or early in April, before they begin to grow at all. It is letting them grow on in the boxes that brings the disease and rust. Every year we sow a small patch of both kinds out of doors in June or July, and these young plants survive the winter perfectly. Dear youth! What a power it is to those that have it, even among plants! In spring these plants are put where they are wanted to flower. If they are in a dry place, I am bound to say they require plenty of water when once they really begin to grow. They look very well in autumn growing out of a fine spreading base of Mrs. Sinkins Pink, which must be divided in the autumn, leaving spaces for the planting of the Lobelia in spring.

This is the time when the plants before named, which were put into the reserve garden in the spring—early Chrysanthemums, Phloxes, Michaelmas Daisies—are brought to fill up bare places in the border. If the borders have been planted as before advised, the colours must be arranged according to the several groups. Two plants of the Daisy tribe—one blue-violet with a yellow middle, called *Erigeron speciosus*; the other a bright yellow, though some are paler than others, called *Anthemis tinctoria*—are invaluable in dry borders. They grow easily from seed, and are very amiable about being moved.

July 27th—Watering outdoor plants not in pots or tubs is a question about which people differ much. Gardeners as a rule are against it, and it certainly kills perennial plants and small shrubs if begun and left off, or even if improperly done. But in a dry soil many a plant is saved by watering it thoroughly once or twice a week, more especially if the flower-buds are formed. My experience is that under those circumstances watering hurts nothing, but it has a tendency to draw the roots to the surface, which is very undesirable with perennials, both for heat in summer and cold in winter. With any precious plant newly planted, and which looks thirsty, a very good and safe plan is to sink a flower-pot in the ground, just above the plant if the ground slopes at all. Fill this with water, and let it soak gradually away, to the cooling and refreshing of the roots. After the plant has been well soaked, one filling of the pot a day, in the morning, is sufficient. All plants that have been planted out, after being removed from a reserve garden or seed bed, must be watered; and once you begin, whether in kitchen or flower garden, you must go on till it rains steadily and well; a slight shower is no good.

A very good shading protection for small plants or delicate seedlings is to get the village blacksmith to make you some flower-pots—he will understand that—in perforated zinc such as would be used for larder windows, &c. Reverse one of these over the plant, to protect it from sun and wind.

The mention of blacksmith reminds me that the parings and raspings of horses' hoofs, which can be purchased for very little, put into a tub of water and allowed to decompose, make a very excellent and nourishing liquid manure. It should not be applied too strong.

July 30th—Two shrubs are now flowering in the garden which in this month of the year are valuable. One is called *Clethra* (Sweet Pepper Bush), mentioned in May for pot-cultivation, and useful, as it stands pulling about and changing; it is quite hardy, but in dry places it is the better for watering when coming into flower. The other is called Pavia or *Æsculus parvifolia* (Dwarf Horse Chestnut), a handsome and valuable hardy tree from North America. It does not grow fast, and takes little room; it has long spikes of flowers with bright pink stamens, is refined and sweet, and very pretty when gathered and wedged (*see* Appendix), though it would not look well in a room in any other way. I have had it several years, and it flowers every year; its handsome and yet restrained growth is a great advantage in a small garden.

AUGUST

Gilbert White—The decline of vegetable culture in the Middle Ages—
Preserving French Beans and Scarlet Banners—Scotch gardens—
Tropælum speciosum—Crimson-berried Elder—The coast of
Sutherland—The abuse of coarse Creepers.

August 1st—I cannot allow a summer to go by without
referring to that dear old classic, Gilbert White's 'Natural
History of Selborne.' Even now I do not quite know why I
am so fond of these letters, except that they show strongly
the observant eye and the genuine love of Nature which are
so sympathetic to me. When I was young my mother gave
me the book to read, and it bored me considerably. I thought
the long speculations about the hibernating of birds—Swifts,
Swallows, and others— so tiresome; especially as I knew for
sure that they migrated. I, almost a child, knew that. In those
days I just panted for what was coming; the saying 'old days'
to me meant the present, which was older than the past and
growing each day, as I grew myself, to greater maturity, I did
not understand what people meant by referring to the days
which were behind as 'the old days,' for they represented to
me the youth of time. I longed to live the day after tomorrow

before it came, if only that were possible. Everything new interested me; I thought the world was moving so fast; and now that my life is nearly over, it is as if nothing had happened. Progress is indeed like the old Greek pattern, a continuous unbroken line, but curling back and inwards for long periods before it starts a new development. Just now even the enthusiastic and the young are trying to live in the past—a whole generation conservative in its youth. I suppose it is all right, but it seems to lack the generous impulses of the generation nourished on the teachings of Mill and Bright. How true it is that Liberalism is not a principle, but an attitude of mind! And the old Greek pattern will start its long line forward again some day.

Now that hope is over for me, the old times, with their edifying lessons, interest me most; and so I try to understand the evolution of the present as taught through knowledge of the past, rather than breathlessly to grasp the future. My mother was so kind and sensible with me. So many parents are apt to be irritated by daughters who bound forward in life as children pick flowers in a field, always thinking there are many more and much finer ones just a little further on.

Though it is now little over a hundred years since Gilbert White died, his pictures of the change within his memory in the general condition of the poor, and of the improvement in agriculture, gardens and health, seem most strange. Leprosy still existed in Selborne, though it was much on the decline. He attributes this partly to improved food and partly to wearing clean linen instead of dirty woollen garments. As to the produce of a garden, he adds, 'Every middle-aged person of observation may perceive, within his own memory, both in town and country, how vastly the consumption of vegetables is increased. Green stalls in cities now support multitudes in a comfortable state, while gardeners get fortunes. Potatoes have prevailed in this district, by means of premiums, within these twenty years only, and are much esteemed here now by the poor, who would scarce have ventured to taste them in the last reign.

'Our Saxon ancestors certainly had some son of Cabbage, because they call the month of February "Sprout-cale"; but long after their days the cultivation of gardens was little attended to. The religious, being men of leisure, and keeping up a constant correspondence with Italy, were the first people among us who had gardens and fruit trees in any perfection, within the walls of their abbeys and priories. The barons neglected every pursuit that did not lead to war or tend to the pleasure of the chase.'

It seems to me from this exceedingly probable that gardens declined very much in England after the Reformation, and no doubt the eating of vegetables, like the eating of fish, may have been considered Popish. Even in my childhood I can remember that salad was rarely seen at any but the tables of the very wealthy, who had foreign cooks, and then it was covered with a rich cream sauce, full of mustard, which was supposed to make it digestible. This superstition of the day was pointedly brought forward in some letters I found of my grandmother's to my father at Oxford, strongly recommending him to take mustard-seeds before his meals as very helpful to digestion.

I am far from suggesting that the Reformation had, on the whole, an injurious effect on England, but indirectly in many ways it seems to have led to curious and even pernicious results. Among the most peculiar of these was the increase of piracy in Elizabeth's reign. The following account, given in Froude's 'English Seamen in the Sixteenth Century,' will explain what I mean:—'In harbour there were still a score of large ships, but they were dismantled and rotting; of artillery fit for sea work there was none. The men were not to be had, and, as Sir William Cecil said, to fit out ships without men was to set armour on stakes on the seashore. The mariners of England were otherwise engaged and in a way that did not please Cecil. He was the ablest Minister that Elizabeth had. He saw at once that on the Navy the prosperity and even the liberty of England must eventually depend. If England were to remain Protestant, it was not by Articles of religion or Acts of Uniformity that she could be saved, without a fleet at the back of them. But he was old-fashioned. He believed in law and order, and he has left a curious paper of reflections on the situation. The ships' companies in Henry VIII.'s days were recruited from the fishing smacks, but the Reformation itself had destroyed the fishing trade. In old times, Cecil said, no flesh was eaten on fish days. The King himself could not have license. Now to eat beef or mutton on fish days was the test of a true believer... The fishermen had taken to privateering because the fasts of the Church were neglected. He saw it was so. He recorded his own opinion that piracy, as he called it, was detestable, and could not last. He was to find that it could last, that it was to form the special discipline of the generation whose business it would be to fight the Spaniards. But he struggled hard against the unwelcome conclusion. He tried to revive lawful trade by a Navigation Act. He tried to restore the fisheries by Act of Parliament. He introduced a Bill recommending godly abstinence as a means to virtue, making the eating of meat on Fridays and Saturdays a misdemeanour, and adding Wednesday as a half fish day. The House of Commons laughed at him as bringing back Popish mummeries. To please the Protestants he inserted a clause that the statute was politically meant for the increase of fishermen and mariners, not for any superstition in the choice of meats; but it was no use. The Act was called in mockery "Cecil's Fast," and the recovery of the fisheries had to wait till the natural inclination of human stomachs for fresh whiting and salt cod should revive in itself.'

I have made this long extract because it seems to me to throw an exceedingly interesting side-light on the non-cultivation, and above all on the bad cooking, of vegetables, which extended to a great degree into my childhood. Even to-day, in spite of the increased quantity of vegetables and their comparative cheapness, it is rare to see them in any variety in English family life; and I am told that at ordinary clubs Potatoes and Brussels Sprouts represent in winter the vegetable kingdom. What is still more remarkable is that the absence of vegetables has now extended to all the principal foreign hotels, with the probable notion of suiting the English taste.

In the early Protestant days meat was no doubt eaten with a religious zeal, and the cultivation and cooking of vegetables was utterly neglected. The old gardens of the monasteries ran to ruin even quicker than the fish-ponds. It became a point of national honour to disregard the methods of cooking vegetables which had been brought by the monks, who were men of taste, from France and Italy. Proper cooking alone makes ordinary vegetables palatable, and improves even the very best. The extraordinary development of the vegetable, fruit, and flower trade is one of the most marked changes of my lifetime. When I was young, it was impossible in the West End of London to buy any flowers at all in the streets or shops. If we did not winter in the South of France, but remained in London, we had to go to some nursery gardens that lay between Rutland Gate and Kensington in order to buy a few Violets.

Froude says, about another strange effect of the Reformation, 'It probably, more than any other cause, stopped the development of painting in England. Holbein had no pupils. Zuccaro left the country in disgust. All portraits that remain were painted by foreigners.' Then worst kings from the political point of view have been the best from that of painting. Charles I. was no exception to the rule, and his magnificent gallery was sold by Parliament in 1645 for 38,000*l*., apparently without protest.

Of all the months in the year, this is perhaps the one in which the keenest amateur can best afford to leave home; and if I do not go away, it is the one I can best spare to my gardener for his holiday. In August hope, as far as the year is concerned, is over. There is nothing that imperatively requires doing; nearly all there is to do can be as well done in July or September. After deciding to leave home I gave instructions that the young French Beans and Scarlet Runners should be picked over, almost daily, so that none should grow coarse and old; and that the cook should lay them separately, as they were brought in, in large earthenware pans—a handful of Beans and then a handful of salt, and so on till the pan was full. This is an excellent method; and I have eaten them, preserved in this way, all through the winter. I believe this is done everywhere abroad, but never in England, where the waste, both in the kitchen and the garden, is, as we all acknowledge, a national vice. Of course the Beans in the salt must not be allowed to get touched by frost in the autumn. When wanted, they are taken out, well soaked (to prevent their being too salt), boiled in the ordinary way—cut up or whole, as we like them best—then drained, and warmed up in fresh butter, a squeeze of lemon and a little chopped Parsley on the top. They can also be cooked with a white cream sauce. All this is well described for fresh Beans in 'Dainty Dishes.' I think these salted Beans have more flavour than the tinned ones, or than those that come from Madeira in the winter. Besides, the principle of utilising everything in a garden should never be lost sight of. This year fate took us to the North, to Northumberland, the home of my maternal family, from which my mother in her youth, with the whole large family, travelled twice a year on the old North Road to London and back in carriages and coaches. One of my mother's aunts used to tell a story of how in her youth she had had her hair dressed in London to appear at a Newcastle ball, and she added with pride, ' When I entered the ball-room I had my reward.'

I was surprised to find that the great changes that have come over our Southern gardens by the re-introducing the old-fashioned flowers and the old methods of cultivating them are much less noticeable in the North. Apparently changes work slower in the North than around London. I wonder why this is? People there have the same books, the same newspapers, and the same climatic advantage as in Scotland, which makes the herbaceous plants grow to great perfection, and flower much longer than in the South. One would have thought the fashion which has so influenced us would have influenced them. I saw in many places long borders planted with rows of red, Violet, white, yellow, and purple—vistas of what used to be called ribbon-borders, very unpicturesque at the best, and nearly always unsatisfactory. Why they ever came in, and why they have lasted so long, it is difficult to understand. The gardens of rich and poor, big house and villa, were planted on the same system—perennials in lines, annuals in lines, Mignonette in lines; and where long lines were not possible, the planting was in rows round the shrubberies, which is, I think, the ugliest thing I know. If shrubberies are planted with flowers at all, I like large holes cut back, which makes a good protection, and plants introduced in bold groups. I did not see one garden while I was away—whose owners ought to have known better—where things were what I call well planted, in good bold masses of colour; whereas near Dublin more than two years ago I found the best herbaceous border I have ever seen. The way of planting in this Dublin border, with all the reds in one place, and the blues, the yellows, and the whites kept apart as much as possible, was as superior to the dotted arrangement as the dotted system is to the line, in my opinion. I even saw in some places this year what I as a child had remembered as old mixed borders, turned into that terrible gardening absurdity, carpet-bedding—the pride, I suppose, of the gardener and the admiration of his friends. This is never to be seen now in Surrey, I think, except in certain beds at Hampton Court; and why it is continued there I find it hard to understand, unless it is that it really does give pleasure to Londoners, and certainly in its way it is carried out to great perfection.

I had always heard of the brilliant beauty of Scotch gardens, and the moment I saw them I understood why it was. The seasons are so late that all the summer flowers bloom together; May and June of the South merge into July and August in Scotland, and everything is in flower at once. No wonder the gardens look bright; besides, the damp air makes the colours more beautiful and the scent stronger.

It is, I think, very interesting to the gardener, where-ever he goes, to see how the common everyday things flourish more in one place than another. The Highlands seem to be the home of the Gooseberry—such old and hoary bushes, more or less covered by grey Lichens, but laden none the less with little hairy Gooseberries, both red and green, and full of flavour. There, too, the beautiful *Tropæolum speciosum,* South American stranger as it is, flames and flourishes and luxuriates everywhere, growing too, as it will not do in the South, in full sunshine. The seed is so lovely in Scotland, almost as beautiful as the flower itself—three dark steel-blue seeds set in the dying flower, which turns a rich brown. Was ever anything more daintily beautiful to be seen? It can be grown up strings, as in the picture in the 'English Flower

Garden'; but I do not think that is as pretty as rambling with its delicate growth over some light creeper, such as Jasmine or Rose, as I recommended before. I did not see in the Highlands, rather to my surprise, though I believe it is planted in some places, the beautiful crimson-berried Elder, *Sambucus racemosa*. This was the one remarkable plant-feature I saw in Norway last year. I was there too late to see the wild flowers. It had not been imported very long, they told us, and it adorned all the stations (there is only one short railway in Norway), throwing out long branches covered with bunches of crimson berries, which are shaped like the black bunches on the Privet rather than like the flat berries of the common Elder. At a distance the plant looks, when covered with ripe berries, like a beautiful Crimson Rambler. It is singularly effective, and I have never seen it in England. I imagine this must be because, if it grew and berried ever so well in damp places, the birds would soon clear off all the fruit. In Norway there seem to be no small birds, for there the berries hung for weeks and weeks, in crimson loveliness. The shrub is about the height of Lilac bushes; the berries grow on the old wood, and the growth of the year is a most brilliant green. It is a plant that more people should try to grow in damp situations.

We were far North, up in Sutherland, where the great storm of two years ago laid bare miles and miles of forest. I never saw a more curious sight—pathetic and sad too, in a way. The poor trees, which had from their youth up been accustomed to storms from the south and west, had sent out long roots, and buried them deep under rocks and stones, which gave them firm hold to resist the blast. But on this November morning two years ago the snow was on the tree-tops, which made them heavy, and the furious gale swept on them from the north, and down they fell in thousands—whole hillsides laid bare, without one tree left standing, all torn up by the roots. It will be many years before the countryside is cleared of its own fallen timber.

We lived a mile from the sea. The Sutherland coast is tame enough, but beautifully desolate—no travellers, no tourists, nothing to disturb the solitude. I am not very fond of the East Coast, as there in the afternoon one is only able to enjoy reflected sunshine. It always reminds me of friends as they grow cold; they expect us to be warmed by the sunshine of yesterday. Once I went down alone to the shore; it was a beautiful evening, with hundreds of shades of pearly greys and pinks reflected on sand and wave—an evening to make mean things noble and costly things ridiculous, an evening that humbles one down to the very dust, and yet lifts one clean off one's feet with enthusiasm and exultation. I remember years ago a friend of mine telling me she had met Jenny Lind, who had then just left the stage, at a quiet South Coast seaside bathing-place. Jenny Lind was sitting on the steps of a bathing-machine, and my friend began talking to her and asking her 'if she did not think she would miss terribly the excitement of acting.' 'Very likely,' she answered, 'but I had ceased to be able to admire that,' pointing to the great gold sun going down in its glory,' and I had ceased to be able to read this,' tapping a Bible that lay on her knees. 'Don't you think it was time to give it up?'

I had not been five minutes on this lonely Sutherland shore before I counted quite ten wild sea-birds of different kinds flying around, screaming to each other, and floating about on the tiny waves that broke gently on the sand. I suppose few can hear that sound of the waves without thinking of Tennyson's 'Break, break, break.' A little poem of Emerson's, much less known, is a great favourite of mine, full as it is of a tender double meaning:—

The delicate shells lay on the shore;
The bubbles of the latest wave
Fresh pearl to their enamel gave,
And the bellowing of the savage sea
Greeted their safe escape to me.
I wiped away the weeds and foam,
And brought my sea-born treasures home;
But the poor, unsightly, noisome things
Had left their beauty on the shore
With the sun and the sand and the wild uproar.

I feel these lines reproach me for my many quotations. Have we any right to pick beautiful things out of books and quote them without their context? I suspect not, and I beg you all to consider, if you find them deficient, that it is I who have taken them away from 'the sun and the sand and the wild uproar.'

In the grounds of the great castle we were near was a very interesting museum. What an excellent thing is a private museum in a large place! It would be a great advantage, I think, if it were started on many estates, or even in villages, as then the barbaric things and various specimens of natural history which different members of a family bring home might be kept where they are of distinct interest, instead of crowding up a modern sitting-room, where they look totally inappropriate and even ugly.

There had always been a tradition that one of the ships belonging to the Spanish Armada had been wrecked off this coast, but no treasure had ever been found. Two years ago, when the river was low, a cow went into the mud to drink, and came out with a splendid Spanish old gold coin of the time of the Armada stuck in her hoof. Nothing more was discovered, but as the river was tidal it was a curious confirmation of the old tradition. On our way South we could not help noticing how far more beautiful Scotland is than Norway. The Heather was unusually fine this year. We stayed a night in Edinburgh, which gave me an opportunity of seeing the pictures in the National Gallery. I wonder if many tourists visit it? The morning I was there I did not see two people in the gallery. Besides the Raeburns, which are of world-wide fame, several pictures stand out with peculiar interest, especially the life-sized Gainsborough of the young Mrs. Grahame. She sat for this picture as a bride, but before it came home she was dead and her husband had gone to the wars. When he came back, he never had the courage to open the case which contained his young wife's portrait. On his death, many long years after it was painted, it was opened by his heirs, and inside the case was the little white slipper she had left with the painter to help him to finish his picture. The portrait was given to the Edinburgh Gallery, and the slipper was kept by the family. It is worth noting that an oil picture should have remained so long shut up and apparently not deteriorated in any way. There is a lovely Greuze, one of the prettiest I have ever seen, a child of about fourteen crying over a dead canary; an exquisite little Boucher of Mme. de Pompadour; a large picture by the eighteenth-century Venetian painter Tiepolo, whose works are rarely seen out of Venice. The picture gives one more impression of his power and cleverness than it delights one with its beauty. The expression, character, and sex are described by the power of the brush as completely as by the word-painting of a Paul Bourget novel. What added to my interest in Tiepolo was the revival of admiration his works have lately had among young French painters. I was immensely pleased at seeing a portrait of the painter Martin, by himself—a red-haired youth, with the cold dreamy eyes of the artistic temperament, a mouth rather sensual than passionate, a fine brow, and a slightly receding chin, which gave a touch of weakness to the face. All my life I have so admired his wildly imaginative illustrations of the Bible, Milton, &c. The impression given by the portrait is of a touching, interesting face, with that look of sorrow which so appeals to one, especially in the young. The gods do not always remember that those whom they love should die young. Poor Martin did not die till middle life, and went mad, I believe.

On leaving Edinburgh we returned to Tweed-side, where we saw several of the old Border towers and the really fine 'stately homes' of England. Here I was struck by the same mistake which prevails in the South. The walls and shapes of fine old houses are ruined by allowing, even on the southern and western aspects, a rampageous growth of coarse creepers, such as Ivy, the common Virginia Creeper, and *Ampelopsis veitchii*. This last is the most insidious and destructive of all, as no kitten compared to a cat, and no baby donkey compared to an old one, could ever more completely change its character from youth to age than does this creeper. When first planted, the tiny, delicate growth that creeps up the mullioned windows is as pretty and harmless as anything can be; but in a year or two all this turns into a huge mass of green leaves of an even shape and size, smothering up any less strong-growing creeper and destroying all outline of the house itself, its tiny feet sticking so fast to the stone or brick work that, if you try to pull them away, small particles of the wall itself come with them. Besides the temptation of its beautiful early growth, one must admit that for ten days the red and bronze and gold of its autumn tints go far to compensate for its many defects during the rest of the year. But this pleasure is easily retained by allowing it to grow over some ugly barn or northern wall, which has no architecture to injure or hide, and where flowering creepers would not flower. No one who has ever been to America and seen Boston can forget the dreary effect of house after

171

house covered from cellar to roof with this luxuriant, overpowering 'Vine,' as every Creeper is called in America. The true name of the Ampelopsis is *Tricuspidata*; but the Americans call it Japanese Ivy, in memory of where it comes from. If anything could accentuate the ugliness of the general effect, it is the square holes cut for the windows in this evenly green foliage. Everything is worth having in London that will grow there, but, with this picture in my mind, may I urge all who have any influence to make some protest against the fashionable use of this creeper, which seems to prevail from South to North of Great Britain? Just before I left home I saw with consternation that every delicate brick turret of Hampton Court Palace had been carefully planted with Ampelopsis. For the present it looks harmless enough to all but the prophetic eye of a gardener, but in a few years the sharp lines of the delicate masonry will be entirely veiled by its luxuriant and monotonous growth. Surely fine and historical buildings are very much better left without creepers. In the case of ordinary modern houses with bare walls it is infinitely better to cover them with some of the endless variety of shrubs, creepers, and plants, which can be chosen to flower in succession through the whole year—from the *Chimonanthus fragrans,* which pushes forth its sweet-scented brown flowers in January, to the bare branches of the *Jasminum nudiflorum,* whose yellow stars light up a December fog.

Returning from Scotland, we spent a few days near Lancaster. The town is picturesquely situated. It is full of sketching possibilities for those who delight, as Turner did, in the glorification of commonplace objects by the veiling and unveiling of smoke, and in the constant colour-changes produced by the same. A very handsome bridge crosses the broad Lune, and carries the Preston and Kendal canal. This is one of the curious historical records of the waste of a people's money, and absolutely dead speculation. This canal was just finished, with its magnificent engineering, at great expense and with high hopes of its usefulness, immediately before the railways came and rendered it almost useless. Sleepy barges glide along it, profiting by its dignified engineering, and creeping under its countless bridges as they never could have done had it been ceaselessly ploughed by small steamers, as was intended. I do not exactly know why, but it brought back to my mind—from a consecutiveness of idea, I suppose—the elaborate fortifications of Quebec, the pride of George III.'s heart, upon which had been spent the nation's money and labour, and which were scarcely finished when the developments of modern warfare rendered them useless. Not very far from Lancaster, at Levens, is the famous example of topiary gardening which figures in the last edition of the 'English Flower Garden.' I was unfortunately prevented from going to see it by deluges of rain.

pointed leaves, its red square stems, its seed-vessels shaped like buds, which burst with a crack and scatter the seeds far and wide. Were the plant difficult to grow, no garden or greenhouse would be without it. It deserves a place, even if reduced to one plant, in every moderate-sized garden; it looks especially well grown as a single plant in good soil. To add to its perfections it has a delicate, sweet smell, and does well in water. Gardeners will always look upon it, with a show of reason, as a horrid weed; but flower-lovers will never be without it. The little yellow Fumitory is invaluable for walls and dry places and under shrubs, always looking fresh and green and flourishing, however dry the weather or apparently unfavourable the situation. It is a weed, but it keeps away other weeds, which, as the old nurse said, was the great use of mothers—they kept away stepmothers. Another low-growing, fast-spreading small plant I strongly recommend is the *Polygonum affine.* It has pink flowers, which continue in bloom many weeks; it can be increased with the greatest facility by division, and it is a good border plant, as the leaves take beautiful colours in the autumn. The hardy *Plumbago larpentæ* is a first-rate plant for a sunny, dry place, and its bright-blue flowers continue till the frost comes. *Tradescantia virginica* is a plant constantly turned out of borders, as it spreads so fast; but all it requires is severe thinning in the spring, and again sometimes in the summer. I have four shades—the ordinary blue, a deep red-purple shade, a pale grey, and a pure white; they are lovely flowers, and interesting through their unusual shape. All these last-mentioned plants are well worth growing in even the smallest gardens.

September 15th—I have flowered out of doors this year for the first time the beautiful *Amaryllis belladonna.* Anyone who has a garden, or a wall or a corner near a greenhouse, where the conditions for growing this Lily can be carried out, ought to spare no effort to make it successful. The instructions have been clearly given in the 'English Flower Garden,' but I have found two other things helped the growth—one is planting them by the wall of the greenhouse where the warm pipes run; and the other is, when the leaves have died down in June, and the earth is weeded and raked, to cover the beds where the bulbs are planted with pieces of glass, so that the rains of July, which are so frequent, should not damp the bulbs before they are ready to start into flower in September. When the flower-buds appear, a dose of liquid manure may be given them; and a little fern to protect their leaves in early spring is desirable. I know nothing more beautiful than the fine, pink, Lily-like flower on its thick, rich brown stem when brought into a room.

September 16th—About this date is when we look, here in the South, for the first sign of cold, or even for frost. The weather must be watched, and any half-hardy things that have not done flowering are best taken up, potted, and encouraged to go on flowering. The drought this year kept many things back. My Tuberoses and the sweet-smelling white Bouvardia—the one best worth growing, especially outside—I must now take up, and they will go on flowering in the greenhouse. The pink and red Bouvardias are pretty, but have no sweet scent, like the white; the pink ones are a true pink, and that is always worth cultivating for a greenhouse, where every shade of magenta should be excluded. I am sure many of the eye-shocks we receive with regard to colour—both in dress, in rooms, and in the arrangement of flowers—is not so much owing to what would be called bad taste as to various degrees of colour-blindness. An inability to see colours at all, much less to see the shades truly and correctly, is far more common than we imagine, and is one of the things that should be tested in children, as—though probably the defect cannot be cured, any more than short sight, which is now so much helped by glasses, &c—any good oculist would give advice as to the best method of cultivating the eye to be true as regards colour. The improvement in the arrangement of cut flowers in the last twenty years is very great indeed, and in almost every family there is one member at least who gives it real love and attention; but I hardly ever see a greenhouse, large or small, that is not left entirely to the tender mercy of the gardener, who thinks of nothing, and quite rightly, but of his plants being healthy. He spots everything about—red, white, blue, grey, yellow—and often in the very midst he places some well-grown but terrible blue-pink or magenta Pelargonium, which puts everything out of tone. In the greenhouse, as in the garden, two things are to be aimed at—form and colour: and in a greenhouse one must be sure to add plants that give forth a sweet smell. To get the colour good, you must keep the plants in groups, the same colours as much as possible together, a bold mass of yellow, red, or blue, dividing them with green or nearly-green plants. *Cryptomeria japonica* makes a charming greenhouse shrub, and will grow in very small pots, and not grow quickly; it is, however, only one of many. Another small green growth that is very pretty, and easy to grow and increase by division, is *Pilea muscosa.* For smell I know nothing more delicious than the mixture of *Lilium auratum* and *Humea elegans*; but lately I have had to give up that tiresome though charming half-hardy biennial, as, like the Hollyhocks, it is so apt to get a disease, its leaves growing spotty and falling off. In the 'English Flower Garden' it is said that this happens from sowing it too early the previous year. A thick-leaved plant called *Rochea falcata* I find a useful greenhouse plant. It has to be two or three years old before it flowers, but is easy to increase from cuttings in July. I tried drying it off like the Cactuses, but that does not answer; it requires a warm greenhouse all the winter and a little water. For baskets in the greenhouse I use *Fuchsia procumbens*; it has a lovely little miniature flower, and later a pretty fruit three times as big as the flower. *Campanula garganica* (blue, and the white one too) and *Convolvulus mauritanicus* are lovely basket plants. The last-named, nearly hardy, is from North Africa, and easy to increase from division or cuttings. The Cape Mesembryanthemums are pretty basket plants, and do well in a sunny greenhouse. Small, old-fashioned Ivy-leaved Geraniums grow prettily in baskets. But the flowers are endless that can be grown in this way; some require a saucer to keep in the moisture, others do not. Nothing, however, will teach all this but experience and constant reference to the books.

Among the immense mass of annuals advertised in catalogues it is often so difficult to make up one's mind what to have. I live, luckily for me, not far from Mr. Barr's Nursery at Long Ditton, and this gives me a chance of seeing a variety of plants and annuals for which no private garden would have room. Two little half-hardy annuals that flowered this year for a very long time seem to me well worth growing, *Alonsoa linifolia* and *A. Warscewiczii*. I do wish such small flowers would have less break-jaw names. They are low-growing (about a foot or a foot and a half high), rather delicate-looking little plants; but so bright in colour, one scarlet and the other scarlet and orange. They are very effective if grown in a good large clump. *Bartonia aurea* is a picturesque-growing yellow summer annual, which does well in this light soil.

Limnanthes Douglasii, a Californian annual, is much loved of bees in spring, and, if sown early in the autumn, flowers in May. Wallflowers require sowing very early for the following year; also all the Primrose and Polyanthus tribe are all better sown in April. I know nothing more puzzling in gardening than the times of sowing annuals and biennials to make them successful, and I imagine they must have different treatment in different soils and climates. Constant practice and study are required. All the autumn things do best here sown late in April or at the beginning of May; otherwise they come in too early. Early annuals and late annuals are worth growing in this light soil; but Poppies, Salpiglossis, Mignonette, and Sweet-peas are, I think, almost the only summer annuals we make room for every year. Eschscholtzias and Musk sow themselves; and only have to be thinned. The common Hemp (*Cannabis sativa*) is a lovely foliage-plant when well grown and not crowded up.

It is all-important to remember in the sowing of seeds from January to September, be it in heat or out of doors, and whether perennials, biennials, annuals, or greenhouse plants, that what we want is not a quantity of seedlings all germinating into life in masses, but a few fine healthy plants. The larger and cheaper the packet of seed, the more thinly they should be sown. In the case of rare and delicate plants it is well to sow only one seed in each pot, the smallest that can be got (I have never seen any so small as the French ones), sink them in a box with cocoanut fibre, which prevents the necessity of constant watering. Seedlings, like all other plants, are the better for using nothing but rain-water, if possible. If the sowing is done in a seed bed out of doors, and if the weather is very dry, it is best to soak the ground well first before sowing, and then cover the tiny seed beds with fine gravel, leaving the small stones in, as they give great protection to the seeds from the heat of the sun. We have all noticed the vigour with which self-sown seeds grow in a gravel path. Towards the end of this month, or at the beginning of the next, is the time to take the early layers off the Carnations and to re-make the beds, or, at any rate, to plant them in clearly-named rows in the kitchen garden, so that they may be carefully moved in the spring with a ball of earth. I find that the beds made up in early autumn do much the best, though one is loath to disturb Carnations which may go on occasionally throwing up a flower, or whose foliage, in any case, is so very beautiful half through the winter if the weather keeps mild.

September 15th—Everyone who lives at all in the neighbourhood of suburban residences must be struck with the extraordinary sameness of the shrubberies which surround these houses and gardens, especially those which are almost invariably planted along the approaches. First of all you generally find the road waving and twisting—to give, I suppose, an impression of greater length—edged by a foot or two of grass, ugly in itself and laborious to keep tidy. The shrubs are roughly clipped back, chiefly at the bottom, while as they grow upwards the top branches out of reach are left to overhang the road. This clipping, without any regard to the good of the shrub, whether evergreen or deciduous, all treated in exactly the same way, makes a hideous hard wall of green, more or less imperfect. A still uglier way, though more modern, is to keep the shrubs apart by cutting them back in round, pudding-shaped nobs. This method has not one redeeming quality, to my mind. When you arrive in front of the house, the road terminates in a most unmanageable and impracticable circle, surrounding a green plot of grass with more or less the same clipped shrubs all round. This plot of grass is sometimes broken up with standard Rose-trees, or small beds with Geraniums, or basket beds, all very inappropriate, adding much to the gardener's labour, but not contributing in any way to any beauty of form or colour. Instead of this drive round a grass plot or the circular bed of shrubs, I think most people would find their approach more simple and dignified if that road were straightened where it is possible, and ended in a large square or oblong of gravel at right angles to the house, sufficiently roomy for carriages to turn with ease. The sides could then be planted with borders or shrubberies, or merely turfed, according to the taste of the owner and the space at his command. Where the soil is light, and the drive up long enough, it is well to plant it with the wild growth of the neighbouring common—Box, Holly, Broom, Ling, Honeysuckle, Blackberries. These will never grow into a wall, and require very little weeding and attention.

Now a word about the original planting. When you take a new house, it generally happens that the first wish is to gain privacy by planting out a neighbour or a road. In light soils the common Rhododendron grows nearly as quickly, if planted in peat, as the Laurel or the Portugal Laurel. It is decidedly prettier, and does not suffer in the same way in severe winters from frost. I believe that some people prefer Laurels to other shrubs; but it must be remembered that Laurels make root-growth like trees, take all moisture out of the soil, and starve other shrubs near them. Rhododendrons, on the other hand, grow very much on the surface, are easily transplanted at any time during the summer, and can be increased by layering. Where screening is necessary, the first object must, of course, be quick-growing shrubs, and these three—the common Rhododendron, the Laurel, and the Portugal Laurel—are, we must admit, the most satisfactory. They must be planted in bold masses, not mixed, and thinned out in a few years by taking out alternate plants. Where this screening is not wanted, choicer shrubs should be planted, with knowledge, according to their growth, their requirements of aspect, their size, their colour, their time of flowering, their hardiness or delicacy and so on; all to be learnt from the 'English Flower Garden.' A good deal of what I have said on the planting of herbaceous borders applies here—namely, the necessity of grouping colour in masses, and not speckling the kinds about at random. The amateur must not be disappointed at finding that a good shrubbery, however well planted, will not make much effect under five or six years. This kind of planting is very much better understood by the landscape gardeners sent out by nurserymen now than it was some years ago.

If, instead of a new house, we buy a place that has been planted for some twenty or thirty years, the amount that has to be thinned out is incredible. People in England are so afraid of thinning out; if they would only try-it with greater boldness, they would soon realise how very quickly the gaps are filled up again by the improved strength of the plants. Short of destroying protection from winds, I should say it is hardly possible to do any harm if, where two plants are crowded together, the Laurel is always sacrificed. But remember that severe clearing of shrubs must be done in the summer, as when delicate shrubs that have always been surrounded by strong growers are exposed late in the year, they are apt to be killed if the winter is severe. Wherever Hollies or Yews have been crowded, they look very ugly, after clearing, for a year or so; but if well cut back, they soon recover, and make better plants than young ones would do in many years. It is quite superfluous for me to give a catalogue of desirable shrubs, for there is an admirable list of all the hardy flowering trees and shrubs in the introductory part of the later editions of the eternally-mentioned 'English Flower Garden.' Their cultivation and propagation are all given in the body of the work. Where edging is necessary to keep the soil separate from the gravel road, I should advise, instead of the grass, flat pieces of stone, where it is possible to get them, or bricks put in edgeways, or drain-tiles, tiles, or flints. There are all sorts of low-growing things which may be planted behind this edge, according to situation and aspect, such as Periwinkles, St. John's Wort, London Pride, and other Saxifrages, Heuchera, *Tiarella cordifolia,* and the hybrid Megaseas (large-leafed Saxifrage) in many varieties.

However many or few of these varieties are chosen, each sort must be planted together in groups, never dotted about. Beside the more picturesque effect produced by masses, there is a practical necessity for this: the stronger-growing plants crowd out the weaker. Some want replanting or dividing every year, others thrive best left alone.

What I have said above refers to moderate-sized places, but I think I can especially help people with regard to much smaller gardens, which I have so often seen ruined by coarse-growing shrubs, not one of which should be admitted. I should not allow anything coarser-growing than the green and variegated Box, the golden Privet, Bay-tree (which can be constantly cut back), Daturas, *Viburnum plicatum,* Irish Yewa, Cotoneaster grown as a bush, *Choisya ternata,* Berberises, *Buddlea globosa.* If you have room, and can get the special soil, Azaleas and other of the smaller American plants are very desirable. I may mention now that for a very small garden no turf is advisable. Do not try to copy the Manor House garden, but rather take the cottage garden for a model, improving and beautifying it. Make the background of shrubs take the place of the background of cabbages of the cottager, and have only one paved path down the middle, and a narrow earth one round the outside. If you have a little spare space on one side or at the back, then turf that over and plant it with Apple-trees, spring and autumn bulbs, Columbines for summer, together with Snapdragons and Foxgloves—all of which grow well in grass. The grass must then only be mown once a year, in July.

Many of the houses built round the neighbourhood of London in the early part of the century were built close to the road, and have a ludicrous and pompous approach of a drive passing the front door, with two gates—one for entrance and one for exit. Surely this is a great waste of ground with no proportionate advantage. Most places of this kind would certainly be improved if the two gates were blocked up, the drive done away with, and a straight paved or bricked path made from the door to the road, with a shelter of wood, or even of corrugated iron, painted to match the house, and creepers planted along the posts that support it. The space on either side of this path could be planted with low-growing shrubs, or in some instances laid with turf.

In spite of all the charming things Mr. Robinson says about it, 'wild gardening' is, I am sure, a delusion and a snare. I live near one of the most beautiful so-called wild gardens in England, but it requires endless care, and is always extending in all directions in search of fresh soil. What is possible is to have the appearance of a wild garden in consequence of the most judicious planting, with consummate knowledge and experience of the plants that will do well in the soil if they are just a little assisted at the time of planting. I saw the other day the most lovely Surrey garden I know, though it is without any peculiar natural advantages from the lie of the land—a flat piece of ground on the top of a hill, a copse wood of Spanish Chestnut, Birch, Holly, and Fir, Even in the original thinning of the wood the idea had been formulated that certain plants and trees had better be kept together as they grew, and broad open spaces had been cut, broken up with groups of Holly for protection. The paths were laid with that short turf that grows on Surrey commons, and only wants mowing three or four times a year. The planting had been done with the greatest skill, almost imperceptibly getting more and more cared for and refined as it got nearer the house. Here I saw, among many other things, the finest specimens of the smaller Magnolias, *Stellata* and *Conspicua*. This surprised me, as I thought they required heavy soil. The ground had been thoroughly well made, and they were well away from any trees that could rob them; but in the lightest, dryest soil they were far finer plants than the specimen plants in the grass lawns at Kew. This whole garden was such a beautiful contrast from the usual planning and clearing-away of all the natural advantages that generally surround a place which is being built or altered. The land, as a rule, is dug over and made flat, and planted in the usual horrible shrubbery style. I have seen such wonderful natural advantages thrown away, a copse laid low to extend a lawn, a lovely spring, which could have been turned into a miniature river, made into a circular pond, with Laurels, Rhododendrons, and other shrubs dotted about, and twisted gravel paths made round it. Another lovely natural pond I knew, into which the rains drained, though nearly at the top of a hill, where water was precious and scarce. Now it is cemented all round with hard, cold cement, on which nothing can grow, and into which, in the wettest of weather, the water can no longer drain. The pond never fills, and nothing can grow around it. I know few things more depressing than an utter want of feeling for Nature's ways of playing the artist, as she does at every turn. I cannot understand anyone walking down a hilly road after rain without admiring the action of the water on its surface, with the beautiful curves and turns and sand islands that Nature leaves in playful imitation of her grandest efforts—the St. Lawrence, for instance, cutting its way to the sea through its over two thousand miles of flat plains in North America. It has long been said, 'God sends the food, and the Devil sends the cook.' I am sure the same might be said of the owners, the nurserymen, and the landscape gardeners, who most carefully, as a rule, throw away every single natural advantage of the piece of ground they are laying out, and believe they are 'improving'! What would give me the greatest pleasure would be to have the laying-out of a little place on the side of a hill with a fine view to the south and west, and the land sloping away and gently terraced till it reached the plain at the bottom. But for this kind of garden clever terracing and a good supply of water are absolutely necessary.

September 20th—Towards the end of this month we take up the double Violets—old Neapolitan and Marie Louise are the ones we grow—exchanging runners with friends and neighbours in the spring, as it is not well always to go on growing from the same plants, especially in a light soil, as they deteriorate. In April the old plants are broken up and the runners planted in a good, well-made bed of loam and leaf mould, not much manure, under a wall facing north, to keep them cool and shaded all the summer; they must be watered if the weather is very dry. At this time of year we make a deep hole in the full sun in the kitchen garden, fill this in with the ordinary stuff for making a hot-bed, putting the frame over this, with the sides a little sunk to keep out the cold, and fill up the frame with good mould. It is of supreme importance that the Violets should be planted quite close to the glass of the frame, touching at first, as the mould always sinks a little. If the winter is cold, it helps the Violets very much to put some rough boards a foot away from the outside of the frame, and fill up the space with leaves or manure. We find nitrate of soda useful for many things, and especially so for Violets. For Czars and other outdoor Violets it is useful to cut a ditch running north and south, and plant both banks with young runners of Violets in April. The position is more natural to the plants than on the flat ground, and they are shaded during part of each day; this makes a great difference to so many plants. *Ophiopogon spicatus* is a small herbaceous plant which no one would grow merely for its unshowy little lilac flower, which appears late in the autumn, but it is well worth growing in every garden, because its pretty foliage is in its prime about December and January, and is most useful for mixing with small greenhouse flowers.

September 25th—The plants moved from the reserve garden

in July have done very well. The Michaelmas Daisies are unusually good. There are a great many dwarf kinds, very suitable for small gardens. Little shapely trees covered with starry white or lilac flowers are, I suppose, to be got anywhere now; mine came from my neighbour, Mr. Barr, who has a grand collection. I can only repeat what I said before, how easily these plants can be divided and replanted in spring, and in large and roomy places a Michaelmas Daisy garden can be made for the late months. *Boltonia corymbosa* is a charming plant, more restrained than the Michaelmas Daisy, and better suited to small gardens. It is very pretty picked, but its fault is that it comes in rather early.

The wet weather has suited one of the handsomest of autumn flowers, the tall white Pyrethrum. Salvias do well here, but they like it dry and hot, and are not so good as usual this year, though flowering well now. *S. patens,* the dark-blue, and *S. splendens,* the beautiful scarlet one, are the two that no one should be without. They grow most easily from cuttings every year, though we keep the tuberous roots of *S. patens,* as we do Dahlias, from year to year. There are other Salvias quite worth growing, but none I know so good as these two. Things are keeping on well in the kitchen garden with the wet and the absence of frost. We have still some excellent late-sown French Beans. As a rule gardeners stint the slightly uncertain crop of French Beans by not sowing them in succession, depending for the kitchen supply on the Scarlet Runners, which are not nearly so delicate, and have not half the flavour of the true French Beans. Late Peas completely beat us. We have never had them but once; they damp off. This must be, I should think, from the western aspect of the garden. I will try sowing them the first week in June next year in an open field we have, exposed to the full sun and wind, to see if in that position they will do better.

September 30th—We have tried for the first time just lately the baby chickens, which were a fashionable and expensive luxury last season in London. Roast them as you roast a quail, or they can be boiled and served cold with a covering of delicate white Mayonnaise sauce. They should be killed when five or six weeks old, cooked the same day, and each person should have one. This sounds very extravagant, but a chicken the day of its birth is not worth much more than the price of an egg, and feeding them six weeks is no great expense. I can strongly recommend anyone who keeps poultry to try them, as we found them very delicate and tender.

For those who keep pigeons and want to kill them off—which, of course, must be done—I do not advise you to roast them and place them on the *menu* as 'Bordeaux pigeons' (which a friend of mine did, to the indignation of her sons), but to cook them as they do ptarmigan in Norway:—Stew them quite fresh in an earthenware stew-pan (with the livers, &c., chopped up, inside them) in good stock, with a lot of vegetables cut up, especially onion and a bunch of herbs, which is removed before serving. If more details are wanted, the receipt for jugged hare in 'Dainty Dishes' will supply them. Serve with a hot compote of Cherries, dried or bottled, or Cranberries or Bilberries or Barberries, instead of the usual Red Currant jelly. If you have a great many pigeons, they could be boned and made into the French Pie, according to the recipe in 'April.'

We grow a great many Morella Cherries on the east and north side of the wall. These ripen enough to be used for compotes in July, but by covering up the trees they can be kept on till now, or even later, and this is the best time for making them into Brandy Cherries, as follows:—Cut the cherries off the trees, leaving a little stalk, and let them drop straight into the bottle. When the bottle is half-full, shake in some powdered white sugar. Fill up with more cherries and more sugar. When quite full, pour in brandy, and leave it till next day. Then fill up the bottle with brandy, and cork it down. Seal the cork as in receipt before given. The brandy cherries are better if kept for two years before eating.

All gardens at this time of the year are full of unripe green Tomatoes; they are generally left hanging on the plants till the frost touches them, and then thrown away. If picked and stewed in a little butter in an earthenware dish, they are excellent. They have not quite the same flavour as the ripe ones, but still they are very good, and some people think them nicer than the red ones when cooked.

Carrots are a very neglected vegetable in England, and yet they are good in so many ways. The following is a Belgian receipt:—Cut the red part in to thin Julienne strips, boil for fifteen minutes, drain, then put them into a stew-pan with a nice piece of butter, a little sugar, and cover with light stock. Stew for about half an hour; then set over the fire, and boil till they are nicely glazed. Young Carrots are good done in the same way, but only take about half an hour's boiling. Carrots are excellent purée'd like mashed Turnips. French Beans and Scarlet Runners are very much better boiled whole, if not too old, only partly drained, and butter added at the last; they should be boiled enough to break up when the butter is stirred in. To be served very hot. For a second-course dish cream may be added as well as butter. When French Beans are old and the seed ripe, they cook as well as the real white Haricots.

Every year I grow Red Cabbages, and cook them as recommended in 'Dainty Dishes.' I also make large jars of pickled Red Cabbage, most useful in the winter. The following is a German receipt, and also good:—Cut the cabbage as for *choucroute*. For three or four large cabbage heads take ¼ lb. of butter, put it into an earthenware saucepan on a coal fire. When melted, add the cabbage, salt, pepper, and a little flour and a large cupful of good broth; cover well, and let it cook for about an hour and a half, turning it from time to time. During the last half-hour add a glass of strong red wine.

Some years, and this has been one, the Siberian Crabs ripen in great quantities. They look so lovely on the tree, one hates to pick them; but the moment they are ripe the missel-thrush clears every one off, with the same rapidity with which he leaves us without a single berry on the Mountain Ash in the summer. So we harden our hearts, and gather them to make into jam, according to the following receipt (the fruit of the *Rosa rugosa* can be utilised in the same way):—

Remove the stalks and well wash the fruit, put this into a preserving-pan with just enough water to cover them; boil until quite tender; then rub through a brass wire sieve, and for every 1 lb. of pulp add 1 lb. of sugar. After bringing to the boil, simmer for three-, quarters of an hour and put into jars. It will become firm as it cools. It is, although not so clear, almost as good as Currant jelly.

An immense improvement to stewed Apples or Apple tart—if the crust be baked apart, as recommended in 'March'—is to put in four or five Peach leaves, fresh from the trees, and take them out before serving; it gives the Apples a most excellent flavour.

OCTOBER

Autumn mornings and robins—Italian Daturas—The useful 'Myticuttah'—Nerines—Three Cape greenhouse plants—Sweet Chestnuts—Other people's gardening difficulties—Making new beds— The great Apple time—French White Haricot—The stewing of chickens and game—Re-planting Violas and Saxifrages—'St. Luke's summer'—Plants for August, September, and October— London gardens.

October 1st—Once more we are back in the month when the robin sings so much. The robins, I find, are the tamest of all the birds in a garden; and as we fork over the beds, or dig new ones, they follow us all about, enjoying much the newly turned-up earth. Almost the prettiest lines in the 'Christian Year' are about the Robin Redbreast, and were written by a friend of Keble's. I wonder if the 'Christian Year' is read now, and is as well known as it used to be? I will risk it, and recall the two favourite little verses:—

TO THE REDBREAST

Unheard in summer's flaring ray,
Pour forth thy notes, sweet singer,
Wooing the stillness of the autumn day;
Bid it a moment linger,
Nor fly Too soon from winter's scowling eye.
The blackbird's song at eventide
And hers who gay ascends,
Telling the heavens far and wide,
Are sweet. But none so blends
As thine
With calm decay and peace divine.

The following four verses are, I think, very pretty, and not likely to be generally known (I do not know who wrote them); and how we do, all of us, 'love the sweet fall of the year'!—far the most beautiful of all the seasons in England:—

I wondered this year—for the autumn was in,
The acacias were dark and the linden leaves thin,
And the south wind in coming and going was loud,
And odorous and moist, like the breath of a cloud—

I wondered and said, 'Then the autumn is here.
God knows how I love the sweet fall of the year;
But the feeling of autumn is not in my brain;
My God, give me joy in Thine autumn again.'

I woke in the morning, and out in the air
I heard the sweet robin his ditty declare,
And my passion of autumn came down from the skies,
And I leapt from my bed with the tears in my eyes.

Ah! robin, sweet robin, dost thou know the power
That comes on the heart with the fall of the flower,
The odour of winds, and the shredding of trees,
And the deepening of colour in skies and on seas?

October 2nd—How beautiful are these early autumn mornings! Here, at any rate, they have qualities unequalled all through the long year. The flowers shine with colour out of the grey mists, as they do at twilight in the long summer evenings, and the gardens now are all filled with dewy gossamer.

Two new autumn Crocuses have lately been brought to my notice; one, *C. speciosus,* is very pretty standing up straight and strong on a border or rockery. It is of a very blue colour, with a centre of lovely stamens and stigma forming a bright orange tassel. These species of Crocus are much more satisfactory to grow in borders than the pale Colchicums of the Swiss meadows, as they are true Crocuses, and only form in spring slight narrow leaves instead of the despairingly coarse growth of the Colchicums, which, dying down in the end of May, make such an eyesore in the borders; it seems best therefore to plant the latter in grass. My double and single Italian Daturas are later this year than usual, owing to the wet weather; but they are covered with blooms now, and very sweet. The double ones will last longer in water, scenting a room, than the single ones. We plant them out at the end of May; and when they have been out three weeks or so, a spade is passed round them to cut the roots, and a ditch made, which is filled in with manure. This generous treatment makes the whole difference in their flowering well. I cannot say whether it would be necessary in a damper soil, but I think it would, as cutting their roots in spring stimulates them to flower earlier, before the frost comes. The old plants are taken up and put into pots, and housed for the winter. This is such a happy time of the year for a gardener. There is a sense of power about it; all the planting and planning and changing are done now. One is loth to disturb beds till the frost comes and kills things down; but it is most desirable not to put off planting, and to get everything done one can before any real cold comes.

I am gradually clearing away nearly all the Laurels I found on the place, only keeping those growing under trees, and others that form a protection against the north-east wind; but even those few that are left want constantly cutting back, as they soon encroach and choke everything else. At the stores they sell a most excellent instrument for pruning, called the 'Myticuttah.' There are some with long handles and some with short; they cut through quite big branches like butter, and are really indispensable. The work is not too tiring for any woman to do herself, and everyone should have a strong pair of French nippers as well, for cutting back smaller shrubs and plants. One is always seeing in catalogues that this plant or that will do for the borders of shrubberies. My experience is that no summer herbaceous plants do in the borders of shrubberies at all, though spring and autumn things may do fairly well; and many of the smaller shrubs like Lavender Cotton, Rosemary, and Brooms of sorts, will hold their own in front of larger shrubs.

October 4th—The Nerines (*see* Johnson's 'Gardener's Dictionary') have flowered well and been charming this year. *N. Fothergillii* is the finest colour, but all are most useful autumn bulbs, and last a long time in water. They are easy to manage, and, like many Cape bulbs, flower before the leaves are produced. During the growing of the leaves they must be carefully attended to and watered; and even, now and then, a small dose of liquid manure does them good. They are best not re-potted, except very rarely; and as the leaves die down they must be laid on their sides and dried and well baked in the sun, just like the Freesias, only not shaken out and re-potted, as recommended for them. The bulbs, too, should be planted, like Vallotas or Hyacinths, well on the top of the pot. I never can understand why these very ornamental bulbs are not grown in larger quantities especially as they increase and improve, instead of being almost useless, as is the case with the spring bulbs after forcing.

A Cape family of small, very sweet-smelling shrubs called Diosma (*see* Johnson's 'Gardener's Dictionary') are well worth growing; in fact, no greenhouse ought to be without some of them. Their charm is principally in their foliage and scent, as the flowers are insignificant. They are easily increased by cuttings in spring under a bell-glass. The growing of Cape plants is always interesting. Small Cape Aloes have charming pink flowers in spring, which last long in water, not unlike the Lachenalias (*see* catalogues), all of which are worth growing.

Leonotis leonurus has not flowered out of doors with me this year at all, either in large pots or planted out in a bed. The plants were covered with buds, and so we lifted them at the end of September, and put them into the heat, where they have flowered well. This would be worth while for anyone with plenty of room, as it is such a handsome unusual flower when picked. Like the Daturas, they may be extra late from the excessive dryness of May and June, and the wet afterwards. It is a Cape plant; there it forms large bushes covered with bloom. Another African greenhouse plant well worth growing is called *Sparmannia africana*. The covering of the bud is white, and shows, when the flower opens, between the four petals, forming an unusually pretty star-shaped flower with a brush of yellow stamens tipped with red.

We have a good many fine Sweet Chestnut trees, and they ripen more or less well every year. We cook them in a great many ways: boil them and shell them, and warm them up in butter or with a little stock, as a vegetable. They are very good made into a puree with butter and cream, to eat with cutlets; or boiled and rubbed through a wire sieve, to serve round whipped cream well flavoured with sugar and vanilla. Of course the cheap Chestnuts sold in London can all be cooked in the same way, but only the best Italian Chestnuts are good for roasting.

October 8th—I have been lately on the East Coast. One cannot help being amused to find that gardening is so like life, each one has his own difficulties. I was suggesting to my friend to plant her Violets in leaf-mould, when she said: 'Why, we have not a single leaf. The few there are on the dwarf trees blow away into space.' Oh! what a fight the poor plants have with the salt-laden winds! But some things thrive and flourish by the sea as they do nowhere else. I think the sunk Dutch gardens, before described, will be found most useful by the seaside.

October 14th—It is a very good plan, when you want to cut a new bed or alter the shape of an old one, to shuffle along the wet dewy grass on an October morning —and this leaves a mark which enables you very well to judge of size, shape, and proportion—before you begin to cut your beds out. I am taking up and replanting—in the way before described of massing all the plants of one colour together—my long herbaceous borders. These borders run right across what was once a fair-sized lawn, and the principle of the garden is to have it all beds and low-growing shrubs, except the paths, which are turf; the main paths are left gravelled for the sake of dryness in bad weather. I only replant the herbaceous borders every four or five years, mulching them well every winter; and even then it is best only to replant them partially, as certain fine plants are much injured, if not killed, by moving at all, and these plants remain as landmarks both as regards height and colour for the replanting of the borders. Keeping colours together and some empty spaces for annuals or filling up in spring or summer out of the reserve garden, makes it much easier to prevent the borders looking dull and shabby at any time during the summer months.

The large square beds are planted now with all kinds of spring-flowering things, not formally, but in broad patches— Wallflowers, Forget-me-nots, Tulips, Silene, *Limnanthes douglasii* (a Californian annual much loved by the bees), sowing a large patch of Love-in-the-mist and the annual *Gypsophila* (for early flowering, sown in September), Spanish Iris, Pinks and Carnations, Madonna Lilies, a large corner of Anemones, and another of *Scabiosa caucasica* (*see* 'English Flower Garden'), both these grown originally from seed. And as the spring flowers pass away, their places are filled up from autumn-sown plants, Snapdragons, &c., which are quite hardy when young and in the seed bed, but which get killed and injured by cold winds in the open. Let everyone read what is said in the 'English Flower Garden' on the giant Saxifrages, Megaseas. There are several varieties, all worth growing, and they are most useful, satisfactory plants for all sorts of purposes, not nearly grown enough for covering the ground and making fine masses of low-growing foliage. To keep out weeds by planting low-growing and spreading plants is a great secret of gardens that are to have a picturesque appearance, and, in fact, be a cultivated wilderness rather than a tidy garden.

October 15th—This is the great Apple time. All the windfalls that take place in September and October we collect, and either eat or stew down into Apple jelly. It is very useful through the winter in many ways, and injured Apples never keep.

Quince jam and jelly we also find good. This is an old-fashioned receipt:—First boil the Quinces till soft, for about half an hour; take off the outer thin skin. Cut the Quinces in half, removing the core, and pulp them. To every pound of Quince pulp add half a pint of the water in which the Quinces were boiled. Peel carefully and cut up some Blenheim Apples; add half a pound of Apples to every pound of Quince pulp, and three-quarters of a pound of sugar to every pound of fruit. Boil for three hours.

We find the ripe Beans of the Scarlet Runners very good if well boiled, and then served with a little of the water and a good bit of fresh butter stirred in just before dishing up. Many years ago Mr. Bright, in the 'Lancashire Garden,' wrote: 'One excellent vegetable I have generally grown I would recommend to anyone who has space to spare—the French White Haricot. It is not often seen with us, though it is so very common in France. It is a species of French Bean, of which you eat the white bean itself instead of slicing up the pod. I suspect that, taking England through, there are very few gardens where the White Haricot is found.' This was true nearly twenty years ago, but the astonishing thing is that it is true still. It is wonderful how rarely the *Haricot blanc* is to be seen at English tables. Is this the fault of the gardener or the cook? I suspect both. It is very disheartening to grow vegetables the cook does not know how to use. English housekeepers, so extravagant about many things, are often curiously economical on the subject of butter. To use that horrid, fatty, adulterated stuff called 'kitchen butter' with vegetables is fatal; it must be good fresh butter. There are only two economies that generally rather wasteful people try to practise—one is in coals, and the other is in butter. Neither makes much difference in the year, and many other things could be so well done without. Compared to the expense of wine and meat, they are really nothing at all. Vegetables should not be cooked in butter except when really fried; they should be boiled, and drained, and warmed up, and cold butter stirred in just before serving. Vegetables should not look or taste greasy, or rice either.

In the autumn those who keep fowls always have some to get rid of that are better stewed than roasted. The following is an old family receipt I have not seen elsewhere:—

Poulet à la Turque—Truss a chicken as for boiling, put it in a deep fricandeau-pan, spread it thickly with butter, and lay therein a dozen pieces of raw ham, some carrots, onions, parsley, and a little nutmeg, pepper, and salt; cover with a buttered paper. Braize it for one hour. When it is dished, place round the chicken in groups stewed rice, sultanas, and prunes. Pour a lightly seasoned curry sauce over the chicken, and serve more sauce in a sauce-boat apart, if desirable—especially if there are two chickens.

People who have a good deal of game get rather tired of the eternally roast pheasant or partridge with bread sauce. The following is a good receipt to make a variety:—

Partridge or Pheasant a la Sierra Morena—Take a brace of partridges properly trussed. Cut into dice 1 inch thick a little less than ½ lb. of bacon, put them into the stew-pan; cut 2 large onions in quarters, take 6 whole black peppers, a little salt, 1 bay-leaf, a ½ gill of vinegar, 1 gill of port wine, 1 gill of water, 1 table-spoonful of salad oil. Put all these ingredients into the stew-pan with half a sheet of kitchen paper; stew on a slow fire for 2 hours. Then take out the partridges and dish them, and put round some of the quarters of onions which have been stewed, pass the gravy through a sieve, and send to table.

Just now the greengrocers' shops in town and country are full of very cheap large melons brought from abroad. I find they make a very good compote if the hard outside is taken off and the pulp cut into pieces the size of a plum. Make a syrup of sugar flavoured with the melon-peel, spice, bay-leaf, and a little powdered ginger; boil this up, and pour it over the pieces of melon.

Turnips are often strong and hard with us. This year they are delicious, and we have had a very pretty dish—much appreciated—of small round Turnips boiled tender, and served with a white sauce made of milk boiled till it thickens, into which has been stirred a little butter and cream.

Carrots, too, are delicious done in this way with the addition of a little parsley and sugar.

The following is a good cake:—The weight in flour of four eggs; beat to a cream, butter, sugar, rind of lemon grated, a few Sultanas, and citron; then add the yelk of each egg, one by one; then add the flour, and beat the white of the eggs to a froth just before putting it into the oven. Bake for half an hour in a flat tin dish.

October 18th—I have at last succeeded in flowering the *Schizostylis coccinea*. I am relieved to see that in the new edition of the 'English Flower Garden' this is pronounced a great difficulty in a light dry soil. It is probably owing to the very wet autumn we have had that these little Cape bulbs have done so well. They were planted in fairly good garden soil, under the protection and shade of a wall facing east; so they did not get much sun except early in the year, when at rest; and when they began to grow, they were watered till the rain came. When the flower-spikes began to colour and nearly open, as the nights were very cold, I cut them and put them in water in a warm room, and they bloomed quite well. Two or three sticks as a support, and mats or newspaper thrown over them, help these late-flowering plants in prematurely cold weather, which often lasts only a day or two.

October 24th—This is about the time we replant the Violas and Saxifrages in the sunny beds, taking them out of the shady border in the reserve garden. London Pride is better taken up and divided every two years. As Saxifrages do not mind the dry springs, it is well worth while to grow a quantity of London Pride, the bloom of which resembles in colour a faint pink evening cloud; this is not only a satisfactory plant when picked, but it will travel well, and makes a lovely support for Iceland poppies and other flowers.

October 27th—I have been taking up to-day the *Lobelia cardinalis* and *L. fulgens. Cardinalis* is the one with the dark leaves and the handsomer grower; the other flowers rather the earlier.

October 28th—With all the weeks and weeks of wet we have had this year we have waited long for our 'St. Luke's Summer'; and now it has come at last, it is not with its usual still, lovely warm days. It has come fine and lovely, yes; but hand-in-hand with Jack Frost, and the garden is cleared for the present of nearly every bloom that was left.

A first foggy day! How beautiful it is in the country, and what an endless pleasure when, at midday, the sun conquers the mist!—reminding one of Milton's simile at the end of his description of his hero, Satan:—

... As when the sun, new risen,
Looks through the horizontal misty air
Shorn of his beams.

And how useful are days like these in the country! There is no such time for noticing the shapes of the groups of shrubs and forms of plants, and what ought to be cut away and what left as it is. Some low-growing plants luxuriate so in the wet autumn days, they make us believe no winter is coming— such as the foliage of Pinks and Carnations, Sweet Williams, Golden Feverfew, and last, but not least, another of the treasure weeds of a garden, the common Marigold. Down the kitchen garden I have a patch of border given up to the Marigolds, and they sow themselves over and over again, and flower at all sorts of unexpected times. As they proudly defy early frosts, they become really precious with their grand glowing orange faces. As is so often the case, the single ones, with their varieties of dark and light centres, are prettier than the double ones, though both may be grown to suit all tastes, the colour always being good. No garden, however small, should be without this patch devoted to Marigolds. I do not dislike their pungent smell, as many do.

The wet has kept the leaves long green and fresh on the trees, but the cold of last night brought down at once the great succulent leaves of some young Horse Chestnuts not far from here. Just about this garden they will not grow, as they so dislike the sand. As I passed them to-day I noticed the leaves all lay in heaps, freshly fallen round the slight stems, on the green grass, fold on fold, in the low autumn sunshine. Very beautiful, like Keats's description in 'St. Agnes' Eve' of fair Madeline unrobing:—

Of all its wreathèd pearls her hair she frees,
Unclasps her warmed jewels one by one,
Loosens her fragrant bodice; by degrees
Her rich attire creeps rustling to her knees,
Half hidden, like a mermaid in seaweed.

So the trees stood up this afternoon, with all their summer clothing round their feet.

I always long at this time of the year to have been to Japan to see one of their Chrysanthemum shows. I am told our individual flowers are far finer, but their method of arranging the shows is so superior to ours, and the effect produced is naturally much more lovely. They arrange them in bands and waves of colour, from the darkest red to the palest pink, fading into white; and up again from pale lemon, yellow, and orange to the darkest brown. I am sure, even in small collections, picked and unpicked Chrysanthemums look far better if the colours are kept together in clumps, and not dotted about till the general effect becomes mud-colour, as English gardeners always arrange them, only considering their height or the size of their unnaturally disbudded blooms. They are, I admit, most beautiful and useful flowers. What should we do without them? But owners of small places, and I think even large ones, should guard against too much time, attention, and room being given to them. For putting into vases, there is no doubt Chrysanthemums look better allowed to grow more naturally and not so disbudded. A huge Chrysanthemum that is nearly the size of a plate, though it may have won a prize at a local flower-show, looks almost vulgar when picked. Bunches of Chrysanthemums with their buds will go on blooming a long time in water, and make in a room a natural and beautiful decoration, instead of painfully reminding one of the correctness of the flower's paper imitations.

A kind gardening friend living in Lancashire has written me out the following list of ornamental shrubs and flowering plants which, for one reason or another, look well in August, September, and October. I think, though I mention several of the plants elsewhere, it useful to give it in its entirety, as many are of opinion that in those three months it is necessary to be entirely dependent on bedded-out plants for colour and beauty.

Trees for autumn leaves and berries:—Ash (Mountain), Cherry, Siberian Crab, Buckthorn (sea), Elder (golden), Filbert (purple), Hawthorn, Hornbeam, Maple.

Creepers and shrubs for autumn:—*Aristolochia sipho*, Arbutus, *Azara microphylla*, *Berberis thunbergi*, Clematises of sorts, *Clerodendron*, *Colutea*, *Cotoneaster*, *Cydonia japonica*, Dog-wood, *Eccremocarpus scaber*, *Escalonia macrantha*, *Euonymus* (both European and *latifolius*), *Genista*, Heath, *Hibiscus*,

Honeysuckle, *Hydrangea paniculata*, *Hypericum*, *Indigofera*, Jasmine, *Laurustinus*, Lavender, *Leycesteria formosa*, *Mahonia*, *Olearia haasti*, Pernettyas, *Lithospermum*, *Pyracantha*, *Prunus pissardii*, *Rhus laciniata*, *Rosa rugosa,* Roses (autumn), Rosemary, *Rubus* (Brambles), *Skimmia*, Snowberry, *Spartium junceum,* Tamarisk, Virginia Creeper, Vines of sorts.

Plants—*Achillea ptarmica flore pleno*, *Aconitum* (Monkshood), *Adonis autumnalis*, *Anemone japonica* (most useful, three shades), Asters, Michaelmas Daisies of sorts, *Ageratum*, Antirrhinum, *Armeria cæspitosa* (Sea Pink), Bergamot, *Calendula*, Marigold, *Callistephus* (China Aster), Campanulas of sorts, Campion (Rose), *Cannæ*, *Centaurea,* Chrysanthemum, Colchicum (autumn Crocus), *Convolvulus tricolor*, *Coreopsis lanceolata*, *Cucurbita* (Gourd), *Cuphea zimpani* (good annual), Dahlias of sorts, Datura, Dianthuses of sorts, Desmodium, *Diplopappus*, *Echinops*, Erigeron, Eryngiums of sorts, *Exogonium purga* (Jalap plant), Fuchsia, Funkias of sorts, Gaillardia, Gaultheria, *Geum coccineum*, Gladioli of sorts, *Gypsophila paniculata*, *Harpalium rigidum*, Helenium, Helianthuses of sorts (Sunflowers), Helichrysum (Everlasting), Heliotrope, Hollyhock, *Hyacinthus candicans*, Hypericums of sorts, *Ipomæa* (Convolvulus), *Lathyrus* (Sweet Pea), *Lengogium autumnale*, *Lilium tigrinum*, Linaria, Linum, *Lobelia cardinalis* and *fulgens*, *Lunaria* (Honesty), *Mathiola* (Stocks of sorts), Oxalis, Pentstemons of sorts, *Physalis alkekengi* (Winter Cherry), *Phytolacca decandra*, *Plumbago carpentæ*, Polygonums of sorts Poppies of sorts, *Pyrethrum uliginosum*, *Reseda* (Mignonette), *Rudbeckia neumani*, Scabious of sorts, *Statice latifolia Tagetes* (Marigold), Tansy, *Tritonia tropæolum*, Nasturtiums of sorts, *Vinca*, Periwinkle, Viola, Verbena, Yucca, Zinnia.

It seems hardly necessary to mention that many of these plants flower earlier further South than they do in Lancashire.

October 26th—The French proverb, 'La variété c'est la vie,' always appeals to me in many things, especially domestic ones. I know nothing such a test of a good housekeeper as a periodic change of biscuits. Everybody tires of the best biscuits in the world, and the new shape and the old biscuits of better quality should ring the changes. All through the summer a slight surprise and pleasure comes at the end of a little dinner if a buttonhole of sweet-smelling flowers and leaves are carefully tied up (fine wire does them the least clumsily) and dropped into the water in the finger-bowls. Nothing should be used but what is really sweet—Lemon-scented Verbena and Geranium leaves being the principal foundation; and in summer there ought always to be plenty of these two in the smallest gardens.

I think it may be a little amusement or help to some of you if I make a list of a few of my dinner-table decorations during the six months in the country:—

April—White Allium with greenhouse Asparagus, red Geranium in low vases between, with no green. Various spring flowers and blossoms arranged, each separate, in small narrow-necked vases, having the effect of a miniature spring garden.

May—A Japanese arrangement of *Clematis montana* and greenhouse Asparagus. Parrot Tulips in narrow glasses all about the table. Pink ivy-leaved Geranium, called Souvenir of Charles Turner, in a large flat glass in the middle, and a pretty pink Pelargonium all round. Oriental Poppies, no green. In the middle an arrangement of German Iris of four or five different shades. Perennial herbaceous Lupins, white and blue, with their own lovely leaves; they must never be allowed to droop, but go at once into water. Lilies of the Valley and *Narcissus poeticus. Narcissus poeticus* and *Stachys lanata.*

June—Iceland Poppies (three colours), Cornflowers and London Pride; no green; very pretty, like a Frenchwoman's bonnet. Herbaceous Peonies, white and pale pink. *Lilium thunbergianum* and green. *Gloire de Dijon* Roses floating in water in flat vases, and greenhouse Maidenhair Fern. Mrs. Sinkins Pink and *Gypsophila elegans*. *Gypsophila* and pink Shirley Poppies. Yellow Snapdragons and *Gypsophila*; this was pretty and uncommon. Mixed Roses. White Madonna Lilies with various white flowers, and pale green.

July—Yellow French Daisy and *Gypsophila paniculata*. Small vases with blue *Campanula turbinata*. *Calceolaria amplexicaule*. *Gypsophila paniculata*, Nasturtiums, and leaves of variegated ground Ivy. Clematis (Travellers' Joy) trained up a Bamboo in the middle, wedged. Mixed Carnations and *Gypsophila paniculata*. Carnation (Lady Agnes) with own green, or from Mrs. Sinkins.

August—White Sweet Pea and *Gypsophila paniculata*. Branches of the Everlasting Pea laid on the tablecloth. Salpiglossis and *Gypsophila paniculata*. Sweet Geranium leaves and pink Ivy-leaved Geranium (Souvenir of Charles Turner).

September—Eed Virginia Creeper leaves and Geranium (Henry Jacoby). Single Helianthemums and Carrot leaves of various shades. Red Virginia Creeper leaves, Nasturtiums, and a large tray in the middle piled up with fruit—apples, pears, peaches, grapes, &c.

October—Single Dahlias and Venetian Sumach. Greenhouse Chrysanthemums.

October 30th—It is an excellent plan, if you have a very sunny window that you are glad to have shaded in the summer and not in winter, to put two bars of wood like a bracket out from the wall as a support for one long bar; or if your window is high, and so requires more width to shade it, have two, or even three, bars across the top. You plant on one side a Vine or a Wistaria and train it over this kind of wooden eyebrow. If you have a Wistaria, the flowers hang through in spring; if you have a Vine, the little bunches of grapes hang charmingly along the top of your window in autumn. In both cases the branches become quite bare at the first frost, and so your room is not shaded at a wrong time of year. I think this method of growing certain plants usually grown against walls will please many plant-loving people.

I have been so often asked about London gardens and in two cases have taken real and active interest in them—one a small square piece of ground behind an old house in Westminster; and another much larger very near the Addison Road Station. In all cases in and ner London I say, emphatically, 'Avoid evergreens.' They get black and miserable, and look horrid, even in winter; though, if syringed and pruned, I think both Aucuba and Box, and especially the latter, might be kept clean and flourishing, and even prove useful for picking. Ivy, too on a wall facing north is often preferable to the bare wall. I have said a great deal in August against growing Virginia Creeper and *Ampelopsis veitchti*, because of its spoiling and hiding beautiful old houses; but in London, and where we want to hide, they are the most useful and, indeed, invaluable Creepers that can be planted. They have every merit, are quick growers in any soil, graceful if pruned and cared for, and yet doing well if left alone. Their growth in the spring and early summer is full of beauty, and in London they hasten to lose their leaves without colouring them.

On the back of a house my parents built in '41, in Rutland Gate, was planted, I think, the first Virginia Creeper I ever remember in London. In those days beyond this house it was all fields and nursery gardens. London was not then quite so black as it is now—not in that part, at any rate. I well remember the beauty and glory of this Virginia Creeper. It was never pruned, Mid hung from top to bottom of the house in lovely masses of falling foliage. Virginia Creepers, like

many other things, vary a little in their growths; one that has
its leaves out early in the spring is the best for London. The
Ampelopsis is prettier for being very much starved, as the leaves
keep smaller, and less like the redundant growth at Boston,
which I so condemned before. But on the whole, even for
London, I prefer the growth of the common Virginia
Creeper.

Autumn effects need never be thought of in London at
all. When people come back to the West End, after the
holidays, it is nearly winter. The poor leaves, choked and
smothered in soot, have fallen sadly and greyly to the ground,
leaving all their autumn glory to their more fortunate country
brethren; and all can be swept clean and tidy before anyone
comes back. Amongst deciduous shrubs all the ordinary
common ones do very well, and only want attention and
pruning, and pulling-off of suckers, as the same plants require
in the country. Privets, being half-deciduous, do very well
also. Bamboos we useless, as they are never in full beauty,
even in the Country, till the autumn and winter. In all small
gardens it is my advice to avoid turf, and especially in London.
It never looks well, and is expensive and troublesome to
maintain, which is one reason the day-gardener likes it. Have
as wide a border all round the wall as you can afford, and
some red gravel or a bricked or tiled square in the middle of
the garden to sit on.

Have a sunk tub, in the sun, under a tap, from which to
fill a watering-pot, to water more delicate things; and do not
hose too much, especially if your soil is damp, except in very
warm weather. On the walls have *Ribes sanguineum* and
Forsythias, as they flower very early. Vines and Fig-trees,
white Jasmine, and *Jasminum nudiflorum*, all do well in
London. Wherever there is room on the walls facing south
put the deciduous Magnolias (*see* 'English Flower Garden').
The *Magnolia grandiflora* has such polished and very shiny

leaves; it grows very well near London. I remember some very fine plants of the same that used to grow in gardens at Walham Green and Fulham, where in my youth people gave what are now called garden-parties and used then to be called 'Breakfasts'—why, I do not know, as they never began till three o'clock in the afternoon. Perhaps the French refugees brought in the fashion of such entertainments, full of the recollections of the *déjeuné champêtre* of Louis XV. and Louis XVI. and their Courts.

I know a Magnolia in Addison Road—I think it must be a *M. conspicua*—that, though crowded up and apparently neglected, flowers most beautifully every spring, nearly as well as the famous one which is such a marked ornament every year in the Champs Elysées. A Forsythia at the corner of Marlborough House garden in the early spring has often excited my admiration. I quote these examples to show that plants will grow and flower in London still, if well chosen and cared for.

For the borders, I recommend no edging; it is expensive and useless. The gravel is enough; and it is, I think, prettier to disguise the fact of a line than to accentuate it. Plant what you have in bold clumps— the tall plants, of course, at the back; but rather in waves of height, with bays of the front low-growing things, running back towards and under the wall. Anything looks better than a row of plants all the same, or nearly the same, height. There are the line of the wall and the line of the path. Your object must be, not to repeat these, but to work into your border that which makes either beautiful form or beautiful colour, or both at the same time. Do not repeat your clumps over and over again. For instance, if you have a good number of German Irises (many of which grow admirably in London), put them into two large groups—one facing east or south (which is the best) and the other facing north or west. In this way you may hope for a succession, an object that anyone who plants for flowering reasons ought never to have out of their mind. Spanish Irises would, I believe, do very well in a London garden if planted every year in a sunny corner in October. They are not expensive (*see* catalogues). Buy no double or even single Dutch Hyacinths; they are not worth it. They last a very short time, are often injured by the weather, and can be seen in the Parks in mournful and irritating regularity and perfection. Buy Snowdrops, Crocuses, Scillas (*see* 'English Flower Garden'), especially *S. hispanica*, blue, white and pink (though the pink one is rather the least pretty), *S. bifolia*, *S. sibirica*, *S. italica*, and our own common Blue-bells (Wood Hyacinths), *S. nutans*. I think the only real Hyacinth worth trying would be the early Roman. The only seed I would recommend sowing in place is Mignonette, and that would want watering. For all other annuals, and many other things that are not annuals, I would pocket my gardening pride and act in the following manner:—In April, and again in May, make out from the books a short or long list of plants, those common things that you would like to have, which flower early. Send or go to Covent Garden, taking a basket with you, and buy the seedlings there two or three inches high; bring them back, plant them at once, and water them and watch them. Plants are just like children; it is a keen, watchful, ever-attentive, thoughtful eye they require—not, figuratively speaking, pulling up by the roots to see how they are getting on. If you cannot go to Covent Garden, go to the nearest nurseryman, and try and get there what you want. I would buy Daisies, Forget-me-nots, Violas, Pansies, common Marigolds, Nasturtiums, blue Lobelias, Geraniums, Sweet Verbenas—in fact, nearly all the things you see. Only make notes year by year as to what does best, and try to learn for yourself what likes full sun and what likes half-shade, and what can be planted in April and what not till the end of

May. I believe in this way a very bright London garden might be seen—during May, June, and July, at any rate—at a very small expense.

Sowing your own seeds takes too long, and is too uncertain without a hot-bed. Do not put off planting all the hardy plants too late. London is warmer than the country, and your great object ought to be to get things early. All Pinks, Saxifrages (especially London Pride), Ferns, and all the hardy perennials you like to try, ought to be planted in October, at the same time as the bulbs. The Campanulas named in June would do well in small London gardens; the shade of the walls and the moisture would suit them excellently. Perhaps they might want water, if the weather was very dry, to help them to flower.

There are often a few cold nights at the end of May, when the icebergs are floating South—those wonderful, beautiful ice-mountains, once to have seen, never to be forgotten; they have eight times their height below the water, and this keeps them straight as they float onwards, glittering in the sunshine. Beautiful as they are to those who see them, they are cruel destroyers of our poor uncertain spring weather. A very good plan on cold nights is to throw over your plants some newspapers, held down by stones; or if you cover up some wicker or wire hen-coops with muslin, they will keep out five or six degrees of frost. These protections can be removed in the morning. All spring-watering should be done in the morning, not in the evening; and it is better to add a very little warm water than to use very cold water out of pipes. The handsomest, easiest-grown, hardiest, most useful plant for London gardens is the *Polygonum cuspidatum* (there is a lovely drawing of it, by Mr. Alfred Parsons, in Mr. Robinson's 'Wild Garden'); but its whole beauty and utility, as I have said before, depends on taking up the suckers as they appear in early spring. Without that, the plant is a useless weed; but treated as I recommend, I am sure no one can be disappointed with this strong-growing herbaceous plant. The larger-leaved kind, *P. sacchalinensis,* is very good also, if you have room for both, but it has not quite such a beautiful up-standing and yet graceful growth.

I think the *Bocconia cordata* would also do in London gardens, as it is a very handsome herbaceous plant, and comes to perfection early, throwing up its feathery blooms in July. None of the Primrose family are any good in London; the leaves are too woolly.

Do not allow the beds to be dug over or pulled about in the autumn; it is a very bad plan. Consciously or unconsciously the man digs everything up, and I believe many a gardener thinks it is good for trade!

No Roses are worth trying in or near London, though a few are growing in Holland House Gardens that look fairly healthy; but that is a very large open space, and they are old-established bushes, which have been there a long time. I think that most beautiful shrub, *Hydrangea paniculata*, might do well; it is best cut down every March, and is such a beautiful thing. It likes a strong soil, but flowers rather late for those who leave London early. Lilies of the Valley do very well in London if planted under a wall; facing east is the best position, and they should be left alone. Most of the hardy Lilies would thrive if planted in October, especially the scarlet Lily, *Lilium chalcedonicum*, which flowers early. One reason why London gardens do so badly very often is that they are neglected in September and October. Wallflowers are best planted in September; and I am afraid many beginners fail to realise what are annuals and what are not, and the greater the difficulties the greater the care necessary. I saw once in a review of an American book on gardening that the late springs and the early heat in parts of America made the growing of many of the larger annuals a great difficulty, as they could not be sown out of doors early enough. The reviewer quoted the author of the book's statement of how she ingeniously devised the following method:—Determined not to be beaten, she grew the single seeds in empty egg-shells stuck into boxes of sand; when the time came for planting, and the little seed had grown, the shell was just broken and the whole thing dropped into the ground where it was to grow. In this way she got Poppies, &c., to flourish—plants that will not bear moving at all, as a general rule. I mention this as an example of the whole spirit of gardening, a patient conquering of difficulties. Riding on the crest of the wave that tries to submerge us is one of the phases of our existence that makes life most satisfactory and worth living, and it is the secret of all progress. If gardening were easy, even under favourable circumstances, we should none of us care to do it.

It must strike everyone when driving through the streets of London in the summer how elaborately ugly is the planting of many of the window-boxes. What seems to me to look best is to keep the flowers as distinct and as Unmixed as possible. To set out plants that are not really hardy before the end of May is waste of money, and gives me a feeling of unloving ignorance of plants which is as the murdering of the innocents to those who are fond of them. A pretty mixture is the yellow French Marguerite with two or three— according to the size of the box—little upright *Cryptomeria japonicas*, either in the middle or at each end of the box, according to the shape of the window. White French Daisies do just as well, if preferred. Calceolarias and white Daisies are also pretty. I have lived so little in London in the summer of late years that I am more prepared to criticise than to suggest. One day I saw outside a dining-room window some large, heavy, oblong Japanese flower-pots planted with single plants, and they looked very well, as one was able to see the growth of the plants. These Japanese pots are glazed, and much thicker than the ordinary flower-pot, and thus lessen evaporation and the risk of being blown over. No plants can possibly succeed on balconies or windows in ordinary English flower-pots unless they are sunk in boxes or other pots as a protection from the sun and wind.

NOVEMBER

Letting in the autumn sun—Jerusalem Artichokes—Hardy Bamboos—*Potygonum cuspidatum*—Autumn flowers—Small Beech-trees—Last day in the country—Some gardening books of this century.

November 2nd—I recommend housekeepers to take down about the end of October all muslin curtains, silk blinds, &c., which shade the windows, only keeping such curtains as are drawn at night for warmth. The difference it makes in the appearance of the room is very pleasant. In all manner of ways possible—in our house and gardens, in our cooking and dress—the adapting ourselves as well as we can to the changing seasons is sensible and desirable; it gives point and variety to existence, especially for those who live most of the year in one place. In the case of the south windows in our sitting-rooms the pouring-in of the low winter sun is delightful—'le soleil de Saint Martin,' as the French play had it, comparing it to the love of an old man, 'qui échauffe et ne brûle pas.' It is only just now we enjoy this very low sun. It is a great delight to watch the changing year, and how differently the sun affects the house and garden. In summer he shines high above our heads, beating and burning on the roof; and in, winter he bows and smiles at us just above the tree-tops.

November 8th—To-day we have had our first dish of preserved French Beans out of the salt pan, before described; and they are really delicious, just as if they had been freshly picked in August.

I suppose everybody knows that Jerusalem Artichokes are much better if left in the ground and only dug up as they are wanted, though before hard frost they must be dug up and housed. This vegetable is amongst the most useful ones we have in the winter, as it can be cooked in such a great number of ways. It is one of the things much improved by growing from fresh seed, and not planting the old tubers over and over again. The Artichokes can be made into soup, can be purée'd like Turnips, or fried in thin slices like Potato chips. 'Dainty Dishes' has one receipt for cooking them. The only way in which they are not very good is the ordinary English way—plain boiled, with a floury butter sauce. The best way of all is *au gratin*, like the Maccaroni-cheese in 'Dainty Dishes'; only they require more sauce. Everything *au gratin* is very much improved by using half Parmesan, half Gruyère, and a very small piece of shallot. I used to think this plant, from its name 'Jerusalem' being derived from the Italian *Girasole*, with its curious English amplification into 'Palestine Soup,' was perhaps the only Sunflower (*Helianthus*) that had not come from America, and might have been brought here by the Crusaders; but all this is not the fact. It does come from America; and a curious confirmation of the same is that the French name is *Topinambour*, a corruption of Topinambout, a native tribe in the Brazils, whence the plant comes.

November 6th—The last few days there has been quite a hard frost, and last night our garden thermometer registered ten degrees. This means, of course, death to everything not quite hardy; and even the hardiest hang their heads, and flop their leaves and look dying, though we know it is only affectation, and that a steady rain, bearing in every drop heat from the tropics, will revive many things again. I confess I like these sudden deaths in Nature. When the time comes, it is better that things should go, than linger on, as they do in very mild autumns. Never since I have lived here have the berries of the Pyracanthus and Holly been so fine; the latter are covered with berries. In old days they used to say it meant a cold winter and a providential providing of food for the birds. Now we say it means a fine spring and a wet autumn, which is just what we have had this year; but a wet autumn may mean a cold winter.

November 9th—One or two hardy Bamboos should be in all gardens, because of their appearance just now, apart from all other reasons. The 'English Flower Garden' gives the best kinds, which must be selected according to the size of the garden and the situation in which they are to be placed. They by no means require to be planted in wet places—in fact, I imagine it is that which kills them in winter—but a few cans of water daily in dry weather, at their quick-growing time of May and June, helps them very much to throw off sooner that shabby appearance in spring which is one of their drawbacks. Another drawback is that they live such a short time in water after they are picked. The Japanese have many devices for preserving them; the simplest of these is burning their ends in the fire before putting them into water. This answers with many flowers. In a small garden, Bamboos look much better for thinning out every year; and the long canes make very useful, tidy sticks for pot-plants. At this time of year, when all else is dying or dead, they are healthfully and luxuriantly green. I have found by experience that, if Bamboos are really injured by frost, it is best to cut them down entirely the following spring. It requires some courage to cut out the tall, well-grown canes; but, once nipped by frost, they do not recover, and they make better plants the following year if cut right back.

It is well worth while for anyone walking round the kitchen garden in November to pick the few remaining frost-bitten pods of the Scarlet Runners. When gathered and opened, what a treat of colour they display!—recalling wet shells on the seashore, mottled and marked, and of a rich deep purple, and no two alike grow Scarlet Runners singly, or two or three together, between the Apple-trees; and it is a good plan, as they bear much better than when planted in rows in the open, and look much prettier. They creep up into the branches of the Apple-trees; the growth is so light it does no harm while it protects the late pods from frost.

The dear, bare branches of my favourite *Polygonum cuspidatum*, here planted in a hole in the grass, look lovely now at this time of the year, red in the sunshine against a background of evergreens. I have now on the table before me—cold and grey as it is out of doors—Marigolds, Tea-rose buds (that are opening in the room, and looking so pretty with a shoot of their own brown leaves), Neapolitan Violets, some branches of small white Michaelmas Daisies, and of course Chrysanthemums— those autumn friends we are half tired of, and yet we could so little do without. Another striking feature in the garden just now are some small Beech-trees, quite small, grown and cut back as shrubs are pruned. In a soil where Beech-trees do not grow naturally, it is well worth while to have them in this way, because of their peculiarity of retaining on their branches the red dry leaves more than half through the winter, causing a distinct point of colour against the evergreen shrubs.

November 14th—This is my last day in the country, calm and warm. I eat my luncheon by the open window. All Nature is very, very still, the silence broken now and then by the chirp of a bird and the distant crow of a cock in some neighbour's yard; the sky is pearly and grey, and soft light-grey mists hang about, just enough to show up the glory of some autumn bush or leaf. In front of the window there are some little delicate leaves of one of the shrubby Spiræas, planted on purpose to shine, coral and gold, late in the year. It does not matter about its being planted in a choice bed, as its growth is not coarse; if it looks a little dried up in summer, it is not noticed when all the flowers are about. The dear little black and white pigeons—'Nuns,' they are called—with outspread wings, are flying down to feed. The flight of a pigeon is so beautiful; no wonder Dante immortalised it in the famous lines in the Paolo and Francesca episode. That old cynic, Voltaire, used to say that Dante's fame would always grow, because he is so little read.

As I sit and watch, the low yellow winter sun bursts out, illuminating all things. Tomorrow he will not shine for me, as I shall be in that horrid dark London.

One other morbid little poem, appropriate to this time of year, I think I must give you, for it used to be a great favourite of mine in past days, before the cheerfulness of old age came upon me. If I ever knew who was the author, I have forgotten it now:—

LA MELANCOLIE

Que me dis-tu, morne vent d'automne—
Misérable vent?
Toi dont la chanson douce et monotone
Jadis charmait tant?

Tu me dis, hélas! qu'amour et jeunesse
M'ont fait leurs adieux...
Et du fond de l'âme un flot de tristesse
Me déborde aux yeux!

Tu me dis, trop bien, où le sentier mène
Que l'espoir a fui...
Et ton chant piteux, traduisant ma peine,
Triple mon ennui.

Ce mal qui courbait sur mon foyer vide
Mon front désolé—
Ta complaints, O vent, et ton souffle humide
Me l'ont révélé;

C'est le mal des ans—c'est la nostalgia
Des printemps perdus:
Et ton vieux refrain n'est qu'une élégie
Sur ce qui n'est plus!

Modern Gardening Books—In the month of March I finished noticing the books in my possession up to the end of the last century. I begin again with this century, and shall carry them down to the present day.

1803. (An XI.) 'Le Jardin de la Malmaison.' By Ventenat. Illustrated by P. J. Redouté In two folio volumes. This is one of my great possessions—a handsome book, sumptuously produced, as was likely to be at the time, dedicated as it is to Madame Bonaparte, just at the height of her power and influence. The implied flattery in the dedication to her is as large and magnificent as the paper is beautiful and the printing perfect. On the title-page is a little motto in Latin, saying that if the praises of the woods are to be sung, the woods should be worthy of the Consul. The book is an obvious imitation of Jacquin's 'Flora Schoenbrunnensis.' The illustrations are, I think, less artistic and certainly less strong than Jacquin's. They are not hand-coloured, like his, but are very fine examples of the best and most delicate (then newly discovered) method of colour-printing. The reason why Redouté's work is artistically inferior to Jacquin's is, that in his delicate rendering of the flowering branch he always puts it exactly in the centre of the page, without reference to its size or growth. The plates are at the end of each volume, and the descriptive text, which is in French, at the beginning. Poor Joséphine! She was so fond of her gardens; and I am told there is still an order preserved in our Admiralty that, when French ships were captured in the war, any plants or seeds that were on board for Madame Bonaparte were to be expedited. That was a gracious order; and gardening in those days meant so much more than it does now. A flower blooming then was an interesting event all over Europe, and the gentle perfume of it rose and permeated through the smoke and din of the Napoleonic wars. Nevertheless, there always have been, and there always will be, those who would rather sing the old French rhyme:

Jardiner ne m'amuse guère,
Moi je voudrais faire la guerre.

Redouté, the artist, in this fine Napoleonic book plays only a secondary part to Ventenat:

1805. (An XIV.) 'La Botanique de J. J. Rousseau, ornée de soixante-cinq planches d'après les peintures de P. J. Redouté.' Apparently Redouté brought out this book to please himself, for it is a reprint of Rousseau's 'Elementary Letters on Botany to a Lady.' It has sixty-five such beautiful illustrative plates, exquisitely drawn and colour-printed like the last. Were ever such beautiful things done for those who wished to adapt natural flowers to chintzes, needlework, or wall-papers? French artists, no matter of what school or of what period, always excel all others in the beauty of their actual draughtsmanship. Among these illustrations there is a very fine old-fashioned dark-red single Chrysanthemum called *Astre de Chine*: I have never seen anything in the least like it growing. The Daisy and the Dandelion, too—were they ever more beautifully or more sympathetically rendered? Everything done is in honour of botany, nothing as a representation of a flower worth growing. The text is in French.

My other Redouté book is a very charming one, though my large octavo edition is, alas! not the best, which is a folio in three volumes. The title-page states that the drawings have been reduced, re-engraved, and coloured under the eye of Monsieur Redouté, 1824. He had now become famous. The title is 'Les Roses, par P. J. Redouté, avec le texte par C. A. Thorry'—the order of the artist and author being just reversed from that in the work of his early days, 'Le Jardin de la Malmaison.' The book begins with the following charming sentence:—'Les poètes ont fondé dans l'opinion les seules monarchies héréditaires que le temps ait respectées: le lion est toujours le roi des animaux, l'aigle le monarque des airs, et la rose la reine des fleurs. Les droits des deux premiers établis sur la force et maintenus par elle avaient en eux-mêmes la raison suffisante de leur durée; la souveraineté de la rose, moins violemment reconnue et plus librement consentie, a quelque chose de plus flatteur pour le trône et de plus honorable pour les fondateurs.'

Anyone who cares about Roses ought to try and see this book at the Botanical Library of the Natural History Museum at South Kensington, as it is very full of suggestions. Had I a soil that suited Roses, and room to grow them in, I should try and make a collection of the wild Roses of the world and the roses figured by Redouté in 1824, many of which I have never seen. The Banksia Rose, which now covers the walls all along the Riviera, is here called *Le Rosier de Lady Banks* (wife of the botanist Sir Joseph Banks). There are Moss

Roses and China Roses, and every form and kind of Eglantine; but nothing larger or more double than the Cabbage Rose. The Malmaison Rose, though called after Josephine's garden, must have been a much later introduction. In fact, in 1824 there were no Roses and no Strawberries in our sense of the word. Even what is now called the Old Maiden's Blush is not in the book. The *R. lucida*, which I grow successfully in Surrey (for it is easy of cultivation, and has a lovely foliage), the York and Lancaster, and the Centifolia are all in this book. Even my small edition I look upon as one of my chief treasures; it is bound in an old-fashioned bright-green leather. I suppose few people have seen this book, otherwise I cannot imagine how anyone has ever had the courage to publish the modern illustrated Rose books with pictures that look so coarse and vulgar in comparison with these delicate coloured prints.

1804. 'Exotic Botany, by James Edward Smith, President of the Linnean Society; figures by James Sowerby. Two volumes in one.' This book is, of course, an English one, but on the title-page is the following quotation from Rousseau's seventh 'Promenade.' I copy it, as it expresses the feeling of the times:—

'Il y a dans la botanique un charme qu'on ne sent que dans le plein calme des passions, mais qui suffit seul alors pour rendre la vie heureuse et douce: mais sitôt qu'on y mêle un motif d'intérêt ou de vanité... tout ce doux charme s'évanouit. On ne voit plus dans les plantes que des instruments de nos passions, on ne trouve plus aucun vrai plaisir dans leur étude... On ne s'occupe que de systèmes et de méthodes; matière éternelle de dispute, qui ne fait pas connaître une plante de plus... de là les haines, les jalousies,' &c.

I wonder if it will strike anyone on reading this that the

sins of the botanist have been inherited in some degree by the modern gardener?

The book is dedicated to William Roscoe of Liverpool. Rare and interesting plants from all parts of the world are figured here, and many of them are uncommon to this day. Some are familiar garden plants, such as Rosemary-leaved Lavender Cotton, which, the author tells us, 'Clusius says he met with on the sloping sides of some hills near Narbonne, in the year 1552, when travelling with his friend, the celebrated Rondeletius, from Carcassonne to Montpellier. It is said to grow in other parts of the South of France, as well as in Spain, chiefly on open hills near the coast. It bears our climate in the open border, flowering, though very rarely, in August. We receive it from the Botanic Garden of Liverpool by favour of Mr. John Shepherd.'

Such a passage, one of many, seems to stretch a hand across the centuries, and explains the kind of charm these old books have for those who like them. The plates are carefully drawn and well coloured. This book contains many plants from New Holland which must then have been rare; some are noted as grown in gardens at Paddington, some as never having flowered in Europe at all. It is certainly an interesting book.

1810. 'The Gardener's Kalendar,' by Walter Nicol. This is the earliest of my gardening directories, and it is not illustrated. It is an excellent little book, but one learns nothing from it except that nearly all we know now was known then.

1810. 'A Small Family Herbal,' by R. J. Thornton, M.D., interesting as it claims to be illustrated by Thomas Bewick. The little woodcuts of plants and flowers are charming. The arrangement of the book is sensible and clear, and has, at the end of the medical part, some receipts for currant wine, elder wine, &c.

1812. 'A Family Herbal,' by Sir John Hill, M.D. The

illustrations are coarse, and not well drawn, though hand-painted. It is a typical book of the day, when there were so many of the same kind.

1812. 'The New Botanic Garden. Illustrated with 133 plants, engraved by Sansom from the original pictures, and coloured with the greatest exactness from drawings by Sydenham Edwards.' There is considerable boldness and character about these drawings of ordinary garden plants and flowers, but the colour has changed on several of them. Like other books of the period, the flowers are illustrated and described in an absolutely chance and desultory way; the only exception is when the authors confine themselves to one family, like Andrews' 'Heathery,' or Jacquin's 'Oxalises.' What is striking in all these books is the beautiful paper and printing. The drawing and painting are just beginning to decline.

1814 (about). 'The Botanic Garden,' by B. Maund. I think this the most useful, from a modern gardener's point of view, of all the old books in my possession. Nothing approaches it for instructiveness in herbaceous plants till we get to Robinson's 'English Flower Garden.' The complete set, consisting of sixteen volumes, is difficult to find, though odd volumes or broken sets are often advertised. This lovely 'Botanic Garden' is arranged on an entirely new system. It is purely gardening and botany, no medicine at all. The volumes are quarto, and the illustrated page is divided into four. Each square is filled with an illustration from a flowering plant every one of which—from the tallest Hollyhocks to the smallest Alpine—is drawn exactly the same size, to fill the space. This, to my mind, is a grave fault, continued to this day in flower illustration.

In some of the old Dutch books which I have seen, but, alas! do not possess, they had a plan of drawing the flowering branch, life size, in the middle of the page, with a small drawing in the corner representing the growth of the whole plant. This is a sensible and instructive method. I should like all flower illustration to be exactly the size of a fine specimen in Nature, quite regardless of filling or non-filling the page. To give a correct impression of the lant illustrated is very much more important than attempting to make uniform or even artistic pictures.

But to return to Maund. The letterpress follows the illustrations, one page to each plant, and the following characteristics are given above the drawing in every case:— (1) Name of country the plant comes from, (2) height, (3) when it flowers, (4) duration of plant, (5) when first cultivated. This gives, at a glance, a comprehensive idea of the plant. There are constant allusions through the book to Parkinson, Gerarde, and other old botanists. The earlier plates are far superior, better drawn, and more delicately coloured than those in the later volumes. In the twenty-five years which were covered by the serial issue of this publication the decline of flower-painting marched apace.

1814. 'Flore Médicale. Décrite par F. P. Chaumeton, Docteur en Médecine. Peinte par Madame E. P—et par P. J. F. Turpin.' This is a lovely book in eight octavo volumes. The illustrations are most delicate and fine, and in the Redouté manner. He influenced all flower-painting at that time in Paris, professional as well as amateur. Flower-painting only ceased to be good when it was no longer considered the handmaid of botany and medicine, which necessitated quite a different order of merit and precision from what was required for mere flower illustration for gardening purposes. One of the useful and uncommon idiosyncrasies of this book is that at the top of each page describing the plate the name of the plant is given in seven European languages. The curative properties of various medicines are named, but there are, alas! no cooking receipts. This is what is said about

Cardoons, the vegetable so little used in England because the cooks do not know how to dress it:—

'Le Cardon *Cynara cardunculus* dont les feuilles, prodigieusement amples, deviennent, en blanchissant, une de nos meilleures plantes potagères. La culture en a fait des variétés et des sous-variétés, dont deux dépouillées d'épines sont plus faciles à manier, cependant on préfère au cardon d'Espagne, tout inerme qu'il est, le cardon de Tours, armé d'épines longues et très aiguës. Celui-ce est moins sujet à monter; ses côtes sont plus grosses, plus tendres, et beaucoup plus délicates. Le professeur Gilibert a connu un médecin qui depuis dix ans prenait tous les matins un verre de décoction des feuilles vertes de cardon, avec la persuasion intime que ce remède l'avait guéri d'un engorgement au foie, et en prévenait le retour.' It is curious how, in these old books, the faith seems always to have been in what was put into the water, not in the good tumblerful of any hot liquid—plain water being perhaps the best of all, though no doubt in any decoction of vegetable there would be small quantities of soda. The book is full of all kinds of interesting information, and there are constant allusions to the use of vegetables in all sorts of illnesses, especially gout and stone. There is an article in the 'Edinburgh Review' of November 1810 on the uses of vegetarianism for the cure of stone. It seems now as if we were once more tending towards the system of Abernethy, who lived in the early part of the century. The recommendation he gave to his patients was: 'Live on sixpence a day, and earn it.'

1824. 'The Universal Herbal,' by Thomas Greene. This is an ambitious book in two large fat volumes. It professes to contain an account of all the known plants in the world, adapted to the use of the farmer, the gardener, the husbandman, the botanist, the florist, and country housekeepers in general. Mine is the second edition, revised and improved. The frontispiece is coloured and very funny; it is called 'Wisdom and Activity collecting the various treasures of the Vegetable Kingdom.' Wisdom is represented by an old woman in the background under a hedge. In the foreground on the left is a youthful Flora, and on the right Activity is represented by a middle-aged husbandman, who does not look active at all. On the title-page is an extraordinary collection of young women without too many clothes, which I should have thought represented the elements or the seasons, only there are five of them. Surrounding these is a wreath of vegetation and flowers, held up at the top by fat winged Loves. The book is alphabetically arranged, and every now and then there is a page with four coloured flowers on it, only moderately executed. Compared to those gone before, these are not worth noticing, but they are not so bad as those about to come. This book certainly contains an extraordinary amount of detailed information and instruction; its comprehensiveness may be imagined when I note that sixty-seven Oxalises are described in separate paragraphs. It is exceptionally interesting for the botanical account it gives of garden plants and flowers. The medical properties of many plants which hitherto have been spoken of as certain panaceas are here alluded to in a comparatively doubtful tone. The treatise on gardening, at the end of the second volume, is very amusing; and the prints enable me to realise the date and origin of our characteristic villa plantations, approaches, drives, &c. There is an illustrated page of ornamental flower-stands, which, ugly as they are, I think might be improved and adapted so as to be rather pretty and useful in some greenhouses and windows.

The lists of plants, bulbs, and seeds are useful even now, and would have been exceedingly so to me some years ago. The way these books fell out of knowledge and fashion is quite extraordinary. The botany they contain was constantly superseded by newer books; faith in herbalism died out; and the beautiful herbaceous plants were swept away from our gardens. I suppose I did not look out for these books, knowing nothing of them; but I never saw one of them till I began to be interested in them and to collect them five or six years ago.

1825. 'The Manse Garden,' which has long been out of print, I have. Canon Ellacombe praises it most warmly and justly at the end of his 'Gloucestershire Garden,' published last year. It has no name and no date, but he says it was written by the Rev. N. Patterson, at that time—nearly seventy years ago—Minister of Galashiels and afterwards a leading member of the Scotch Free Kirk. 'It is altogether,' Canon Ellacombe adds, 'a delightful book, full of quaint sentences, shrewd good-sense, and quiet humour; and the cultural directions are admirable.' This praise I entirely endorse. The chapter at the end, called 'The Minister's Boy,' is especially human, in the modern sense of the word. It is a modest, non-old-fashioned-looking little book, and is, I expect, to be found hidden away in many an old Scotch house.

1825-1830. 'Cistineæ: the Natural Order of Rock Rose,' by Robert Sweet. This, once more, is a book entirely confined to one family, the extent of which is such a surprise to most of us. Who would have expected that there are thirty-five Cistuses, seventy-eight Helianthemums, and about a hundred Rock Roses? The drawings are good; but the colouring, though still by hand, compares very badly with Redouté's lovely Rose book. Cistuses are such charming plants, opening their papery blooms in the sunlight; they do very well in the light Surrey soil, but very few of them are really hardy. *Cistus laurifolius* is hardy with me, and *C. florentinus* only dies in very severe winters. Mr. Robinson gives a list of them, and they are such pretty little shrubs that they are well worth any trouble. The mixed Helianthemums (Sun

Roses) are best raised from seed, and it is very easy to keep any specially good ones from cuttings made in the summer, when they strike freely. I take potfuls of cuttings of the shrubby kinds every year as well, in case of accidents. There are several other books by Mr. Sweet, all of which must be well worth having.

1826. 'The Gardener's Magazine,' conducted by J. C. Loudon. This publication, of which I have seventeen volumes, was, according to his biographer, Mr. Loudon's own favourite, into which he put the best of his ideas and work. It is only illustrated with small wood-cuts in order to explain the text, but is crammed with interesting information, well-arranged lists of plants, and descriptions of country houses, the culture of fruit and flowers, green-houses, and stoves. I repeat, the especial use of these older books is to help us to the knowledge and cultivation of non-hardy exotics—a subject which the great authority of the day, Mr. Robinson, does not touch upon. They, however, require to be read with understanding, as in Mr. Loudon's day gardeners were much more afraid than they are now of treating plants as hardy—the risk of losing them being then too great, whereas now it is only considered as being good for trade. In nearly all private gardens of the present day it is almost forgotten that plants can be easily reproduced by layers, cuttings, and seeds. Modern gardening shares in the common fault of our generation, which is so prone to waste and to buy, rather than to produce.

Mr. Loudon seems to have been an upright, hardworking and educated man, who was rather forced by ill-health into the life which he took up. There is an interesting portrait and biography of him in a little book of his, published after his death, called 'Self-Instruction for Young Gardeners.' As is frequently the case with men whose whole mind is taken up with some absorbing intellectual occupation, he neglected his own money affairs, and at the time of his last illness he had to make an appeal to his many friends and admirers fpr funds to enable him to publish his great work, which has not yet been superseded, though it calls for re-editing, the 'Arboretum Botanicum,' of which more hereafter. Mr. Loudon died on December 14, 1843, before he heard of the kind way in which his friends had come forward and responded to the appeal. His wife states that he died on the anniversary of the death of Washington, thus linking us on by an allusion to older times, which seem to us so very long ago.

The story of Mrs. Loudon's marriage is rather interesting. As a girl (1825) she wrote what she herself describes as 'a strange, weird novel,' called 'The Mummy'—perhaps the first of the prophetic stories that have been so common in my time, the scene being laid in the twenty-second century. Mr. Loudon was struck by a review of this book, and read it. It made so deep an impression on him that two or three years afterwards he expressed to a friend his great wish to know the author, whom he believed to be a man. An introduction was brought about, which in a short time resulted in their marriage. They lived in a charming house at Bayswater, which was then quite in the country, and 'The Gardener's Magazine' alone brought him in 750*l* a year. Soon after their marriage they saw at Chester, in 1831, the first number of Paxton's 'Horticultural Register,' the earliest rival to 'The Gardener's Magazine,' which gradually declined from that time, and was given up immediately after Mr. Loudon's death. The impetus given by Mr. Loudon's books and periodicals to landscape gardening and greenhouse cultivation, for pleasure and beauty alone, and for the ornamentation of the houses of the wealthy, must have been immense. But from that time the books assumed the deteriorated character from which they are only now

beginning to emerge. Cheapness became a desirable object—
necessary for the propagation of the instruction. This change
greatly enhances the interest and value of the older books.
The illustrations only served to elucidate the text, and in the
case of coloured plates several plants were often crowded
into one page for the sake of cheapness in reproduction. The
gardener was no longer a botanist and an artist, but employed
inferior draughtsmen to illustrate his instructions.

The original debt on the 'Arboretum,' published just after
Mr. Loudon's death, was 10,000*l.*, which seems a very large
sum, considering how poor the illustrations are. It is a book
of immense study, great interest, and valuable instruction.
The work is in eight volumes—four letterpress and four
illustrations.

1842. 'Ladies' Magazine of Gardening,' by Mrs. Loudon,
published just before Mr. Loudon's death, has some rather
good illustrations of flowers, some certainly not commonly
grown now. What she calls the Golden-haired Anemone is
quite unknown to me. The illustrations for gardens and
rockwork are elaborately descriptive of all which should be
avoided; but in every book of the period there is much for
the student to learn. Failing income induced Mrs. Loudon,
no doubt helped by her early efforts in literature, to publish
books on gardening for the use of amateurs. When she and
her little daughter were left very badly off, her efforts assumed
a more ambitious line.

The first edition of 'The Lady's Companion,' which I have,
was published by William Smith in 1841. It is a delightful
little book, alphabetically arranged, with a few useful
illustrations, light to hold, and beautifully printed. It always
mentions the country from which the plant or flower comes,
and it often suggests, most usefully, the soil or locality where
the plants do best in England. This is a point too often
omitted in modern gardening papers. The book was

afterwards enlarged. It went through several editions, and had many imitators. Mrs. Loudon's earlier books are often to be picked up, very cheap, at secondhand shops, and I strongly recommend all ladies interested in gardening to buy them whenever they can lay their hands on them, either for themselves or to give away. It is not that they are really better for the advanced student than the modern books, but that they are more simple. They begin more from the beginning, they teach more what amateurs require, and they are not complicated with the immense variety which in modern books and catalogues drives unfortunate young gardeners to despair. A good deal of this applies as well to the many imitators and humble pupils of the Loudons' school who published between 1840 and 1850. One book I have is called 'Every Lady her own Flower Gardener,' by Louisa Johnson (seventh edition!), published by W. S. Orr, 1845. Any lady with a small villa garden would find most useful instruction in this little manual. The gardening matter in all the books of this time is excellent; where they fail, like the Loudons themselves, is that they are permeated with that early Victorian taste now thought so execrable—baskets and vases, summer-houses and seats, are all tortured into frightful 'rustic' shapes. The planting and laying-out of grounds are equally bad; they constantly recommend both kinds of Laurels, which time has taught us are the most destructive of plants, killing all other shrubs in their neighbourhood with their insolent and devouring roots.

Those who have larger gardens would do well to try and get Mrs. Loudon's six quarto volumes, illustrated with coloured pictures. Though artistically bad as flower-paintings, and inferior to those published now in the weekly gardening papers, they resemble the flowers enough to be recognisable. They most usefully illustrate the text for the ignorant amateur, who learns far more quickly when pictures and letterpress are combined than by any written instruction alone, however good.

Mrs. Loudon's quarto volumes are now rather difficult to get complete. There are two volumes on perennials, one on annuals, one on bulbs; this one is perhaps the most valuable of the lot, as it gives many of the best-known bulbs as they arrived from the Cape, before they were so over-cultivated and hybridised by the modern nurseryman. Perhaps the volume on greenhouse plants is the least interesting, as so many things are recommended for cultivation under glass which have since been proved to be hardy, or nearly so, and grow very well out of doors—at any rate, through the summer months. The volume on English wild flowers, which completes the set, is a little superficial, but helpful. It has rather good pictures of many of our native plants, some of which are now very rare. The best of these wild flowers can be cultivated from seed, even in small gardens, giving us most beautiful effects with very little trouble and expense.

1828. 'Mémoires du Musée d'Histoire naturelle.'

1834. 'Mémoires sur quelques Espèces de Cactées.' These are portions of two books with most beautiful and curious illustrations of Cactuses, the only examples of old botanical drawings of Cactuses I have been able up to now to procure. They are not coloured, but delicate and precise in drawing to a high degree.

1829. 'A History of English Gardening—Chronological Biographical, Literary, and Critical—Tracing the Progress of the Art in this Country from the Invasion of the Romans to the Present Time,' by George W. Johnson. This little book is so comprehensive in subject that it is rather dry reading, though Mr. Johnson's introductory chapter abounds in interesting information about the gardens and vegetable cultivation of the ancients. Cato's description of the cultivation of Asparagus is very much the same as what is now recommended. Gardening, at no time in the world's history, seems in any way to have been the especial property of the good and simple, in whose hands alone 'it is the purest of human pleasures.' To sit about gardens in summer sunshine, to listen to the birds, and to enjoy the scent of the flowers cultivated by others may be very enjoyable, but in no sense does it deserve to be called 'the purest of human pleasures.' No one who does not actually work in his own garden can ever really realise the pleasure of having one, and the enjoyment of a garden entirely worked by others is merely a form of idleness and luxury. The title does not accurately describe the book, as the gardens of the ancients are confined to the introduction, and the history of English gardening begins only from the accession of Edward III. The main part of it is a detailed account of all the books that have been written on the art of gardening. Mr. Johnson most critically describes the letterpress of gardening books, but very little notice indeed is taken of any illustrating, and when he reaches Curtis's beautiful 'Flora Londinensis' he gives it no more praise than to any little short gardening essay that may have appeared at the time. Anyone going to the Museum Library with this comprehensive catalogue would have but a slight idea of what are the best books to ask for. Till the appearance of Miss Amherst's book in 1895, I believe this was the only existing book of reference on the history of English gardening.

1830. 'On the Portraits of English Authors on Gardening, with Biographical Notices,' by S. Felton. A curious and really valuable book of reference. Mr. Felton, in his preface, pays high tribute to the 'History of English Gardening,' just described, and says: 'Mr. Johnson's work is the result of original thought and of an ardent and extended scientific research. Mine is a compilation "made with a pair of scissors," to copy the words of Mr. Mathias, which he applies to a certain edition of Pope. I content myself, however, with the reflection of Mr. Walpole, that "they who cannot perform great things themselves may yet have a satisfaction in doing justice to those who can.'" This reminds me of the flippant newspaper critic who called Sir George Cornewall Lewis's 'Influence of Authority in Matters of Opinion', 'a book to prove that, if you did not know a thing, you should ask some one who did.' There is a delightful wisdom in this remark.

1830 (about). 'The Florist's Journal and Gardening Record.' I have two volumes of this publication. The plates are well drawn and coloured, and are more delicate than those in Mrs. Loudon's books. One volume contains a fascinating picture of that rather rare flower, which I have failed as yet to bloom, called *Zauschneria californica*. The two volumes are good specimens of the books of the period.

1834. 'The Magazine of Botany,' by Joseph Paxton. In this year the intelligent gardener at Chatsworth started his 'Magazine of Botany,' which was finished in 1849. I have the complete set of sixteen volumes. The first volume contains a somewhat fulsome and yet touchingly hearty dedication to his master, the Duke of Devonshire. Each of the succeeding volumes are dedicated to more or less exalted members of the peerage—some men, some women. The 'Magazine' to this day is interesting, useful, and full of instruction as regards the cultivation of desirable and uncommon greenhouse and stove plants. The title-page is quite simple. Evidently the fashion for adornment, allegorical or otherwise, hitherto so much in use, seems to have entirely died away, and plainness rules the day. The page has nothing on it but the title and the famous Bacon quotation, which can never be too often repeated: 'God Almighty first planted a garden, and indeed it is the purest of human pleasures: it is the greatest refreshment to the spirit of man, without which buildings and palaces are but gross handiworks; and a man shall ever see that, when ages grow to civility and elegance, men come to build stately sooner than to garden finely, as if gardening were the greater perfection.'

Bacon is delightfully solemn, but one cannot help remembering Adam found it so very dull till Eve came that he even sacrificed a rib for the sake of a companion.

There is a sad falling-off in the plates, both wood-cuts and coloured ones, though they are executed by different people, and some are much better than others. Paxton must have studied hard, as he constantly refers to the older books. What is of chief interest about him is that he was the greatest unconscious instrument in the movement he helped to develop, which altered the gardening of the whole of England, and consequently of the world. He used the old patterns of Italy and France for designs of beds, filling them, as had never been done before, with cuttings of tender exotics, which were kept under glass during the whole winter. Endless sums of money were at his disposal, and everything was done which could facilitate his efforts to make the terraces of Chatsworth a blaze of colour during the months of August and September, the months when his master came from town. From his point of view this was a most praiseworthy object, and no doubt gave great satisfaction. It was copied, for the same reasons, by most of the great houses in England. But what was really unfortunate, and can only recall the old fable of the ox and the frog, was the imitation of this system in all the gardens of England, down to the half-acre surrounding a vicarage, or the plot of ground in front of a suburban residence. The ox, as we know, was big by nature; and when the frog imitated him, it was flattering to the ox, but the frog came to grief. So I think to this day, if bedding-out is ever tolerable, it is on the broad terraces facing large stone houses, with which we have nothing to do here. Where it becomes intolerable, and perhaps it is hard to blame

Paxton for this, is in the miniature Chatsworths, with their little lawns and their little beds, their Pelargoniums—often only coloured leaves, like the Mrs. Pollock—their dwarf Calceolarias, their purple Verbenas, and their blue Lobelias; where the lady is not allowed to pick, and where the gardener, if he is masterful and gets his own way, turns the old herbaceous border in front of the house into that terrible abomination called 'carpet-bedding.' Paxton was a very remarkable man in his way. When taken up by the Queen and the Prince Consort, he built in 1851 that wonderful and ever-to-be-remembered glass case, in Hyde Park, the first general International Exhibition, which enclosed two large elms. Poor trees! how they hated it! Their drooping autumnal appearance is my strongest childish remembrance of that Exhibition. Paxton was knighted by the Queen, and partly built the Crystal Palace at Sydenham with the remains of the Hyde Park Exhibition.

1835. Culpepper's 'Complete Herbal.' A republication of his original 'Epistle to the Reader' is dated from 'Spitalfields, next door to the Red Lion, September 5, 1653.' The frontispiece has Culpepper's portrait—a sharp amiable face, with long hair, a white collar, and a Puritan dress. Below is a little picture of the upright, modern-looking London house, surrounded though it is by fields, in which he lived and died.

The instructions for 'the right use of the book' are so curious that I may as well copy them: 'And herein let me premise a word or two. The herbs, plants, &c., are now in the book appropriated to their proper planets. Therefore, first consider what planet causes disease; that thou mayst find it in my aforesaid judgement of diseases. Secondly, consider what part of the body is afflicted by the disease, and whether it lies in the flesh, or blood, or bone, or ventricles.

'Thirdly, consider by what planet the afflicted part of the

body is governed; that my judgement of disease will inform you also.

'Fourthly, you may oppose diseases by Herbs of the planet opposite to the planet that causes them, as diseases of *Jupiter* by Herbs of *Mercury*, and the contrary; diseases of the *Luminaries* by the Herbs of *Saturn*, and the contrary; diseases of *Mars* by Herbs of *Venus*, and the contrary.

'Fifthly, there is a way to cure diseases sometimes by *Sympathy*, and so every planet cures his own disease; as the *Sun* and *Moon* by their Herbs cure the Eyes' *Saturn* the Spleen, *Jupiter* the Liver, *Mars* the gall and diseases of choler, and *Venus* diseases in the instruments of Generation.

'(Signed) NICH. CULPEPPER.'

The whole book runs on the same lines. Of course it can only have been re-published as late as 1835 as a curiosity.

1835. 'The Language of Flowers, with Illustrative Poetry.' Inseparable from a collection of flower-books of this period is one example at least of the curious childish sentiment— or, rather, of the sentimentality which was the fashion of the day. The frontispiece is a little bouquet of flowers which means, being interpreted, 'Your beauty and modesty have forced from me a declaration of Love.' It is always the woman's fault, somehow, in all times. The little book is dedicated to the Duchess of Kent. The 'illustrative' flower-writing is curious, and the dictionary of the language of flowers very arbitrary. How utterly the whole thing has passed away! The outside of the little book, bound in stamped green silk, is rather pretty.

1837. 'Amaryllidaceæ,' by the Honourable and Reverend William Herbert, and dedicated to Leopold, King of the Belgians. This book is very botanical, and dry to the ordinary reader, though, I should think, comprehensibly descriptive and interesting to the student. The drawings are good and delicate, and very slightly coloured.

1839. 'Pinetum Woburnensis, or a Catalogue of Coniferous Plants in the Collection of the Duke of Bedford, at Woburn Abbey, systematically arranged.' This is a very handsome book, unfortunately not large enough to show off the really fine plates to advantage, as they are all folded in half in the middle. I imagine it is the only work of its kind, and seems, so far as I can judge, to be very complete. Considering how late was the date of publication, the plates are-very well drawn and coloured by hand. The introduction, dated 1839, is written by the Duke of Bedford. In it he gives such an amusing anecdote of his grandfather that I cannot resist quoting it:—'In the year 1743 my grandfather planted the large plantation in Woburn Park known by the name of the "Evergreens," to commemorate the birth of his daughter, afterwards Caroline, Duchess of Marlborough; it was something more than one hundred acres, and was, before that time, a rabbit-warren, producing nothing but a few blades of grass, with the heath or ling indigenous to the soil, and without a single tree upon it.

'In the course of a few years the Duke perceived that the plantation required thinning, in order to admit a free circulation of air, and give health and vigour to the young trees. He accordingly gave instructions to his gardener, and directed him as to the mode and extent of the thinning required. The gardener paused, and hesitated, and at length said, "Your Grace must pardon me if I humbly remonstrate against your orders, but I cannot possibly do what you desire; it would at once destroy the young plantation, and, moreover, it would be seriously injurious to my reputation as a planter."

'My grandfather, who was of an impetuous and decided character, but always just, instantly replied, "Do as I tell you, and I will take care of your reputation."

'The plantation, which ran for nearly a mile along the road leading from the market town of Woburn to that of Ampthill, was, consequently, thinned according to the instructions of the Duke of Bedford, who caused a board to be fixed in the plantation, facing the road, on which was inscribed, "This plantation has been thinned by John, Duke of Bedford, contrary to the advice and opinion of his gardener."'

1843. 'Flora Odorata: a Characteristic Arrangement of the Sweet-scented Flowers and Shrubs cultivated in the Gardens of Great Britain,' by Frederick T. Mott. A useful, suggestive, little book, and the only one on the subject that was ever printed, I believe, till the appearance of a book in 1895, 'Sweet-scented Flowers and Fragrant Leaves,' by Donald McDonald. This last often gives the name of one scented variety in a perfectly scentless family, such as the Camellia. *C. drupifera* has scented flowers. I observe that the very faintest odour justifies the inclusion of some plants in both these books.

1846. 'Flowers and their Associations,' and 'The Field, Garden, and Woodland,' by Anne Pratt. I have none of Anne Pratt's books except this curious little one, given me off a Christmas-tree, by a serious old uncle, because I was fond of flowers, when I was a child. It is roughly illustrated, and contains much desultory information.

1848. 'The Rose Garden,' by William Paul. This is a most interesting publication as regards plane growth, increased variety, and the utter collapse and deterioration of the art of illustrating. Viewed by the light of Redouté's Rose book, it is like turning from a Greek goddess to the stoutest of matrons. The poor Rose!—it has swelled and amplified under cultivation to a despairing degree; but the execution of the plates is answerable for much, no doubt. We have now the figure of the *Bourbon* Rose, called '*Souvenir de la Malmaison*.' Roses have increased apace in the quarter of a, century since

Redouté painted them, but many of the Roses in this book are now called old-fashioned. The plans and instructions for Rose gardens are not what are now admired, and, one would say, are singularly unsuited to the spreading wild growth of healthy Roses.

1854. 'A History of British Ferns,' by Edward Newman. Enthusiastic gardeners in the 'Fifties gave a great deal of time and attention to Ferns. Now, people wisely do not attempt them where they will not grow. My other Fern book, published in 1868, is 'Select Ferns and Lycopods, British and Exotic,' by B. S. Williams. A useful book, as Fern-growing in stoves and greenhouses will always be well worth while.

(No date, but I imagine in the 'Fifties.) 'Profitable Gardening: a Practical Guide,' by Shirley Hibberd. A nice old book, full of clear instruction and practical hints. Books of this description are often to be picked up on old bookstalls, and are very helpful, as being the A B C to more advanced modern books.

1855. 'Flora of the Colosseum of Borne,' by Richard Deakin, M.D., with a print of the ruins of the Colosseum before the days of photography. I bought this book, I must confess, out of pure sentiment, as it is too strictly botanical to suit my ignorance. I spent a winter in Rome when I was a little girl, and the vegetation which grew all over the Colosseum, both plants and flowers, was deeply impressed on my mind. I never saw Rome again till about twelve years ago, when the scraped and tidy appearance of the Roman ruins, though no doubt necessary for their preservation for posterity, struck a cruel blow at my youthful recollections. This curious little book gives the botanical description of 420 plants growing spontaneously on the ruins of the Colosseum at Rome. The record of this absolutely vanished vegetation has, I think, a touch of poetry of its own which can better be felt than expressed. The book has some little architectural illustrations of no great merit.

1855. 'Beautiful-Leaved Plants,' by E. J. Stone. This is a book rather interesting to the collector, and illustrative of a peculiarly bad period. Its quotations and general appearance are rather those of a 'Lady Blessington Annual' than of a serious gardening book, but I should think it was a standard work on hothouse foliage plants. It has one great merit: the illustrations are in very bright colours, and the plant in full growth is printed in black and white on the opposite page; this is a first-rate way of illustrating a book of the kind. The letterpress gives a detailed botanical story of the plant illustrated, and the method of its cultivation. A useful book, I should imagine, for head-gardeners whose employers are fond of beautiful-leaved plants.

1869. 'The Parks, Promenades, and Gardens of Paris,' by W. Robinson. This is the earliest of many most interesting books that I possess by Mr. Robinson; a book full of information, branching into many directions. The third, and I believe last, edition, with the illustrations much improved, was published in 1883.

Next comes, in 1871, his 'Sub-tropical Garden, or Beauty of Form in the Flower Garden.' This second title refers to that which, to my mind, is the great value and interest of the book, and to be attained almost entirely as well by hardy plants as by sub-tropical ones. In 1871, however, the idea was new, and is even now but most indifferently carried out or understood in nine out of ten gardens that one sees, in spite of all Mr. Robinson's invaluable teaching both in this and many other of his books.

'Alpine Flowers for English Gardens.' Mine is the third edition. The illustrations are popular, and inferior to those in most of Mr. Robinson's books. How much joy do the Alps recall to thousands of people! Even for those who do not enjoy mountain scenery, there are always the lakes and the flora.

> Avec leurs grands sommets, leurs glaces eternelles
> Par un soleil d'été que les Alpes sont belles!

Some of Mr. Ruskin's happiest lines, I think, are in the 'Mont Blanc revisited':

> O mount beloved, my eyes again
> Behold the twilight's sanguine stain
> Along thy peaks expire;
> O mount beloved, thy frontier waste
> I seek with a religious haste
> And reverent desire.

And who can ever think of Switzerland apart from Matthew Arnold's two wonderful Obermann poems? Do not some spirits still exist who slip 'their chain' with Matthew Arnold?

> And to thy mountain chalet come,
> And lie beside its door,
> And hear the wild bees' Alpine hum,
> And thy sad, tranquil lore.
>
> Again I feel the words inspire
> Their mournful calm—serene,
> Yet tinged with infinite desire
> For all that *might* have been.

De Senancour! how these poems 'To Obermann' have carried your melancholy eloquence from the early years of the century to its very end!

The first edition of the 'Wild Garden' was published in 1881, and of all modern illustrated flower-books it is the only one I know that makes me feel really enthusiastic. The drawings in it, by Mr. Alfred Parsons, are exquisite and quite original. At the time of its publication the method was new, and, to my mind, it has not yet been surpassed. I have also the fourth edition, which came out in 1894, with much new matter and several new illustrations, especially landscapes; but I prefer the first edition—perhaps because we get fond of the particular edition that originally gave pleasure.

I am afraid that the hopeful instructions on 'wild gardening' so cheerfully laid down by Mr. Robinson must be taken with a great many grains of salt when it comes to putting them into practice, especially in dry soils. With care, labour, knowledge, and space, exquisite gardens may be laid out, suitable to the various soils of England; but, in my experience, even the best planting goes off without renewal of the soil This shows itself with the happy possessors of these so-called 'wild gardens' by the constant desire to extend them into pastures new. Mr. Robinson's description of a garden at Weybridge ought to open the eyes of everybody as to what can be done in light soils. All I wish to point out is that merely buying the plants and sticking them in does not make a wild garden. No one can look at Mr. Parsons' beautiful drawings of the Evening Primrose and the Giant Cow Parsley without longing to grow such things. But the first essentials are space and isolation; they are worth nothing if crowded up.

1875. 'The Vegetable Garden,' by M. M. Vilmorin-Andrieux. English edition published under the direction of W. Robinson. This is one of the books mentioned in January as indispensable to anyone who wishes to be up-to-date or to grow special vegetables in the kitchen garden. The illustrations are from the French edition, and, though not artistic, are admirably drawn, and give one quickly an intimate knowledge of the shape and growth of vegetables, whether they be roots or plants.

The first edition of the now far-famed 'English Flower Garden' came out in 1883, and the one published this year

(1896) is the sixth edition. It has been immensely added to, and the present illustrations are among the most beautiful modern wood-cuts I know. It is said that books are now written to be read and understood by the village idiot. If this be so, I must own that the first and second editions, with their quantity of small, gardener's catalogue illustrations of the plants and flowers, are more helpful to the ignorant amateur than is this beautiful illustrating of, let us say, a branch of Hawthorn or a full-blown Tea-rose. This seems a cruel criticism of a beautiful book; and it should never be forgotten that the fault lies with the ignorant amateur, not with the new edition.

'God's Acre Beautiful, or The Cemeteries of the Future' is a strong plea for cremation. My edition is the third, published in 1883. Everyone interested in the subject ought to read it. The picture, at the end of the book, of a section of a pauper corner in a London cemetery is, I think, enough to convert anybody; but it does not seem to me that the practice of cremation is gaining much ground. The recent sweeping-away of West End London cemeteries contrasts badly, even from the point of view of sentiment, with the tombs at Pompeii used for urns; the chapter referring to these is headed 'Permanent, Unpolluted, Inviolate.' That is certainly not the modern cemetery!

In 1892 Mr. Robinson published two lectures of considerable severity, called 'Garden Design' and 'Architects' Gardens.' These lectures were mainly directed against two books; one, that seemed to contradict all Mr. Robinson's work, was 'The Formal Garden in England,' by Reginald Blomfield and T. Inigo Thomas. The fact is, that near large and stately houses there must be some kind of formal laying-out of the ground, even if ever so informally planted (Mr. Robinson himself would be the first to recognise this), unless everything is sacrificed to stateliness, and turf alone is admitted. The whole discussion is full of interest to those who possess large places. The next book on which Mr. Robinson pours the vials of his wrath (I love righteous indignation on one's pet subject) is 'Garden Craft, Old and New,' by John D. Sedding. Of all Mr. Robinson's books, the 'English Flower Garden 'will always remain his masterpiece; and I repeat here, what I said in January, that no modern gardener can get on without it. Every village club should have it, as well as his first-rate little halfpenny paper, 'Cottage Gardening,' which has many useful things in it besides gardening.

Anyone who can remember the gardening of the last thirty years will have no difficulty in recognising all that we owe to Mr. Robinson. His untiring energy, the pains he has taken to bring his books up to the highest and most complete standard of useful knowledge and reference, his newspapers (the coloured illustrations of which come nearer the excellence of the old coloured engravings than those in any other modern periodical), and, above all, the true taste and knowledge he has brought to bear on English gardening are influencing the whole of Europe, America, and our colonies; for he has headed the movement in the right direction, teaching the true principles of the laying-out of gardens and the preservation and cultivation of plants and flowers.

I have (bound) a great many years' numbers of 'The Garden' newspaper. To look over them is endlessly interesting and suggestive, though it is apt to be discouraging, as so many plants are mentioned that we have not got and would like to have.

1872. 'Flowers and Gardens,' by Forbes Watson. This is the only break I make in my resolve to mention no book not in my possession. My reasons for doing so are that it has long been out of print, and that I want to make a short extract from it. So far as I know, this was the first of a long series of books—not so much practical gardening books, as books about the garden as a whole and the way in which the grouping and growing of plants affect the individual writer. An attractive, suggestive, and pathetic little book, written by a sick man to beguile days he knew to be his last. Mr. Watson was perhaps the last of the men who combined the three callings of doctor, botanist, and gardener. What he writes is much in advance of the feeling of the day, and it is full of what we now think quite the right tone about gardening. In the following quotation he expresses better than I can do it what I want to say. He begins: 'Solon declared that to be the best of Governments in which an injury done to the meanest subject is an insult to the whole community.

'This is pretty much the law of a garden.

'Nothing is more objectionable than the manner in which the common plants are often treated to make way for the grandees. Bulbs taken up before they are ready, and dwarfed for next season in consequence; small trees or shrubs transplanted carelessly, and thrust in wherever they will do no harm, because a little too good to throw away, and not quite good enough to deserve just treatment; and many other plants neglected, overshadowed, or in some way stinted of their due, as not being worth much trouble. At times, even worse than this, we see murderous digging and slashing amongst plants in their period of growth. This is not a healthy process for the mind. Whatever is unfairly treated is better altogether away, since we can view it with no hearty relish. And this injustice to the least is felt inevitably in a measure by all, for it affects the spirit of the place. Half the charm of the old-fashioned garden lies in that look of happy rest among the plants, each of which seems to say: "All plant life is sacred when admitted, my own repose has never been disturbed, and I am confident it never will be." You feel this to be a sort of heaven of plant life, preserved by some hidden charm from the intrusion of noxious weeds. The modern garden, on the contrary, is too apt to assume a look of stir and change; here to-day, gone tomorrow. The very tidiness of the beds and the neat propriety of the plants contribute to this impression. We feel the omnipresence of a severity which cannot tolerate straggling. None have been admitted but polished gentlemen, who will never break the rules; and we feel that the most cherished offender would be instantly punished.

'I have been referring here to the herbaceous plants and evergreens of the ordinary beds—Thujas, Junipers, Rhododendrons, &c—rather than to the larger trees and shrubs. To run down the glorious Rhododendrons in themselves would be preposterous; but they always have, however large they may grow, an air of gentlemanly restraint—a drawing-room manner, as it were—which must produce the effect we have described wherever they are very numerous. But the old garden impresses us always by that loving tenderness for the plants. "That wallflower ought not to have come up in the Box edging—but never mind, we must manage to get on without hurting the wallflower;" and it is this spirit of compromise—this happy, genial, kindly character, as contrasted with the sterner and less loving spirit, which you feel is ready to descend upon any transgressor in a moment, that makes the difference of which we speak.'

Mr. Watson is very severe in his condemnation of double flowers, and in a way which, I think, indicates the same nature that could not admire Rubens or the Venetian painters. Surely many people with a sensuous temperament are no more to be blamed therefor than are people who blush to be reprimanded by those who do not. In their power of giving pleasure the strong-scented double garden flowers are superior to the beautiful single ones, and the Neapolitan Violet, the warm, exquisitely scented Tuberose, the tender but full-odoured garden Rose, and the Carnation, give great delight in a harmless way to people of certain temperaments. Why should this be condemned, when that which pleases the eye in the beautiful forms of the single flower is praised? Mr. Watson says, 'Above all, scorn nothing'; yet he himself utterly condemns the cultivator who prefers the double sweet-scented flowers. It is the old story; as Samuel Butler puts it, the damning of the sins we are not inclined to. We all do it more or less. To me some few flowers seem vulgar, partly from association and partly from the unsympathetic harshness of their tint. But surely in gardening, as in all else in life, the broadest view is best, and the wisest attempt is to please as many as we can. The taste of the ignorant and the critical taste of the cultivated never can be the same on any subject, but both are better than indifference and no taste at all. I know one man who dislikes any flowers, and only has stunted Portugal Laurels growing in green square boxes on his lawn. I know another who will not plant anything that does not flower or fruit in the autumn months, because that is the only time he intends to live at his country place. All tastes are respectable, though we may each of us find it difficult to admire the taste of the other.

1872. 'My Garden: Its Plan and Culture.' by Alfred Smee. Second edition, revised and corrected. This book is one I can really recommend to beginners. It is modern in illustration, and yet it retains some of the characteristics of the older books. It really teaches you what to do, and gives a very fair idea of all that a good-sized garden requires; it names and illustrates hardly any plants not worth growing; it includes kitchen garden, flower garden, Alpine garden, greenhouse, stove, and water plants; and it winds up with garden insects, animals, and birds. The illustrations are much above the average. Those who want to buy one single book likely to help them, especially at first, could not do better than get this one, which is often to be seen mentioned in catalogues of second-hand books.

1874. 'Alpine Plants,' edited by David Wooster. This work, which is in two volumes, contains a great many colour-printed illustrations of Alpine plants—not, however, as they grow in the fissures of their mountain slopes, but as they may be seen in Mr. Backhouse's most interesting gardens in Yorkshire. The drawings are rather exaggerated in size and harsh in colour, but the book is distinctly instructive as portraying, among what are called 'Alpines,' the most showy and the best worth cultivating in English gardens.

1879. 'A Year in a Lancashire Garden,' by Henry A. Bright. This little book is the one I alluded to in March, and to which I consider I owe so much. It often gives me pleasure to read it over now. It has qualities like the garden itself. The same flowers come up each year, the same associations link themselves on to the returning flowers, and the verses of the great poets are unchanged; so this little book will always be to me like poor Ophelia's Rosemary, 'that's remembrance.'

The quotations throughout the book are quite unusually original and appropriate.

(No date.) 'Gleanings from Old Garden Literature,' by W. Carew Hazlitt. Of all the recent little book's referring in some way directly or indirectly to gardens, this one, I think, gives me the most pleasure. It has all the charm of a conversation with a clever and sympathetic man on subjects that are dear to him and to oneself. Mr. Hazlitt quotes, from Cowley's preface to his poem of 'The Garden,' the delightful wish which comes home to so many when the strife and toil of life are more or less over and evening is drawing near:—'I never had any other desire so strong and so like covetousness as that one which I have had always, that I might be master at last of a small house and large garden, with very moderate conveniences joined to them, and there dedicate the remainder of my life to the culture of them and the study of Nature.' To anyone who has found any interest in my book-notes I would say, 'Get this little book; you will find pleasure in it.'

1881. 'Notes and Thoughts on Gardens and Woodlands,' by the late Frances Jane Hope. This is a most excellent and helpful work to the true amateur gardener. Though without the unique literary flavour of that book, it belongs in a way to what I would call the 'Lancashire Garden' series, and is not only useful by reason of its suggestive and instructive qualities, but is full of individuality and information. Miss Hope strikes the true note, and one, it seems, of the real difficulties of left-alone half-wild gardens, when she says, 'These two winters and one summer have spoilt our spring beds and borders, and a thorough upturn and change of plan will be requisite. It was impossible to use a fork or hoe in 1879 in our soil; the result of the leave-alone system is a carpet of *Marchantia* and *Hypnum sericeum*. To scrape these pests off does no real good, for the earth is caked below and impervious to air, sun, or rain. So we are longing for our bulb treasures to be up, and to get on to our alterations, do away with rings and surfacings, and whatever prevents us loosening the earth between each plant. Looking at our border, the only real advantage of what is called bedding-out struck me forcibly, being the thorough working and justice done to the soil.' The whole book is simply about gardening, but of the most intelligent and suggestive kind.

1884. 'Hardy Perennials,' by John Wood. An excellent, cheap, instructive little book. Mr. Wood, of Kirkstall, Yorkshire, has a very fine collection of herbaceous plants for sale.

1884. 'Days and Hours in a Garden,' by E. V. B. This is a garden book rather breathing the sweet luxury and joy of a garden than one very full of instruction or practical experience. E. V. B. herself owns one of the most beautiful gardens I know; and the book has, I think, that power which is one of the highest qualities of art, of making one feel beauty. The little pen-and-ink drawings are full of charm; and on the expanse of an inch—for these little headings to chapters are scarcely more—one breathes the pure air of Heaven. As she herself quotes, 'To the wise a fact is true poetry and the most beautiful of Fables.' In 1895 E. V. B. published a second book, called 'A Garden of Pleasure.' It has the same qualities, but is not perhaps quite as good. We are apt to think this of second books on the same subject—perhaps we are prejudiced in favour of our first friend.

1890. 'The Garden's Story, or Pleasures and Trials of an Amateur Gardener,' by George H. Ellwanger. I suppose nearly all readers of garden books have seen this charming, clever, tasteful, little contribution from the other shore; I do not mean the next world, but America. In spite of the constant interchange of books between the two countries, it required an introduction from so well-known a gardener as Mr. Wolley Dod to make the book known here. Let us thank Mr. Wolley Dod cordially, and thoroughly agree that an international exchange of information on so all-absorbing a subject as gardening is most interesting. The climate of America, with its hot summers and long cold winters, makes gardening a much more serious undertaking than it is in our own damp, equable little island. Mr. Ellwanger gives us a most luxurious and opulent receipt for the old favourite mixture called, all the world over, *Pot-pourri*:—'The roses used should be just blown, of the sweetest-smelling kinds, gathered in as dry a state as possible. After each gathering, spread out the petals on a sheet of paper and leave until free from all moisture; then place a layer of petals in the jar, sprinkling with coarse salt; then another layer and salt, alternating, until the jar is full. Leave for a few days, or until a broth is formed; then incorporate thoroughly, and add more petals and salt, mixing daily for a week, when fragrant gums and spices should be added, such as benzoin, storax, cassia buds, cinnamon, cloves, cardamom, and vanilla bean. Mix again and leave for a few days, when add essential oil of jasmine, violet, tuberose, and attar of roses, together with a hint of ambergris, or musk, in mixture with the flower ottos to fix the odour. Spices, such as cloves, should be sparingly used. A rose *Pot-pourri* thus combined, without parsimony in supplying the flower ottos, will be found in the fullest sense a joy for ever.'

1890. 'History of Botany,' by Julius von Sachs, translated by Henry E. F. Garnsey. This book will commend itself to those gardeners, and to amateurs generally, who love knowledge not hard to acquire. The history of the long evolution of botany through so many clever, patient, and painstaking hands, is even more interesting than a smattering of botany itself, now that we take its simple laws unquestioningly as we take the great fact that the earth revolves on its own axis, though we each day repeat the old expressions that the sun rises and the sun sets.

1891. 'The Miniature Fruit Garden,' by Thomas Rivers and T. Francis Rivers. The twentieth edition. This fact proclaims more eloquently than any words of mine can do the excellence and usefulness of this little book. Of all the many changes to be noticed in my life-time, I know none more remarkable than the immense increase that has taken place within my memory in fruit cultivation and fruit consumption.

1892. 'The Garden of Japan,' by F. T. Piggott. A charming little book, the fascinating subject of which is described by the title. The illustrations are very nicely drawn; among them are two or three interesting Japanese flower arrangements. In March Mr. Piggott, writing from Japan, says: 'Every garden is full of the small shrubs [Daphnes], and every shrub is full of flowers.'

1893. 'A Book about the Garden and the Gardener,' by S. Reynolds Hole. This book is well worth having for a modern gardener. It gives a lot of instruction, and is written in a cheerful, parochial, kindly tone, most helpful to those who live rural lives in and near villages. He rejoices, as one would think everyone must, in the allotment system. He suggests in his preface that politicians should send horticultural teachers into our villages. This has now been done, and I am told the lectures given this winter in our own village at home have been most helpful and instructive. I myself should much like to see flower and vegetable shows managed on some other system. I think that prizes should be given for healthy quantity grown in a small space, and for the general clean and healthy appearance of well-stocked gardens. Such things are a great deal more important, for food-producing purposes, than that there should be a few giant Onions, Carrots, or Cabbages; for size rarely adds to the excellence of vegetables. Dean Hole truly remarks that the allotment system will always have two opponents: there will always be idle men who will not have gardens, and ignorant men who will not know how to use them.

1894. 'Italian Gardens,' by Charles A. Platt. This is a book published in New York; it is very pretty, and full of excellent reproductions of artistically taken photographs. The letterpress describes the gardens. Of Villa Lante, at Bagni near Viterbo, there are four illustrations. The book was given to me by two kind American ladies, a mother and daughter, who came to spend a summer's day with me in my garden. They had been all round Europe, studying gardens large and small, and the daughter hoped to lay out some original and typical gardens in America that would be suitable to the soil and the climate; also to try and preserve the beautiful flora of that country, which is in danger of dying away. I thought the idea interesting. In their time and way, under their blue skies and in their lovely situations, nothing, I imagine, will ever come near the beautiful Medician gardens of Italy, which, even in their decay, are never forgotten by those who once have had the joy of wandering in them.

1894; 'The Natural History of Plants,' from the German of Anton Kerner von Marilaun, Professor of Botany in the University of Vienna, by F. W. Oliver Quain, Professor of Botany in University College, London. For the modern botanist this book is deeply interesting. I am, alas! no botanist, and have no scientific knowledge; but to take up the book, and to read a page or two anywhere, opens one's eyes wide with wonder. It refers principally to microscopic botany. The coloured plates are saddening to a degree; they seem to me all that botanical plates ought not to be, and somehow appear to have been affected by Miss North's system of flower-painting. How valuable would have been her untiring energy, if the drawings so generously given to Kew had been either artistic, like Mr. Parsons', or, still better, from the scientific point of view, botanical and delicately true, like Jacquin's or Redouté's, or the drawings in Curtis's books! In the chromo-lithographs of these four volumes we have attempts at the impossible—large plants in the foreground, with skies, distances, and middle-distance all out of tone. The wood-cuts are much better; some are very good and delicate, especially the representations of strongly magnified subjects. I bought the book as bringing illustrated plant-lore down to the latest date. The account, in the third volume, of the distribution of pollen is thrillingly interesting, and is within the comprehension of the aforenamed 'village idiot'; many of our ordinary garden flowers are figured as examples. The saddest attempt at a picture is a Brobdingnagian representation of an Alpine Rhododendron, with pines and snow-clad mountains in the distance. I may be wrong, but to me it seems waste of talent and time and money to illustrate books in this way. These illustrations are printed in Germany; let us hope that the artists were also Germans.

1895. 'In a Gloucestershire Garden,' by Henry Ellacombe. I think most people who are personally interested in their gardens will enjoy this book; there is much to be learnt from it, and the second part is especially instructive. It breathes the true spirit of a garden, independently of the human element or of book-making. Canon Ellacombe names many of the old Roses, now gone out of fashion, but I rather doubt if he has ever seen Redouté's wonderful Rose book. He ends his book with a warning to the clergy against gardening, as being too interesting and too absorbing an occupation for them. I can thoroughly echo this sentiment as a warning to all young people. It can only be perfectly indulged in by the lonely or the old, and by those who do not mind neglecting their other duties, and who say, bravely and honestly, 'I am quite selfish and quite happy.' But of course this is the danger of all absorbing pursuits. I agree with many of Canon Ellacombe's remarks; one especially can never be too often repeated:—'In nothing is the gardener's skill more shown than in the judicious use of the pruning-knife.' His experience of the American Bramble is exactly mine—as far as the fruit goes; it is not worth growing, as the fruit is less in quantity and inferior in quality to our own wild Brambles. But the cut leaf is prettier, and at any rate makes a variety.

1895. 'The Story of the Plants,' by Grant Allen, is a humble, little popular book; but I am sure its perusal will bring pleasure and increased understanding to many who read it. One of his sayings is 'that plants are the only things that know how to manufacture living material. Roughly speaking, plants are the producers and animals the consumers.'

1896. 'The Bamboo Garden,' by A. B. Freeman Mitford, C.B. Mr. Mitford tells us in his preface that his book is simply an attempt to give a descriptive list— what the French call a *catalogue raisonné*—of the hardy Bamboos in cultivation in this country. We ought to be grateful that he has brought within the reach of everybody all that is to be said on this most beautiful family.

1895. 'A History of Gardening in England,' by the Hon. Alicia Amherst. This is by far the most interesting and remarkable book that, I believe, has ever been written on the subject, and far surpasses in every way Mr. Johnson's 'History of Gardening,' before alluded to. The book is full of information, drawn from patient and most diligent research, and will be of real utility to students of the literature and history of gardening and to the owners of large places. It contains little that will practically help people who live in cottages and small villas. It alludes only very indirectly to the beautiful illustrated flower books, especially the foreign ones, which so far exceed our own in artistic beauty and skill. It is rather sad that when the Society of Gardeners wished to illustrate their plants in 1736 they had to engage the services of Jacob van Huysum, brother of the Dutch flower-painter; and to this day the best periodical coloured flower-printing, though painted by Englishmen, is printed in Belgium (*vide* 'The Garden'). Miss Amherst's book is one for constant reference; and the greater one's knowledge, the greater will be one's appreciation of it. I cannot but regret, however, that it has been printed on the disagreeable modern shiny paper, which also makes the book most inconveniently heavy. This paper, I am told, facilitates the reproduction of the illustrations; but these, also, are very hard and ugly, and quite unworthy of the book.

It is almost impossible to keep pace with the Modern books

about gardens, they are so numerous. Just to complete my list I will mention several in my possession, for, as the motto of one of them says, 'It is a natural consequence that those who cannot taste the actual fruition of a garden should take the greater delight in reading about one.'

'Voyage autour de mon Jardin,' by Alphonse Karr, is charming, and has been translated into English.

'The Praise of Gardens,' by Albert F. Sieveking, is a collection of quotations of all that has been written about gardens. The selection is very complete. Unfortunately the book is out of print.

I need hardly mention 'The Garden that I Love,' by Alfred Austin, as it has been such a favourite with the public. It is, of course, a book written less to instruct about gardening than to show what a beautiful and enchanting place a garden is for conversation, especially when the right people come together.

In the 'Edinburgh Review' for July 1896, there is an article called 'Gardens and Garden Craft,' with a long heading of gardening books, which many people will find interesting, as I did.

In the November (1896) number of 'The Journal of the Royal Horticultural Society' is an excellent lecture by Mr. F. W. Burbidge, the Curator of the Botanical Garden in Dublin. In the ' Journal' the lecture is divided into three parts— called 'Garden Literature,' 'Reference Books on English Gardening Literature,' and 'Garden Libraries.' It is interesting, besides other reasons, as being a somewhat new departure in the lectures delivered before the Horticultural Society. I strongly recommend those who care about the subject to read this lecture, as they will get a great deal of most useful information in a very condensed form. Mr. Burbidge strongly recommends garden libraries, in which I entirely agree with him. No large place should be without a room where gardening books and weekly gardening papers are within easy access of all the gardeners on the place, and no village club in England could not afford to take in Mr. Robinson's excellent little weekly paper called 'Cottage Gardening,' which I mentioned before. It costs one halfpenny, and is full of all sorts of useful information. Surely at village shows no better prize could be given than the back numbers (bound) of this most useful publication. Mr. Burbidge says: 'In America and in Germany the library seems to be thought as essential to good gardening and profitable land culture as here with us the seed room or the tool shed; and in England we are beginning to perceive the value of technical education, and to recognise the vital importance of the most recent scientific discoveries relating to our crops and their diseases, and the soil in which they grow. Private garden libraries, while most desirable, really form part of a much larger and wider question. If libraries are essential for the garden, surely they are even more so on the farm.' Mr. Burbidge winds up: 'But to form libraries we must have good and useful books, and I shall give a short list of those I believe to be the best of their kind; and one of the best ways I know of getting the best gardening books into the best hands is to award them as prizes to the cultivators and exhibitors of garden produce at allotment-garden and village flower shows.' With this I most cordially agree. Then follows a list of thirty-eight books.

Another paper of great interest is on the importance of British fruit-growing, from a food point of view, by Mr. Edmund J. Baillie.

DECEMBER

Orchid-growing on a small scale—Miss Jekyll's articles in the 'Guardian'—Winter vegetables—Laver as a vegetable—Advice to housekeepers—Cooking sun-dried fruit.

December 5th—For anyone with a small stove I can thoroughly advise growing some of the more easily cultivated Orchids. For many years all Orchids seemed to me to smell of money, and to represent great expenditure; but this is not the case at all. They only want the treatment suited to them, and the same care and attention required by other plants that are grown in heat. Cypripediums come in most usefully at this time of year; they last well in water, and continue to flower at times all through the winter. There are endless varieties of them to be bought, and some of the least expensive plants are often as good as the costly ones; it is only the new varieties that are dear. Some that I have—green, spotted with brown, and with clear white tips—are lovely. They have looked well lately on the dinner-table, arranged with little branches of a shrubby Veronica, called, I believe, *V. speciosum*. It is a plant well worth growing for the charming light green of its leaves out of doors at this time of year, when fresh green is so rare. Unlike most of the shrubby Veronicas, it lasts well in water. It has a long white flower in July, which is not especially pretty. We also grow very successfully *Dendrobium nobile*, *Oncidium sphacelatum*, and several other Orchids that flower in the early part of the year.

To-day there have come up from the country—not from my own home, which is too dry, but from near Salisbury—some branches cut from an old Thorn or Apple tree, and covered with long hoary-grey moss. I have put them into an old ginger-jar without water, and in this way they will last through the winter. They stand now against a red wall, where they look exceedingly well.

December 10th—There has been in this year's 'Guardian' a succession of monthly papers on a Surrey garden, written by Miss Jekyll of Munstead Wood, Godalming. I give her address, as she now sells her surplus plants, all more or less suited to light soils, to the management of which she has for many years past given special attention. These papers have much illuminating matter in them, and are called 'Notes from Garden and Woodland.' All the plants and flowers about which Miss Jekyll writes she actually grows on the top of her Surrey hill. Her garden is a most instructive one, and encouraging too. She has gone through the stage, so common to all ambitious and enthusiastic amateurs, of trying to grow everything, and of often wasting much precious room in growing inferior plants, or plants which, even though they may be worth growing in themselves, are yet not worth the care and feeding which a light soil necessitates if they are to be successful.

This, to me, rather delightful characteristic of amateurs in every art was severely condemned by Mr. Ruskin in my youth, when he said that the amateur sketcher always attempted to draw the panorama of Rome on his thumb-nail, instead of humbly trying to reproduce what was at his own door. The practice is just as common in gardening as in music and painting.

Every plant that Miss Jekyll names is worth getting and growing in gardens that are of considerable size, and which more or less share her Surrey soil and climate. I trust that before long these articles will be republished in book form, for every word in them deserves attention and consideration.

December 12th—One of the every-day English dishes that is often so bad, and can be so excellent, is the old, much-abused hashed mutton. What I am going to say about it applies equally well to every kind of meat that is warmed up. Make the sauce early in the day with stock, gravy, onions, and other vegetables, or, failing this, a few drops of two or three of the bought sauces, and one or two drops of essence of garlic. Garlic, which is excellent as a flavouring to most sauces, is such a dangerous thing to use in a kitchen that the way I manage it is this:—Put five or six cloves of garlic into a wide-necked bottle and cover them with good spirits of wine. When wanted, stick a skewer or fork into the spirit and use a drop or two. The spirit evaporates and the flavour of the garlic remains. But even in this way it must be used carefully for English palates. To return to the sauce for the hash: avoid flour, or, if it must be a little thickened, let it only be with what is called 'brown *roux*' in 'Dainty Dishes.' The really essential point is to make your sauce first and let it get cold, and then warm up the meat and the sauce together. If you throw meat of any kind into hot sauce, you are certain to make it hard; it contracts the fibre of the meat, and spoils it.

One of the very few ways in which wild duck can be warmed up is to mince it fine and then curry it with some well-cooked curry sauce. This is made on the same principle as the curry mentioned before; that is to say the onion and apple (if you cannot get apples, gooseberries, or rhubarb, or any fruit will do) must be fried together, and the stock and curry powder added, well cooked, and rubbed through a fine sieve, allowed to get cool, and the mince and sauce just warmed up together before serving. For currying fish or vegetables a little milk or cream softens the sauce.

Stewed meats are seldom really good in England. The following is a good way of cooking haricot of mutton:—Set a stew-pan on the fire (an earthenware one is the best) with a little butter in it; put in some pieces of raw mutton, neatly jointed and cut up small; fry till a nice brown colour. Take out the meat, place it on a dish, add some carrots, turnips, onions, celery, and a very little sugar, and fry in the butter. When brown, replace the meat, and pour in some cold water or weak stock—enough to cover all the ingredients. Stew gently for three hours. The stewing can be done in the oven or on the hot-plate. If cooked in an earthenware pot, this stew, as well as many others done in the same way, can be sent to table in the pot with a clean napkin pinned round it.

When vegetables are scarce in winter, and you have cooked carrots, turnips, onions, celery, &c., strained from the soup the night before, it is a good plan to chop them up and warm them in a little butter with a small lump of sugar, some pepper and salt, and serve them for luncheon. If the quantity is insufficient, you can easily add some cold potatoes and cabbage.

Potatoes, now so often forbidden by doctors, seem to me excellent, wholesome food for people who do not eat meat. They can be cooked in such an endless variety of ways, though most English cooks confine themselves, as a rule, to only two or three. The secret of good mashed potatoes is to boil them dry, and beat them up with boiling milk, adding a little butter or cream. Cold milk makes them heavy, and spoils them. Another way is to put in a stew-pan some potatoes and two or three sliced onions, to boil, with only enough water to cover them. When they are done, beat them well with a fork, have ready some boiling milk and a piece of butter, stir these in by degrees as you beat, till the potatoes are like a thick purée. 'Dainty Dishes' has several receipts for cooking potatoes.

A seaweed called Laver is a delicious, wholesome, and uncommon vegetable in London in November and December. It is to be bought at any of the really good grocers', not greengrocers'. The London supply, I believe, comes from Devonshire, prepared and cooked, and requires nothing beyond a little stock and butter to moisten it when it is warmed up. It should be served in a small copper saucepan with a lamp under it, as it is not good unless very hot indeed. For helping it a small wooden spoon is better than a silver one; at least, so it used to be served in old days in the North, when I remember it as a child. Half a lemon is sent up with it. A good many people do not like it, I am bound to confess; but those who do, find it a treat they look forward to—and it is good either by itself or with any roast meat, especially mutton.

The same little copper saucepan is useful for a wild duck sauce which I always make on the table. The saucepan, on a spirit-lamp, comes up with some gravy in it; I then squeeze in half or all of a lemon, according to quantity required, and add a little red wine—Port is the best—and some Cayenne pepper. When warm, I pour it over the slices of wild duck on each plate. Wild duck should be very lightly roasted.

Rice plays a large part in our cooking all the year round; Patna is nearly always the best. Risotto à la Milanese is an original Italian receipt:—Cut up four onions very fine, and fry a nice brown. Throw into the stew-pan 1 lb. of rice, and let it slightly colour; then moisten with good stock, and cook it for 35 minutes. Season with pepper and salt, a little nutmeg, and Parmesan cheese. Serve very hot. Chopped truffles or mushrooms may be added.

An excellent winter salad for serving with wild duck and many other birds is watercress, carefully picked and washed, pieces of orange (cut as described below for the compote), all the juice of the oranges, and a few drops of good salad oil added just before serving.

Orange compote depends almost entirely on the goodness of the oranges, and on the way they are cut. The best plan is to stick them on a fork, and with a sharp-pointed kitchen knife remove, at one cutting, all the peel and all the white. Then, with the sharp point of a knife, cut out all the pieces of orange between the white lines, leaving the white in the middle. Save all the juice, and cut small shreds of the peel without any white, put them into some water with sugar and the juice, and, if the oranges are very sweet, add a little lemon juice. Boil up this syrup, pour it over the pieces of orange, and allow it to cool. This is a good foundation for any winter compote. Apricots, bananas, or pineapple, all can be added, separately or together; and a few dried cherries stewed improve the appearance. Another excellent winter compote is made by cutting up a ripe pineapple (often so cheap), stewing the peel in a syrup, to which is added the juice that runs out of the pineapple, and a little ginger. Strain, and pour it boiling over the pieces of pineapple. A few bananas cut up and added to the pineapple improve it.

Two excellent ways of serving cold chicken for small parties or suppers are the following:—Order the day before from a good baker some extra small dinner-rolls, cut off the tops, and take out the crumb. Mince a little chicken and ham or tongue; it takes a very small quantity of either. Mix with well-made Mayonnaise sauce, a little chopped parsley, and a very little onion. Put this into the rolls, and replace the small round top on each. Finger rolls, cut in half and the crumb taken out, can be done in the same way.

The other way is to make some little open sandwiches—we call them Barrington sandwiches—in the following manner:—Butter some moderately thick slices of a good tin loaf, and cut them into medium-sized rounds. Lay across them, in pieces cut quite narrow, some breast of cold chicken, a quarter of an anchovy, and a thin shred of green gherkin. These form narrow bars of green, white, and red across the slices of bread. Trim the edges, and serve on a plate one laid partly over the other, like cutlets.

I particularly want to say a last word to housekeepers who are anxious to indulge in hospitality. Hospitality should mean, to my mind, not altering our whole way of living, but giving the best of our habitual food. For this nothing is so telling, whether the dinner be large or small, as the procuring of some special seasonable luxury. It is well worth taking the trouble to get any such luxuries, not from the usual shop in your neighbourhood, but from the very best shop you know of for each speciality, whether fish, game, vegetable, Italian goods more especially, fruit (fresh or bottled), dessert, biscuits, or cake. The really good housekeeper is alert to learn where the best things come from, and to take hints wherever she goes. One should never through idleness give up getting the best things. If you go to the expense of entertaining at all, it makes little difference in the way of money whether you deal at a specially good shop or a second-rate one, and the results at your table are very different indeed.

London shops are now full of sun-dried American fruits, principally apples and apricots. These appear to me to be safer and wholesomer, particularly for children, than tinned or bottled fruit. If carefully carried out, the following receipt makes them excellent:—Select the fruit you intend to use, and rinse it thoroughly in clear, fresh water; then place it in a dish with sufficient water to cover it, and allow it to soak for ten or fifteen hours before it is required for use. After this, put it in the vessel in which it is to be cooked (which ought, of course, to be earthenware), simmer it slowly, letting it come just once in a way to the boil, until it is thoroughly cooked. If the water in which the fruit was soaked is thrown away, and fresh water substituted, much of the flavour and nutriment of the fruit will be lost. Sufficient sugar should be added, when the fruit is nearly done, to make it palatable. Dried fruit cooked in this way can be served either hot or cold, as may be desired. As a rule, when allowed to cool, it will be fully as palatable as if eaten warm. By cooking dried fruit according to this method, there will be secured a wholesome and palatable dish, full flavoured, and resembling as near as possible, in appearance, size, and taste, the original fresh product.

This also is good:—Bavarois of fruit, bottled or fresh. Warm the fruit and rub it through a hair sieve, and add just enough isinglass, previously melted in a little water, to set the fruit when cold. Add some cream, and pour into a mould, keeping back a little fruit to make a syrup, which should be poured round before serving. Icing improves the dish.

APPENDIX

JAPANESE ART OF ARRANGING CUT FLOWERS[1]

IT is now some years since Mr. J. Conder's excellent book, 'The Flowers of Japan and the Art of Floral Arrangement,' was first published. But the principles laid down in it have so little penetrated the art of cut-flower arrangements in England that it may be assumed either that the book is still very little known or that its teaching has been set down as unsuited to English flowers and flower-vases. The book is not published in England, but almost any bookseller will get it from Japan; the cost is 2*l.* 2*s.* The coloured plates, to which chiefly this high price is due, do not materially contribute to the expounding of the theory and, although full of character and beauty in themselves, could be omitted without loss to the main object of the book. A smaller and much cheaper edition of the work could then be produced and published in England.[2]

[1] From the *Garden* of October 6, 1894.

[2] Mr. Conder has lately published three articles on the same subject in the October, December '96, and January '97 numbers of the *Studio*—that unusually artistic magazine which is to be had monthly for one shilling. Mr. Conder's articles are beautifully illustrated with numerous plates of Japanese designs, reproduced from photographs; and in the text he sums up many of the most interesting points contained in his book. He does not suggest that the art of which he writes could be applied to the arrangement of cut flowers in England, but it is to be hoped that these articles—which are, unfortunately, already out of print—may be re-published in book form. The great beauty of the illustrations would do more to spread the practice of the art amongst English people than any written theory upon it—C. L., *March* 1897.

In the meanwhile, however, it is my object to spread its teaching and to show how, with but slight modifications and relaxation from the stricter Japanese rules, this artistic science may be adapted to English flowers and English drawing-rooms. It has a strong claim to being adopted by all lovers of the beautiful and the practical combined because, first, these decorations have a quite unique beauty and refinement; secondly, cut flowers and shrubs live long in water when supported by a flower-holder in the Japanese way, to be described presently; thirdly, only very few flowers or branches are required—a great advantage to those who have but small gardens, to people living in towns where flowers are expensive, and for the seasons of the year when flowers are scarce. Also an extremely decorative effect can be produced without making the room airless from the scent of many flowers. Fourthly, the infinite variety of design it is possible to produce with but few branches on the Japanese principle as compared to the English may be likened to the number of changes that can be rung on a few bells when a given system is followed, whereas the different bells rung simultaneously produce only one, and that a discordant, sound.

Roughly speaking, the Japanese art of cut-flower decorations may be classified into three fundamental principles:—

1. Not alone the flowers and leaves, but also the stems or branches should be considered as part of the design—in fact, it is the most important part.

2. The branches are not allowed to lean against the edga of the vase, as in the English manner, but must be firmly supported either by a wooden fixer fitted into the neck of the vase, or by coils of iron if open basin-shaped or flat-

bottomed vessels are used, this giving to the stems the appearance of growth and self-support.

3. Only such flowers and trees as are easily obtainable should be used. Rarity is not considered a merit, and foreign or out-of-the-way plants are only permitted to be used by those who have a thorough knowledge of the nature of their growth, characteristics, &c. The flowers used should be in season, and the design of the decoration suited to its position in the room—*i.e.* if under a picture, on a shelf, in the centre of an alcove, &c—as well as adapted to the vase which holds it.

Although one of my objects is to show how much the English method may be improved without too great a subservience to the strictest laws of the Japanese art, yet it would be difficult to make myself understood by the uninitiated without first giving an outline of that science, which was originally, it is supposed, a religious rite, and which to-day is still a much-reverenced art in Japan. For this purpose I shall quote freely from Mr. Conder's book, as it would be impossible to improve upon his lucid and concise treatment of the subject. The following are selected as the most important rules to be observed:—

The surface of the water in which the flowers are placed is technically considered to be the soil from which the floral growth springs, and the designer must here convey the impression of stability and strength.

The *springing*, or point of origin of the floral group, is of great importance, and the firm and skilful fixing of the stems or branches in the vessel which holds them is one of the most difficult parts of the manipulation. Ordinarily, the stems are held in position by small cylindrical pieces of wood, fitting tightly across the neck of the flower vase, and having a slit, wider above than below, for threading them through. The wedge-shaped form, wider towards the top, which is given to the slit allows slightly different inclinations to be imparted to the several branches. The fastener should be fixed about half an inch below the surface of the water, and should not be visible from the front of the vessel. Some schools affect a rustic simplicity in their appliances, and employ a naturally forked twig to hold the flowers in position. For arrangements in neckless vases, such as sand-bowls or shallow tubs, other sorts of fasteners are necessary. One kind consists of a sheet of copper perforated with holes of different sizes, to receive the extremities of the different stems. Another fastener is made of rings or different sections of bamboo of varying diameters attached to a wooden board, the stems finding lodgment in the sockets thus formed, and being further held in position by pebbles being placed over them.

The direction of the stems at starting need not be strictly vertical; but, if curved, the curves should be strong ones.

The artist studiously avoids an equal-sided or symmetrical arrangement, but obtains a balance of a more subtle kind.

The triple arrangement may be taken as the original model of all arrangements. The *Principal* is the central and longest line of the design, and is made to form a double curve, with the upper and lower extremities nearly vertical and in a continuous line, the general shape being that of an archer's bow. The *Secondary* line should be about half, and the *Tertiary* line about one quarter of the length of the *Principal*, supposing all to be straightened out; and these two lines are arranged on different sides of the *Principal* in graceful double curves of varied character. As a general rule, the *Secondary* has a more vertical and the *Tertiary* a more lateral tendency, the former being on the outside of the arched bow formed by the *Principal*, and the latter making a counterpoise on its hollow side. By changing the direction and giving a different character to the curves of these three lines, a great variety of design is produced.

There is another style of design applied to a large class of flower arrangements, in which the *Principal* line of the composition has a horizontal, or almost horizontal, direction; the intention of such compositions being to suggest floral growth on the edges of cliffs or banks, when used in hanging vessels or vases placed on raised shelves.

The different lines have been spoken of as if existing in one vertical plane parallel to the spectator; but actually these lines have also directions of varying degrees forward or backward. In other words, the extreme points of these lines would require a solid and not a plane figure for their enclosure.

The various directions imparted to plants and branches of trees on the above principles are obtained first by a careful selection of suitable material, then by twisting, bending, building together and fixing at the base, and lastly by means of cutting and clipping off defective or superfluous parts.

Flower arrangements are made sometimes with one species of tree or plant alone, and sometimes with a combination of two or more species. The use of many different kinds of flowers in one composition is opposed to the principles of the purer styles.

In arranging two or more species in one composition, variety must be sought by combining trees and plants. In a three-line composition the branches of a tree should never be 'supported' on both sides by a plant; nor should a plant be placed in the centre with a tree arrangement on either side The two branches of the same kind must of necessity be used, but they should adjoin, not sandwich, the remaining one. For example, a composition with Irises (plant) in the centre and branches of Azalea (tree) and Camellia (tree) on either side would be defective. A correct composition would be one with a Plum branch (tree) in the centre, with a Pine branch (tree) on one side and Bamboo stem (plant) on the other. In cases of variety being obtained by land and water plants, this rule is sometimes violated.

The manipulation of different plants and tree-cuttings with the object of preserving their vitality needs special study. In some cases merely sharply cutting the extremity is sufficient to preserve the succulence; but with other material the charring of the end, or dipping in hot water to soften it, is common. The Bamboo is particularly difficult to preserve. The inner divisions are generally removed, and the inside of the tube filled with spiced water or other stimulants. The object of these methods is to get the water to rise in the stem, so that the vitality of the bouquet may be preserved for days. Other means are resorted to in order to prevent the advanced blossoms falling off or dropping. In the case of some large and heavy flowers, invisible Bamboo spikes are employed to keep them erect. Salt is also applied at the base of certain blossoms, to keep the connection moist, and thus defer the shedding which often takes place owing to dryness.

The flower-vases are made of wood, porcelain, pottery, bronze, brass, iron, and basket-work, with wooden, earthenware, or tin receptacles inside for holding the water. They vary as much in form as in material, the most common standing vessels being broad and flat, or long-necked, opening out to a broad flat surface at the mouth; tall, narrow vases are also used. With the ordinary tall vase, whether of wide or narrow mouth, the height of the flowers is generally fixed as one and a half times that of the vase. In the case of broad, shallow receptacles, the height of the floral composition is made about one and a half times the breadth of the vessel. Vases for hooking on to walls and for suspending from a shelf or ceiling are also frequently used.

Having thus briefly quoted from the main principles of this Japanese art as given by Mr. Conder, I shall now make a few homely suggestions as to how they could be applied by any of us in England.

The following practical directions may be found useful to those who wish to try this system of flower arrangement at once with as little trouble and as little expense as possible:—

Go round your house and collect all the china, earthenware, and metal vessels that can be spared—even a kettle, if nothing else can be found, would do. Earthenware dog-troughs are specially adapted to water decorations; three-legged witch's cauldrons and common salt-jars also do very well; an ordinary earthenware flower-pot, with the hole at the bottom corked up, would lend itself to wedging purposes; and every house contains some ornamental pottery, bronze, brass, or silver vessels of a suitable kind. Glass cannot be used, as the pressure of the wedge would crack it; and for the same reason it is inadvisable to try to fix a wedge in fine or valuable china.

From all these select those of a most suitable shape—*i.e.* either broad and flat for water decorations; or narrow-necked with a wide mouth; or a tall, narrow-necked shape, suitable for supporting only one branch without a wedge. If the vessel be small, and made only of thin pottery or china, it should be weighted by placing stones or something heavy inside to balance the weight of the flower erection; without this precaution a tall arrangement might overbalance the whole thing. If the vessel be heavy in itself—of bronze, brass, silver, or other metals, or if of earthenware, sufficiently large to become heavy when filled with water—then this additional weighting is not necessary.

Your next step should be to procure some narrow wood—fire-lighting wood, or laths of any kind. Measure the width of the vase at the place where the wedge is to be fixed; this should be slightly below the surface, so as to be concealed when the vase is filled with water. Cut two pieces of wood to the required length, and shape them at the end to fit the sides of the vase; then scoop out the inner side of each piece of wood, so as to form an oval-shaped opening when they are placed together, slightly narrower below than at the top surface, so as to allow the stalks a freer play of direction, at the same time holding them firm. Then cut out a small notch at each angle of the wood, at a distance of about half an inch from the ends; place the two pieces together, and tie them firmly with string at both ends in the rut of the notches. The string should first be soaked, wound round two or three times, and firmly knotted; it will then remain quite secure. Wire is even better adapted to the purpose than string.

A yet simpler way is, instead of scooping out an oval-shaped opening, to insert a small extra piece of wood at each end between the two woods that form the wedge, and, by thus keeping them apart, make an opening large enough for the width of the stems.

When the wedge is made, soak it in water for a few seconds to make the wood swell; then fix it firmly in the neck of the vase.

Yet another fastener, and perhaps the most adaptable of any consists simply of a spiral coil made of sheet-lead cut into ribbons. This can be bent about to suit the various sizes of the stems. The weight of the leaden coil will balance flowers and branches of considerable height, and it can always be additionally weighted with stones if necessary. This fastener may be used in almost every shaped vase, of no matter what material; for there is no danger, as in the case of the fitting wooden fasteners, that it will crack glass or fine china. Any plumber will supply the strips of sheet-lead, which should be about 2 ft. long, 5/8 in. wide, and 1/8 in. thick, though the sizes vary, of course, according to the vase. It is quite easy to bend these strips into a spiral coil.

These are simple ways of making flower-holders at home

with the most ordinary materials; but, of course, with more trouble a great variety of fasteners can be made.

The next thing to be done is to get a branch of Bamboo or other thin stick, not too brittle, and cut it up into pieces of about an inch long, so as to have a heap of different thicknesses. Before proceeding to cut or buy your flowers, you must decide in what part of the room to place the decorations, so as to have an idea of what would be suitable as to colour, size, and form. If for the corner of a shelf or mantelpiece, the arrangement might be high on one side of the vase, with a long streamer pendent on the other. If for a table under a picture, it might tend upwards, and the *Tertiary* line form almost a right angle—in complement, as it were, to the shape of the frame when placed to one side underneath it. For any purpose special kinds of flowers are required, as it would be contrary to the fundamental laws of the art to try and make a stiff or upward-growing plant hang downwards, or to try and erect a flower with a limp stem. One place, too, requires a tall, narrow decoration; another a wide or more solemn one. When you have the destined situation of the decoration in your mind, go out and choose flowers and shrubs accordingly, bearing in mind as you pick them the directions the stems will have to take. It is as well always to have a basin of water ready in which to place the flowers immediately after picking them, as in the process of selection, fixing in the wedge, &c—especially until you are practised in the art—the flowers are apt to wither and the vigour in the curves of the stems to get limp, so that it is difficult to carry out any design. The best plan is to place the vase, before filling it, where it will eventually be required to stand, so as to be sure and procure the suitable effect. It is advisable not to put water in the vessel until the composition is completed, as it sometimes tips over in the process of fixing the stems in the wedge.

Before beginning the bouquet, make up your mind, in a general way, what branches and flowers to use and how to dispose them. Then first place the principal ones, fixing each firmly in turn with the bits of Bamboo if not large enough to fill the space, or by pruning the bottom of the stems if too thick, so as exactly to fit the wedge. All tree-branches and shrubs should have the bark peeled off the part which is under water, as this allows a freer entrance to the moisture, and so enables the plant to last fresh for a much longer time. When yon have finished the arrangement, stand at a little distance, and remove all leaves, shoots, or flowers which interfere with the clearness; and beauty of line from various points of view. Then fill the vase with water—slightly tepid is best, especially if the flowers are at all faded. If the wedge is still visible above or through the water, cover it over with a little Moss or other very light leafage or, in the case of a water-plant decoration, with some; small water weed.

The diagrams showing the trilineal arrangement of stems are taken from Mr. Conder's book, and are in strict accordance with the rules of the Japanese art. The other two illustrations of flower decorations are photographed from life, and are merely casual examples of the effect produced by this system of supporting flowers by fasteners, even without conforming with any great precision to the laws adhered to in Japan.

There is hardly a flower, shrub, or tree which is not, at one stage of growth or other, adaptable to this style of arrangement, but some of the most obviously suited are here mentioned by way of suggestion. All fruit blossoms, wild or cultivated: Blackthorn, May, Dog Rose, Bramble, Willow (more especially in bud, known as 'palm'), Maple, Oak, Rhododendron, Azalea, Laburnum, Wistaria, Tree Pæony, Syringa, Berberis, Laurustinus, Holly, and almost all kinds of Fine trees; Irises, Narcissi, Bulrushes, Marsh Marigolds, Water Lilies, Honeysuckle, Clematis, Chrysanthemums, &c.

I have dwelt almost entirely upon the technical side of the art, this being the indispensable means to the end in view. But the goal is one untouched by theory, unmolested by hard-and-fast rules. The wonderful beauty of proportion and balance, the choiceness of selection, the effect of growth and vitality, of dignity and grace, with which the whole of this art is penetrated, are not to be expressed in any doctrinal terms. The tender solicitude which it exacts for the habits and characteristics, tastes and welfare of each plant, endows the least thing utilised by this art with almost a personality. The relative connection of one plant with another—the tall, aspiring *Principal*; the *Secondary*, which seems inclined to follow its lead, yet hesitates half-way with questioning doubt; the *Tertiary* below, in squat contentment—these admit of endless variety of interpretation. To the Japanese every flower has its meaning and associations, as well as every combination of flowers. The force of contrast is ever present in their designs; the opposite sexes ore supposed to be represented, strength and weakness, sternness and tenderness, &c. Without learning the grammar of their complicated flower-language, might we not nevertheless increase our artistic pleasure in flower arrangements by trying to give them a suitableness and a meaning which they have hitherto lacked? The old, long-established English fashion of massing together in a vase may still hold its own for certain kinds of flowers; but, so strong is the fascination of the Japanese principle, that, once it is adopted, it will probably assert its authority even amongst a bunch of Primroses or Violets.

CONSTANCE LYTTON

Flat Feet and Full Steam

Around the world in every way

Christopher Portway

£7.99 paperback

CHRISTOPHER PORTWAY

'His detailed recollections of past experiences add a richness to his storytelling that makes for a delightful read.'

Geographical magazine

From the indefatigable Christopher Portway comes a fascinating account of his journeys around the world.

Christopher spends three months in a dinghy on East Africa's longest and most remote river, avoiding belligerent elephants and rhinos, and jail in Uganda; he treks 1,400 miles across the Andes, following in the footsteps of the Incas; and he escapes German captivity in the Second World War by hitching a train to freedom.

Over every kind of terrain and utilising every possible form of transport, Christopher's experiences couldn't be more diverse: a camel in the Sahara, an elephant in Thailand, dogsledding in Greenland and mule-riding in the Moroccan Atlas Mountains – no one can come close to equalling the extraordinary travel experiences of this remarkable man.

Brit Wit

The perfect riposte for
every social occasion

Susie Jones

£7.99 hardback

'It is a good thing for an uneducated man to read books of quotations.'
SIR WINSTON CHURCHILL

Ever been at a loss for words? Ever wished you had the perfect put-down or wry remark for every socially awkward situation? The great, the good, the intellectual and the downright insulting can all be found in *Brit Wit*.

Densely overpopulated with wonderful one-liners from such formidable figures as Churchill and Shakespeare, to the more recent luminaries of British stage, screen and society, *Brit Wit* celebrates all that makes Britain brilliant.

Essential Beeton

Recipes and tips from the
original domestic goddess

Mrs Beeton

£9.99 hardback

Praise for Mrs Beeton's *Book of Household Management*:

'More wisdom to the square inch than any work of man'

SIR ARTHUR CONAN DOYLE

Beautifully produced and encapsulating the cream of her Household Management Bible, *Essential Beeton* includes pearls of wisdom on housework (and the importance of elbow grease), home hairdressing, child rearing and some of Mrs B's most celebrated recipes.

Mrs Beeton was born Isabella Mayson in London in 1836. She married the wealthy publisher Samuel Orchard Beeton and published her first book, *The Book of Household Management* three years later, aged just 23. Taking four years to compile, it was an instant success, selling 60,000 copies in under a year, and becoming the most widely read of all household advice books in the nineteenth century.

Corfu Banquet

A memoir with seasonal recipes

Emma Tennant

£7.99 paperback

'Full of love for Corfu... delicious recipes... very quirky and absolutely enchanting'

Antonia Fraser, *Front Row*, BBC Radio 4

This charming and personal account celebrates the tastes, smells and colours of an island where the cooking is seasonal and the flowers play changes on the theme of a year-round spring. An island where life follows the sea; from an icy turquoise in March, through autumn's olive darkness when mourga (the mush of discarded olive skins from the village press) clouds the water to a claret wine, as winter sets in.

A memoir set to the rhythm of the seasons of Corfu, the story tells of the house of Rovinia, built in the sixties by Emma Tennant's parents, and of Maria, the 'spirit of the house'.

Corfu Banquet entwines recipes and original photographs with fond recollections in prose.

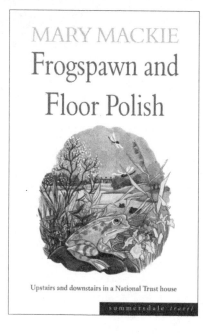

Frogspawn and Floor Polish

Upstairs and downstairs in a
National Trust house

Mary Mackie

£6.99 paperback

'I've never forgotten the photographer who came in as white as a sheet and said he hadn't realised the fence was electrified. Until he was astride it. Nasty.'

Join Mary Mackie and husband Chris as they revisit Felbrigg Hall, the stately home they lived and worked in for several years. Behind the beauty of the gardens, resplendent with apple blossom and wisteria, and beyond the imposing majesty of the seventeenth-century architecture, a constant battle is waged against mould and fungus, over-zealous conservationists, and floors on the brink of collapse...

Mary reveals the quirks and quagmires of living in this wonderful Norfolk National Trust house.

www.summersdale.com